Disability Management and Workplace Integration

Disability Management and Workplace Integration

Disability Management and Workplace Integration

International Research Findings

Edited By

THOMAS GEISEN
University of Applied Sciences, Northwestern Switzerland

HENRY HARDER
University of Northern British Columbia, Canada

Routledge
Taylor & Francis Group

LONDON AND NEW YORK

First published 2011 by Gower Publishing

2 Park Square, Milton Park, Abingdon, Oxon OX14 4RN
711 Third Avenue, New York, NY 10017, USA

Routledge is an imprint of the Taylor & Francis Group, an informa business

First issued in paperback 2016

Gower Applied Business Research
Our programme provides leaders, practitioners, scholars and researchers with thought provoking, cutting edge books that combine conceptual insights, interdisciplinary rigour and practical relevance in key areas of business and management.

British Library Cataloguing in Publication Data
Disability management and workplace integration :
 international research findings.
 1. Disability evaluation. 2. Disability evaluation--Case
 studies. 3. Employee assistance programs. 4. Employee
 assistance programs--Evaluation. 5. People with
 disabilities--Employment.
 I. Geisen, Thomas. II. Harder, Henry George.
 658.3'0087-dc22

ISBN 978-1-4094-1888-7 (hbk)
ISBN 978-1-138-27000-8 (pbk)

Library of Congress Cataloging-in-Publication Data
Disability management and workplace integration : international research
 findings / [edited] by Thomas Geisen and Henry Harder.
  p. cm.
 Includes bibliographical references and index.
 ISBN 978-1-4094-1888-7 (hbk)
 1. Disability evaluation. 2. Occupational health services. 3. Vocational
 rehabilitation. 4. People with disabilities--Employment. 5. Employee
 health promotion. I. Geisen, Thomas. II. Harder, Henry George.
 RC963.4.D57 2011
 616.07'5--dc23

                                                                      2011025336

Contents

List of Figures

List of Tables

List of Contributors

Alison Angleton, psychologist, is National Research and Evaluation Manager at CRS Australia. With 16 years experience working in disability management, she has held a number of roles in both management and direct service delivery. She has conducted research related to the practice and delivery of disability employment services and has interests in mental health, social inclusion and disability management relating specifically to indigenous Australians, solo parents, mature, aged and young people.

Miriam K. Baumgärtner is a research associate and doctoral candidate at the Center for Disability and Integration (CDI-HSG), University of St Gallen, Switzerland. She studied psychology at the Universities of Constance and Mannheim, Germany, and at the University of North Carolina and at Western Carolina University in the USA. She worked at GESIS (The Leibniz Institute for the Social Sciences, formerly ZUMA) as a research assistant for several years. As a consultant at Kenexa, she has gained practical experience in the area of employee surveys and HR management solutions.

Dörte Bernhard (Dr) is a postdoctoral researcher at the National Centre for Work and Rehabilitation, Department of Medical and Health Sciences, Linköping University, Sweden. Dörte holds a Diploma in Work Disability Prevention from Sherbrooke University, Canada. Her background is in rehabilitation science and adult education and she has taught and conducted research into vocational rehabilitation, disability management and return to work at Trier University (2001–2003) and Cologne University (2003–2008) in Germany.

Stephan A. Böhm (Dr), is a senior lecturer and Director of the Center for Disability and Integration (CDI-HSG) at the University of St. Gallen, Switzerland. He holds a master's degree (2003) and a PhD in business administration (2008) from the University of St Gallen. In 2008–2009, he served as a Visiting Research Fellow at the Oxford Institute of Ageing at the University of Oxford, England. His research interests include diversity management, with a focus on the integration of disabled employees and the management of demographic change, as well as group-level and organizational-level processes of categorization, stereotyping and discrimination. He works as a consultant and trainer for several European companies and has gained additional practical experience working at Siemens, Deutsche Telekom and Mercer Management Consulting.

Katrien Bruyninx has a bachelor degree in occupational therapy and is a safety advisor in ergonomics. She currently works at ACT Desiron, an organization that is active in the return-to-work sector. She supports the reintegration/job retention process of individual workers, both in terms of content and procedure.

Nicholas Buys is Professor and Dean of Learning and Teaching in the Health Faculty at Griffith University, Brisbane, Australia and was formerly Head of the School of Human Services and Director of the Research Centre for Human Services at Griffith. He has practised, taught and conducted research into vocational rehabilitation and disability management over a 25-year period. His professional career is in rehabilitation counselling and he has acted as an external consultant on vocational rehabilitation issues for government organizations. He was the founding editor of both the *Australian Journal of Rehabilitation Counselling* and the *International Journal of Disability Management Research* and has produced a number of publications in the area of rehabilitation. His research interests are in the areas of vocational rehabilitation, disability management, vocational evaluation, job placement and career development for people with disabilities.

K.K. Chan, Academic Department, Hong Kong College of Technology, Hong Kong SAR, People's Republic of China.

David J.G. Dwertmann is a research associate and doctoral candidate at the Center for Disability and Integration (CDI-HSG) at the University of St Gallen, Switzerland. He studied psychology at the universities of Mannheim (Germany) and Berne (Switzerland). Before joining the CDI-HSG, he conducted research at San Diego State University, USA, and gained practical consulting experience at Kienbaum Management Consultants GmbH, Germany.

Thomas Geisen (Dr) is a senior researcher and lecturer in the School of Social Work at the University of Applied Sciences Northwestern Switzerland. His main fields of interest are work/labour relations with a special emphasis on disability management, migration, violence and social theory about which he has been widely published.

Henry G. Harder is Professor and Chair of Health Sciences Programmes at the University of Northern British Columbia, Canada, and is a registered psychologist. His research interests are in workplace mental health, suicide and aboriginal health. He is a CIHR-funded scholar and has made presentations and conducted workshops throughout Canada, the United States, Europe and Australia.

Désirée Herbold (Dr) is Director of the Orthopaedic Rehabilitation Clinic Paracelsus-Klinik an der Gande, Bad Gandersheim, Germany.

Daniel Huang is a graduate student in the Masters of Art (Disability Management) program at the University of Northern British Columbia, Canada. His research interest is in the field of human rights and the duty to accommodate in employment. Huang is currently working with the British Columbia government public service on policy for persons with disabilities.

F.K. Ip (Dr) is a consultant in orthopaedics and traumatology. He is one of the founders of the Hong Kong Workers' Health Centre, Hong Kong SAR, People's Republic of China. Since 1984, Ip has been involved in the development of work-injury prevention and rehabilitation services for people affected by work injuries in Hong Kong.

Karen Y.L. Lo-Hui is an accomplished executive with Hong Kong and Mainland China organizations, specializing in work-injury prevention, disability management, rehabilitation counselling and advocacy for the improvement of work-injury insurance. She is the Chief Executive of the Hong Kong Workers' Health Centre and has been appointed as national expert and advisor to the Work Injury Rehabilitation Advisory Committee by the Ministry of Human Resources and Social Security of the People's Republic of China.

Bernhard Koch (Dr) is Chief Occupational Health Physician at SZST Salzgitter Service und Technik GmbH, Salzgitter, Germany.

Birgit-Christiane Leineweber (Dr) is Head of the Department for Special Health Projects at the Salzgitter AG health insurance fund BKK MedPlus, Salzgitter, Germany.

Annette Lichtenauer is a researcher and lecturer in the School of Social Work at the University of Applied Sciences Northwestern Switzerland. Her main field of work is disability research with a special emphasis on disability and employment.

Joachim Maier holds a degree in social pedagogics, with studies in social law and rehabilitation counselling from the University of Heidelberg, Germany. Since 1983, he has been the team leader of the Clinical Social Work and Rehabilitation Counselling department. More recently (since 2001) he has been involved with the Rehabilitation/ Case Management Support and the Driving Ability Centre at the Enzensberg Clinic, a rehabilitation clinic with 400 patients in the south of Germany. He is qualified to teach rehabilitation counselling and is a CDMP (certified disability management professional).

Britta Marfels (Dr) holds a position as a postdoctoral research fellow and the Chair of Labour and Vocational Rehabilitation at Cologne University, Germany, and is involved in teaching and research on integration and disability management. In addition, she has practical experience in the implementation of labour market integration measures. She completed her studies in psychology at Wuppertal University, Germany.

Donal F. McAnaney works with the Work Research Centre and is an associate researcher with the Centre for Disability Studies, University College Dublin (UCD), Ireland. He has worked in the disability field since 1983 and has been responsible for the development of principles of service excellence, assessment systems, individual planning systems and new community-based responses. He established the first postgraduate program in vocational and social rehabilitation in Europe. More recently, he introduced an entry-level NUI Diploma in Community Rehabilitation in partnership with UCD. He has extensive experience in coordinating activities which have EU support, including initiatives funded under R&D 5th Framework Research Programme, Horizon, HELIOS II and Erasmus. He has also acted as an evaluator for the 5th Framework Disability and Elderly program. He has broad international links; he is on the management board of GLADNET, and is very active within the European Platform of Rehabilitation (EPR).

Gregory Charles Murphy is Professor of Rehabilitation Psychology and Head of Department, Health and Social Care, School of Public Health, La Trobe University, Bundoora, Australia. He is a former National President of the Australian Association of Cognitive Behaviour Therapy, and is currently a member of the Technical Advisory Committee (Rehabilitation) for the Australian government's Department of Veterans' Affairs, which develops policy for rehabilitation services for both current members of the armed forces and veterans. His current research program is focused on identifying preventable factors associated with job loss among those who have returned to work following a traumatic spinal cord injury.

Mathilde Niehaus is Professor and the Chair of Labour and Vocational Rehabilitation at Cologne University (the latter since 2002). She is a member of different boards in associations and journals. Her professional career began with her studies in psychology at Marburg and Trier universities in Germany and a position as a research fellow at the University of Oldenburg, Germany. From 1999 to 2001 she held the Chair of Special Education at Vienna University, Austria. She has a number of publications in the area of rehabilitation and the labour market, and has research interests in the areas of vocational rehabilitation, international disability management, transition from school to work, and work health promotion. She is also an external consultant on vocational rehabilitation issues for government organizations.

Mary Alice O'Hare holds a Master's degree in occupational psychology from Massey University, New Zealand, and is currently a doctoral student within the Accident Research Centre at Monash University, Clayton, Australia.

Christine Randall is a rehabilitation counselling lecturer in the Health Group at Griffith University, Brisbane, Australia. Formerly a physiotherapist, her current career is in rehabilitation counselling. She has practised, taught and conducted research into mental health and employment, occupational rehabilitation, and rehabilitation counselling competencies since 2001 and is currently the president of the Rehabilitation Counselling Association of Australasia.

Gisela Riedl (Dr) studied medicine and graduated in 1984. She worked in a hospital surgical unit until 1990. She is currently working at the Enzensberg Clinic, a rehabilitation clinic with 400 patients in the south of Germany. Since 2001, she has lead the Rehabilitation/Case Management Support department which is linked with the Driving Ability Centre. She is also qualified in rehabilitative and vocational medicine and is a CDMP (certified disability management professional).

An Rommel has a Master's degree in history. She conducts research on several work-related health and safety topics (including disability management), at Prevent, Institute for Occupational Safety and Health in Belgium.

Christophe Roulin is a researcher in the School of Social Work at the University of Applied Sciences Northwestern Switzerland. His main fields of work are disability management and migration.

Georg Schielke is a scientific staff member and project leader at the Central Secretariat of the Swiss Conference of the Cantonal Ministers of Public Health, before which he was a researcher in the School of Social Work at the University of Applied Sciences Northwestern, Switzerland.

Mamadouh Shubair (Dr) is an assistant professor in the Health Sciences programs at the University of Northern British Columbia (UNBC), Prince George, Canada. At UNBC, his research and teaching interests have been focused around chronic disease epidemiology, particularly obesity, type 2 diabetes (T2D) and cardiovascular disease (CVD) in rural and Aboriginal/First Nation populations. He is also interested in disability management (DM) issues, such as accommodation and management issues related to obesity, T2D, heart disease, cancer, inflammatory bowel disease (e.g., Crohn's Disease), depression and other chronic conditions in the workplace.

Dan Tang is the Director of Guangdong Provincial Work Injury Rehabilitation Center, People's Republic of China. He has been appointed as national expert and advisor to the Work Injury Rehabilitation Advisory Committee by the Ministry of Human Resources and Social Security of the People's Republic of China.

Elizabeth Tijtgat is an assistant at the University of Ghent (Department of Orthopaedagogics), in the University Centre for Assistance and Training in Belgium. She is active in the strategic development and operational management of scientific projects and has gained experience in projects for people with acquired brain injury and autism.

Lutz Trowitzsch (Dr) is Director at the Institute for Work and Social Medicine at the Paracelsus-Klinik an der Gande, Bad Gandersheim, Germany. He is qualified in work medicine, internal medicine, rehabilitation medicine and social medicine. He is a board member of the federal association EFL of Germany.

Marthe Verjans is a project manager at Prevent, Institute for Occupational Safety and Health, Belgium. She conducts research related to the practice of disability management. She was project manager of the projects Intro_DM and DM@Work.

Shannon L. Wagner (Dr) is an associate professor in the College of Arts, Social and Health Sciences at the University of Northern British Columbia, Canada. Her primary research interests include occupational mental health, disability management and work-life balance. She has a particular interest in workplace-related traumatic stress and has published many articles looking at the impact of traumatic stress on emergency-service responders. She is the Director of the Institute of Social Research and Evaluation and in this capacity completes quality-of-life research. Wagner is also a long-time executive committee member of the Human Early Learning Partnership, the World Health Organization's network hub for researchers looking at issues of early childhood development. In addition to her academic appointments, she is a registered psychologist working in private practice, primarily focused on psychological assessment related to issues of disability management, occupational mental health and return to work.

Ignatius Tak Sun Yu is Professor and Head of the Division of Occupational and Environmental Health, School of Public Health and Primary Care at the Chinese University of Hong Kong, Hong Kong SAR, People's Republic of China.

1 *Disability Management: An Introduction*

HENRY G. HARDER AND THOMAS GEISEN

Since its beginning in the late 1980s, disability management has gained more and more attention in many countries worldwide. Disability management is perceived and understood as an important approach to reduce the negative impact of workers, who are absent due to illness and accidents, on the workers themselves and the company and to assist those with disabilities to enter or re-enter the workplace. Disability management has at its heart the belief that work is central to all of our lives, that individuals, society, employers and governments all value work and want to have all of their colleagues, friends and citizens gainfully employed. An unfortunate reality of work is that some people become injured or ill and have difficulty returning to work, or cannot work to the same extent as before. Some people have difficulty accessing or maintaining work because of existing impairments. Given this reality, disability management says that we should all be proactive in identifying and resolving all factors that prevent persons with any kind of disability from accessing work. Far too often, initiatives to address issues faced by persons with disabilities come as afterthoughts; they react to problems faced by an individual, an organization or a society. Therefore disability management argues on the one hand to give those suffering illness or accident the best support possible to get back to a decent life, which includes getting back to gainful employment. While on the other hand, disability management (based on the case experiences) proposes that we should be thinking about these issues in advance and developing policies and procedures to address them. A clear example of this kind of attitude is: We don't wait to build a hospital until after people are sick. We recognize and accept that they will need medical care. Why don't we do that with respect to disability?

Disability management (DM) in its various guises has now been active for a good decade or more. In some areas, such as workers' compensation, it has made dramatic inroads. In other fields, such as social work, it is much slower in bringing change. DM also appears to be geography specific, being strong in North America and Northern Europe. Indeed, while countries such as Germany, Switzerland, the Netherlands, the USA, Canada and the UK are leaders in DM, other countries, such as China, Japan, Italy and France, have not embraced it to the same extent. Research supporting DM and perhaps shedding light on some issues, such as those mentioned above, appears to be lagging. Government funding agencies appear much more interested in funding new programming rather than research studies which may or may not support existing DM practices and endeavours. As a result, DM appears a bit fractured and not always identifiable as a unique discipline. People are confused by what it is and, perhaps more importantly, by what it seeks to achieve and also what DM has in common with such concepts as 'workplace health promotion' or 'workplace health management'?

So far, disability management has not been developed into a coherent approach. In theory there are some variations under discussion, which typically focus on the usual view that workers with an illness or who have had accident are not able to fulfil their current work duties. Integration, separation, increased flexibility and outsourcing-insourcing (Ulich & Wülser 2009: 192) are offered as strategies to cope with this change in a worker's capacity. However, these disability management strategies represent only a few options for dealing with the negative impact of absent workers. A more cohesive framework, such as the 'comprehensive disability management' approach (Harder & Scott 2005), is preferable so that a range of possibilities and solutions can be brought together rather than separated out. This approach offers a more effective and efficient way to deal with matters arising from absent workers. This is important from the perspective of the worker concerned, as well as for the different stakeholders in a company, e.g., management and co-workers.

Not surprisingly, the question of implementing disability management in companies is a difficult one. Empirical research shows that it takes at least one to two years before DM is successfully introduced and implemented in a company (Geisen et al. 2008). Further a continual and ongoing effort is needed by the company's stakeholders to ensure disability management is a success in the workplace. The reason for this is that disability management is not a pure management strategy that can rely solely on defined structures, procedures and processes. Indeed, personal contacts and interactions are in many cases seen as decisive for success in DM (Geisen et al. 2008). In this regard disability management can be defined as a professional action that needs the capacity to be understood, analyzed and worked on with adequately developed organizational structures. Based on this professional attitude, 'success' cannot be pre-defined by a reduction of absentees or by a short reintegration process, for example. Certainly success in workplace integration or reintegration may not be the best solution for each case. Success in disability management can be defined in an abstract way, such as when the best and most adequate solution has been found for a difficult situation in which many stakeholders are involved. The guiding question for measuring success could be: Does everybody involved in the DM case process see the solution as the best possible for the current situation? Such a process is very demanding for those involved and it can only lead to success if there is an overall commitment to disability management, not only from all stakeholders involved, but also from everyone within an organization.

A strong commitment to disability management when introducing and implementing it in an organization is the result of an intensive process in which the various stakeholders commit themselves to common action and support of disability management. This in turn enhances communication processes between the different stakeholders within a company; social relations also become more open and understanding about social orientations, and expectations improve. This is particularly relevant for decisions that are not likely to be to the advantage of everybody involved. Transparency is necessary to enhance and propel the communication process forward. It is also a pre-condition to reach a fair resolution in difficult and often conflict-ridden situations. Disability management research shows that even if the outcome of the disability management process is far from initial expectations, providing support and seeking a solution as part of a participative process in which all relevant stakeholders are involved generates confidence amongst all involved (Geisen et al. 2008). Not all efforts reach the goal, but the efforts themselves contribute to endow and establish dignity and respect for the person concerned, which can be seen as scarce values in modern capitalist societies (Sennett 2003).

What is relevant at the individual case level is also highly relevant at the organizational and institutional levels. Individual cases can incorporate aspects relevant to the understanding of a more general situation. In a comprehensive DM situation, individual cases are evaluated in order to learn from them and improve health, safety and disability management strategies within an organization. Visibility is the first step to start changes and development at organizational or institutional level. This may lead to changes in conditions and practices that have had a negative effect on the health conditions of workers. Accordingly, comprehensive DM always focuses on the interrelationship between action and practice at the micro-level and within an organization's structure on the meso-level. It is well informed with regards to current social developments relevant to a particular company and workplace, i.e., the macro-level (Bronfenbrenner 1979).

By connecting the micro- and meso-levels within an organization, disability management gives access to a complex knowledge, which supports a company in improving its absentee ratio. In addition, it contributes to cultural change and development that support an overall commitment amongst workers towards their workplace and company by improving working conditions and gives support to a worker in critical and difficult situations. This is the case in Western societies that are typically facing significant demographic changes associated with an aging workforce and an increasing gap between unskilled and qualified workers. Companies need to improve their abilities to support workers more effectively. This means that companies need to enhance workplace conditions and organizational structures according to the heterogeneous need of the workers they have. In the past the strategy to 'hire and fire' was seen as an adequate means for companies to make sure that the labour force was sufficient and of suitable quality. This practice seems to be outdated and a fierce competition between companies for qualified workers is now the norm.

The concept for this book arose from intense discussions on DM that have taken place in recent years, particularly in the European context. Such discussions are closely connected to the transformation of the welfare state into one that supports welfare-through-workfare strategies. During the 1990s DM became established in Canada, Australia, New Zealand and to some extent in the USA. In contrast, European countries have only recently sought to promote DM as a preferred approach to reducing illness-related costs and aiming, in the long run, to avoid unemployment and early retirement and thereby reducing the social costs of the welfare state. Research on DM is still very scarce, therefore findings on the theory, history, research and methods of DM are limited. This book seeks to gather the existing knowledge surrounding how DM has developed in different countries over the last few decades and explore the basic theoretical issues of DM. It also aims to present current research findings in the field of DM, and presents and discusses methodological debates and developments of DM.

The close connection between the implementation of disability management and recent transformation processes of welfare states in Europe has put the spotlight on disability management because it has been accused of being a mere instrument of cost reduction. However, current research shows that disability management has been perceived as very well supported by the workers concerned (Geisen et al. 2008).

In practice, disability management appears to be unchallenged in its relevance and success (Geisen et al. 2008); however, research on disability management has, so far, not been widely conducted and there is an urgent need for research on theory and professional practice. This book therefore seeks to collect the existing knowledge about how disability management has developed in recent decades; to explore basic theoretical issues of disability management; to present current research findings from different countries; and present and discuss the methodological debates about and developments of disability management.

With this book the editors seek to promote current empirical research, the theoretical and historical basis of disability management, the international comparative research findings and methodological approaches of disability management. It includes critical investigations of theory and practice in disability management, especially within the context of the development of welfare states, and it highlights the critical debate around a stricter cost-benefit approach in social work theory and practice. Finally, the book aims to highlight the current state of knowledge and practice in disability management.

An Outline of the Chapters in the Book

The book is organized into three parts: empirical, practical and specific. Part I, Theory and Empirical Research in Disability Management Practice, focuses on examples of research that seeks to show the value of DM in practice. This part starts with the contribution of Christine Randall and Nicholas Buys showing the value and power of using participatory action research to introduce disability management in large organization. They argue that there is a lack of evidence about successful implementation of disability management systems within specific organizations. Action research is presented by the authors as an approach to working with an organization to address occupational stress and occupational rehabilitation issues, taking stakeholder engagement, organizational climate and systems thinking into account. The action research process with the case study organization included a review of organizational background data, 65 individual interviews, six focus groups, and data integration via process maps. Randall and Buys argue that action research is an ideal approach to the development of a disability management strategy within a large organization, and for research.

Dealing with the question of what companies are doing about the introduction of disability management or other health-related programs and activities, Thomas Geisen in his chapter argues that disability management in the workplace has the potential to be an effective instrument for human resources and organizational development to manage new demands for workplace integration and contribute systematically by transforming the company into a learning organization. Currently, companies largely perceive disability management as a strategy to reduce employee absence from work and therefore as a means to keep their illness- and health-related costs to a minimum. The implementation and improvement of casework is therefore the focus of these companies. However, a systematic analysis of the findings at case level compared to the relevance of those findings regarding aspects of work organizations and human resources development are not available, neither on a theoretical nor on an empirical level. In this chapter, recent developments in the area of human resources and organizational development are discussed in relation to their possible links to disability management.

In addition, disability management is presented as a course of action, and the possible connections between human resources and organizational development are presented on a theoretical-conceptual level.

In the next chapter, Gregory Murphy focuses on the micro-level. He provides a review of the literature focusing on the importance of social support in the practice of disability management. Theoretically, the potential of the workplace disability management approach to reduce various problems associated with (preventable) employee incapacity is based on the premise of a positive contribution to rehabilitation and the return-to-work outcomes that flow from the occupational bond that exists between an employer and an injured or unwell employee. This chapter also examines one component of that occupational bond, i.e., *workplace social support*, and, following an analysis of the construct of social support, reviews empirical studies that have assessed the nature and impact of social support on rehabilitation outcomes in general, and on return-to-work achievements in particular. The implications from the findings of this analysis are presented and are especially relevant for those involved in the design and delivery of occupational rehabilitation services.

Of critical importance for social support are the disability management professionals. In their chapter, Dörte Bernhard, Mathilde Niehaus and Britta Marfels show what has been happening with respect to the professionalization of disability management. The participation of people with disabilities in the labour market, coupled with their own desire to take on a more active role in their rehabilitation process, has led to discussions about disability management professionals. By comparing company performance in DM, both internationally and within Germany, this chapter focuses on standardization and quality management for professional actors. The focal point is whether or not the term 'profession' is adequate in the context of the existing disability management practice in Germany. Outlining a need for high quality and effective counselling measures, this chapter states the prerequisites and calls for more research into disability management.

The law provides a base and source of guidance for disability management. Daniel Haung, Shannon Wagner and Henry Harder write in their chapter about the Canadian context and shed some light on the legal issues and developments in jurisprudence that have implications for the practice of disability management throughout the world. This chapter provides a comprehensive overview of Canadian human rights legislation and the duty to accommodate provision in employment law. A history of the development of human rights is discussed along with relevant acts and regulations including the Constitution Act, Canadian Charter of Rights and Freedoms and the Canadian Human Rights Act. In addition, the practice and procedures of human rights legislation are outlined with the interpretation and application of both human rights legislation and the duty to accommodate provision in employment law. It is of paramount importance that disability management professionals understand and have an in-depth knowledge of human rights and have a duty to accommodate this issue in order to: (a) educate employers, unions and workers; and (b) use the legislation and case law remedies to accommodate those who have been discriminated against as a result of their membership in a protected group.

The final chapter in this section examines the discriminated groups by focusing on what disability management and diversity management have in common. Stephan Boehm, David Dwertman and Miriam Baumgaertner argue for the integration of diversity management and disability management and add a broader and interesting perspective to the practice of disability management. This chapter aims at making use of conceptual knowledge from diversity research by transferring it to the field of Disability Management.

Part II, Disability Management in Different Countries, seeks to broaden our knowledge of what is happening in DM around the world. Starting with China, Ignatius Yu, K. K. Chan, Dan Tang, F. K. Ip and Karen Hui-Lo bring us up to date on disability management in this major economy. The chapter examines the development of disability management in both mainland China and in the Special Administrative Region of Hong Kong (HKSAR). The chapter begins with an overview of the economic development and changes in the social security policy in mainland China since the beginning of economic reform in 1978. The original model of social security in communist society is no longer able to deal with the increasing occupational health and safety issues and work injuries accompanying the recent economic reform in mainland China. Hence, reforms in occupational health and safety legislation and changes in the injury insurance system were introduced at the beginning of the twenty-first century. The second part of the chapter summarizes the authors' experience in developing disability management projects in south China and HKSAR. The final part spells out the visions of the authors on the future development of disability management in mainland China and HKSAR.

China can be viewed as a country in which disability management is still very much in the early stages. This is in contrast with Australia, a country in which disability management has become strongly established within recent years. Alison Angelton, in her chapter, brings us a management perspective on disability management in Australia. The chapter explores the notion of disability management within Australia and specifically describes the development and current operational context of Australia's largest provider of disability employment services, CRS Australia. Welfare reform initiatives implemented by government over the last few years have heightened attention to employer engagement and responsibility and represent another dimension to disability management. The ability to join up services and change community expectations of employers with regard to their role in workplace health and well-being will be important to the future directions of disability management in Australia.

In the first of the European cases presented here, Marthe Verjans, An Rommel, Elizabeth Tijtgat and Katrien Bruyninx explain how the disability management approach developed in Belgium. The chapter is mainly based on empirical research acquired during the project Introduction in Disability Management (2005–08). The findings show that on a micro-level there is a need for a professional who coordinates and monitors the reintegration/job retention process from start to finish. On a meso- or company-level, their results indicate that several persons could fulfil the role of disability manager and unite the employer, the outside agencies, the trade unions – the management chain – on job retention and reintegration. Currently, at a macro-level (institutional level), responsibilities are still unclear. Therefore the authors argue that political decision-makers should be encouraged to embrace a more dynamic and integrated approach; they also argue for a rationalization of the existing systems of access to benefits and services.

Thomas Geisen, Annette Lichtenauer, Christophe Roulin and Georg Schielke report on empirical research within Swiss companies that support disability management. Disability management has become increasingly widespread in Switzerland over recent years. The aim of the study was to gather information from companies about the introduction and administration of their in-house disability management programs, and to find out how they rated their success. The findings show that disability management in the workplace implies systematic action on the part of employers. The aim of disability management programs is to assist and support employees who are ill or injured, and should be part and parcel of a company's overall strategy and organization, i.e., DM should not be deployed merely on a case-by-case basis. Disability management can also be seen as the professionalization of workplace assistance for employees who are ill or have suffered an injury. The study also found that some companies implement early identification and prevention measures as part of their own in-house disability management program. Such companies have seen a substantial reduction in health-related costs, as well as significant improvements to their corporate culture.

This section is concluded with the chapter by Donal McAnaney who provides an overview of the position in Europe, a region of increasing importance to disability management issues. This chapter is based on a series of studies incorporating eight EU Member States that was carried out over a 10-year period. All of the studies explored the barriers to, and facilitating factors of, job retention and reintegration. The chapter also addresses the development of disability management within a selection of EU Member States. The RETURN project (1999–2001) (Wynne et al. 2005) and the Employment and Disability Report for the European Foundation (Wynne & McAnaney 2004) both provide a useful insight into the policy and regulatory factors that have inhibited or enhanced the development of disability management in certain jurisdictions. Key findings of the Stress Impact study (2001–03) highlight the experiences of the Land Transport Authority (LTA) workers, their families and professionals in five Member States. Finally, the Re-Integrate project (2007–09) provides an opportunity to explore the views of employers in six countries, some of which are new Member States of the EU. This section, drawing upon quantitative and qualitative research, examines the role that EU legislation and state regulation play in the retention and reintegration of disabled workers and the broader factors that influence a person to return to work.

Part III, Illness, Rehabilitation and Disability Management, looks at more specific contexts within the practice of disability management. Joachim Maier and Gisela Riedl provide a perspective on the practice of disability management from within a rehabilitation clinic in Germany. Based on company interviews and a project with AUDI AG, which linked medical and vocational rehabilitation, Enzensberg (a specialist clinic in Germany) has broad experience in supporting rehabilitation management for companies in cases involving complicated diseases or injuries. The main components of the concept are: a situation analysis, including establishing the potential for rehabilitation; a solution-oriented and interdisciplinary vocational assessment; objective recommendations; vocational and workplace-oriented therapy and training measures; and driving ability tests and driver training. The clinic supports interested organizations and public-body insurance companies with services (seminars and development of programs) to establish return-to-work management, evaluate the functional capacity of workers concerning their work space, and by cooperating with responsible parties for return-to-work programs, get information about social legislation and (financially) supporting offers by the company. This is effective in the reduction of the time required for all processes.

Another case study linking disability management with return-to-work-programs is the chapter by Lutz Trowitzsch, Désirée Herbold, Bernhard Koch and Birgit-Christiane Leineweber, which shows how cooperation between various organizations enhances success when dealing with orthopaedic injuries. From 2005 to 2009, the Institute for Work and Social Medicine (IfWaSM) of the Orthopaedic Rehabilitation Clinic Paracelsus-

Klinik an der Gande (PKadG) in Germany carried out, a disability management pilot project with Salzgitter AG, based on the functional capacity evaluation (FCE) model developed by Susan Isernhagen (1988). The aim of the project was the early provision of rehabilitation and socio-medical services for employees suffering from long-term disability, in order to prevent chronic disabilities, to retain these employees within the company and to provide them with jobs that match their 'new' capacities.

Currently, mental illness is an ever-growing field of work-related health issues. In their chapter, Henry Harder and Shannon Wagner provide insight into the impact that occupational stress and mental illness have in the workplace and how disability management can be applied to assist with these issues. This chapter gives information on the increasingly important area of stress in the workplace. The aetiology of occupational stress is discussed within the context of disability management.

Another important, but more recent topic is presented by Mamdouh Shubair. He explores the issues of people affected by diabetes and how disability management in the workplace can be used to help such workers to stay at work. Type 2 diabetes (T2D) is a significant, disabling, chronic health condition in Canada, the United States and other countries around the world. While the evidence related to the economic burden and costs of T2D in the Canadian and American peer-reviewed literature is abundant, there is no information related to the effectiveness of comprehensive health promotion interventions and strategies targeted towards T2D management in patient populations or employees. Physicians and other health-care professionals are in a very good position to provide support for diabetic individuals. However, clinical guidelines provide little information on how to manage T2D effectively in a workplace environment. Shubair makes some recommendations for employers and employees as to the effective management of T2D in the workplace.

Ultimately, this book seeks to provide a fairly wide overview of disability management current practice. We hope that the information contained within this book proves interesting and encourages discussion and debate. The editors and authors stand willing to engage in such discussion and encourage readers to contact us.

Bibliography

Bronfenbrenner, U. (1979). *The Ecology of Human Development: Experiments by Nature and Design.* Cambridge: Harvard University Press.

Geisen, T., Lichtenauer, A., Roulin, C., & Schielke, G. (2008). *Disability Management in Unternehmen in der Schweiz.* Bern: Bundesamt für Sozialversicherungen.

Harder, H. G., & Scott, L. R. (2005). *Comprehensive Disability Management.* Toronto: Elsevier.

Isernhagen, S.J. (1988). Functional Capacity Evaluation. In S.J. Isernhagen, ed., *Work Injury: Management and Prevention* (139–174). Gaithsburg: Aspen Publishers.

Sennett, R. (2003). *Respect: The Formation of Character in a World of Inequality.* London: Allen Lane.

Stress Impact Consortium. (2006). Integrated Report of Stress Impact: On the Impact of Changing Social Structures on Stress and Quality of Life: Individual and Social Perspectives. Guildford, UK: Surrey University. Available at: http://www.surrey.ac.uk/Psychology/stress-impact/publications/wp8/Stress%20Impact%20Integrated%20Report.pdf, accessed 1 August 2011.

Ulich, E., & Wülser, M. (eds). (2009). *Gesundheitsmanagement in Unternehmen. Arbeitspsychologische Perspektiven.* Wiesbaden: Gabler.

Wynne, R. & McAnaney, D. (2004). Employment and Disability: Back to Work Strategies. The European Foundation for the Improvement of Living and Working Conditions, Loughlinstown, Dublin. Available at: http://www.eurofound.europa.eu/publications/htmlfiles/ef04115.htm, accessed 1 August 2011.

Wynne, R., McAnaney, D., Thorne, J., Hinkka, K. & Jarvisalo, J. (2005) The RETURN Project – Between Work and Welfare: Improving Return-to-Work Strategies for Long-Term Absent Employees. In Mannila, S. & Jarvikoski, A., eds, *Disability and Working Life* (74–100). (Helsinki: Rehabilitation Foundation, Helsinki University Press).

Theory and Empirical Research in Disability Management Practice

2 Workplace Disability Management as an Instrument for Human Resources and Organizational Development

THOMAS GEISEN

Introduction

In the main, companies see disability management as a strategy for reducing employee absence and thereby keeping illness- and health-related costs to a minimum. However, the study Workplace Disability Management in Switzerland (Geisen, Lichtenauer, Roulin, & Schielke 2008) shows that there are not only economic reasons, but also reasons of corporate culture and external incentives for establishing in-house disability management. In the companies examined in that study, the focus of the disability management activities is on the real casework,[1] that is, on the support of employees with an illness or an injury (Geisen et al. 2008: 19–42). Yet until now, the organizational structure aspect was barely taken into systematic account. A comparable practice can be assumed here for external providers who provide disability management services for companies.[2] Most often, in Switzerland, these providers are specialized, private companies, and various public and private social insurance companies, including health and casualty insurance companies, as well as the disability insurance companies. Conceptually, casework in both in-house and external disability management is comprehensive, meaning that the support process takes into consideration the employees' health situation, type of work and workspace, as well as the social conditions outside the workplace, including sociocultural and familial relationships and problem situations. A systematic analysis of the findings from the case studies in terms of their relevance to aspects of work organization and human resources

---

1   The term 'casework' is used in this chapter to mean a systematic approach to the structure of the support process for and activities of injured and ill employees. The usage is synonymous with the term 'case management' in social work.

2   There are no studies of external disability management in Switzerland.

development is not available on either a theoretical or an empirical level, or from the perspectives of either disability management or human resources and organizational development. For this reason – and this is the central thesis of this chapter – disability management's potential is insufficiently realized. Recent developments in the area of human resources and organizational development are discussed in this chapter in relation to their possible connections to disability management. Furthermore, disability management is presented as a course of action, and its possible connections with human resources and organizational development are conceptualized.

Recent Trends in Human Resources and Organizational Development

Human resources development has changed substantially since the 1990s. A narrow understanding, modified according to explicit qualifying measures, has been complemented and extended in many cases (Berthel & Becker 2007: 306), and now a more extensive understanding of its field of activity underlies current concepts of human resources development. Formerly, questions about further education and qualifications were given priority in the narrow perspective of the development of qualification potential; these are now increasingly complemented with questions about team and organizational development. Here, human resources development has become an activity oriented towards fulfilling the company's potential, which combines individual, interpersonal and apersonal (that is, organizational) starting points systematically. Bethel and Becker point out that ideally, 'the systematically initiated human resources development [is dissolving itself] into a learning organization' (Berthel & Becker 2007: 308 (author translation)).

Besides this broadening of human resources development, a new form of corporate personnel policy, known as 'diversity management' (Becker & Seidel 2006), was established in the 1990s. The preoccupation with diversity management in European countries is a result of the internationalization of business activities: 'Internationally active corporations are confronted with objectives and guidelines of a diversity management that draws heavily on North American practices and they function as promoters of the development of a characteristically European diversity management; (Becker & Seidel 2006: (author translation)). Whereas diversity management was based on programs and measures of 'positive discrimination' almost exclusively up until the late 1990s, 'an increasing expansion of objectives in regard to a profound change in corporate culture [is now taking place], in which appreciation and awareness of the singularity of each individual are tied as fundamental values' (Becker & Seidel 2006: 5 (author translation)).

Both developments reveal the increasing importance of human resources and organizational development for corporations. On the one hand, this growing importance takes place against the background of increasing complex work and organizational relationships in corporations. This corresponds with employee requirements that have grown greatly, and to which human resources development reacts, for instance, by offering continuing or further education programs. Health impairments can be a result of growing pressure in corporations. These, in turn, must be met with workplace health promotion (cf. Ulich & Wülser 2009) because corporations have long been aware that absence due to illness is a significant expense. However, workplace health promotion can be characterized as preventive and is directed particularly at employees who have not yet become ill or been injured. Thus, the domains of employment protection and health promotion are merged into an integrative domain in corporate health management (cf. Ulich Wülser 2009). Because of its general orientation towards all corporate employees as a target group, health promotion has rarely been seen as part of human resources development. Overall, health promotion is instead regarded as a domain that has the potential to give a positive boost to employees, but cannot actively contribute to human resources development. This assumption is, however, at least theoretically, barely sustainable any longer if we take a broad view of human resources development. The question of what specific health promotion directed toward individual employees as a concrete human resources development measure might look like still remains.

An answer to this question is provided by the 'comprehensive disability management' approach (Harder & Scott 2005), which considers certain domains – employee, type of work, corporation, and private situation – as a single consistent context of structure and relationship. Here, disability management can be seen as an intervention and counselling approach, the aim of which is to advance and support the integration and reintegration of company employees. Professional (re)integration, as well as social and health integration[3] of employed individuals whose work capacity is impaired because of illness or injury, takes centre stage. Social integration points here to a sustainable network of permanent social relationships in both the work environment and the private domain. Health integration, on the other hand, focuses on access to and participation in existing health-related support systems and resources, including in corporations and the social security systems. From the human resources or organizational development viewpoint, disability management can, as a result, be understood as an approach that responds to the qualifying and performance potential of employees, which has been changed temporarily or permanently. Initially, however, disability management is tasked with detecting demands for change and adaptation on individual, team/unit and company levels. Then, possibilities for realizing these various demands are tested and implemented. The dimension of shifting, changing or the partial loss of service provision and qualifying potential, which can be temporary or permanent, has not been sufficiently considered in human resources development. Only recently has a debate begun about these matters, usually with reference to 'aging personnel'.[4] This topic, however, is regarded as a special case and as an exception in the corporate context of service provision. If we add further groups with existing or potential temporary or permanent changes to work capacity, for instance, disabled individuals, employees with an illness or injury, individuals who care for relatives and individuals who have been victims of discrimination, to the aging personnel category, then the high priority of change in provision of services becomes apparent. It is generally assumed that this potential can be further developed into performance enhancement.

---

3   The term 'health integration' means participation in the measures and resources available for re-establishing and improving health. These include measures and activities conducive to the treatment of illness, as well as preventive concepts and activities. In this chapter, the term is used in its corporate context, that is, the possibility of access to corporate measures for health promotion and care and support in case of illness and resulting health problems.

4   There are, however, some findings about the productive effects of different personnel age structures. Veen, for instance, says: 'Overall, different age structures of employees have productivity effects and these effects need to be treated differentially, according to their tasks. Age heterogeneity is a positive factor, if it is connected to the right task, and if there is a rather creative and innovative task. If there is a favorable corporate view of innovation, then heterogeneity is positive; if the emphasis is on quick coordination, then it is instead homogeneity that is to be given preference' (Veen 2008: 152 (author translation)).

In light of the challenges that corporations will face in coming decades because of demographic change, lack of qualified personnel, the aging personnel phenomenon (cf. Klauk 2008), and the increasing significance of chronic diseases (cf. Maaz, Winter & Kuhlmey 2007), this gap should be closed urgently – not least to secure economic vitality. In this regard, disability management could make an essential contribution. Besides these external influences and contexts, disability management in corporations makes and essential contribution to the better utilization of potentially marketable work capacity.

Hence, disability management can be regarded as a specific approach that focuses on the connection between gainful employment and well-being in the workplace. Since the 1990s, there have been developments that give increasing priority to health-related matters. These developments are discussed in the following sections according to their relevance to disability management.

Corporation, Gainful Employment, and Health

Workplace health promotion (cf. Badura, Ritter & Scherf 1999; Giesert 2008; Meggeneder, Pelster & Sochert 2005) has become a focal point of public interest at various levels in recent years. The company has been defined as a place where employee health must be preserved and advanced. At the same time, this is resulting in a turning away from health policies that are exclusively related to the prevention of accidents and work-related illnesses, as workplace health promotion takes effect in the area of occupational health and safety (cf. Lenhardt & Rosenbrock 2007). Since the 1970s this aspect has been to the fore in debates about the humanization of work, as they have been conducted since the 1970s. But more recently, this perspective has been complemented and extended with a positive focus on resources and qualifications. Accordingly, illness and well-being are no longer perceived as completely antagonistic.[5] In line with the salutogenesis approach, they are perceived rather as 'poles of a continuum' (cf. Antonovsky 1997). In relation to the individual, they are in an ever-specific relation to each other. The salutogenesis approach thereby cancels out the binary coding of ill/healthy, altering the perspective fundamentally; instead of a debate concerned primarily with the prevention of illness and accidents at work, it is now about the configuration and application of proactive processes of comprehensive health promotion. At the same time, the question of how individuals with health-related limitations can be supported and assisted, in order for them to continue to live autonomous lives, takes centre stage.

ILLNESS AND GAINFUL EMPLOYMENT

Gainful employment has a crucial meaning for autonomous life in modern societies. Work does not simply represent a basic human activity.[6] Social integration in modern work-sharing societies is connected fundamentally with the social, cultural and

---

5   Alexa Franke puts this development in the context of changes related to the social state: 'From a medical history perspective, a strict separation between ill and healthy has only become necessary because of western countries' social legislation ... Today, the strict separation between well-being and illness is questioned increasingly: In theories of well-being and illness that have been developed in recent times, "healthy" and "ill" are no longer dichotomous categories, but poles of a continuum, which implies different dimensions of well-being and illness' (Franke 2008: 26 (author translation).

6   Cf. Arendt (1996).

economic conditions of gainful employment. At the same time, (gainful) employment is an important activity biographically, connected to strong self-identifications because successful integration into the work process is a crucial element in an individual's development. This applies especially to adolescence, the transitional phase to adulthood that is characterized through a 'contradiction between work and the delusions of grandeur and omnipotence' (Erdheim 1992: 308 (author translation)). According to Erdheim, 'the integration into the work process [defines] their destiny; the social requirements force the individual to adapt its ego-centred organization to the conditions of employment, resulting here in the transformation of it, ego, and superego into a highly hierarchical structure that is adapted to the relationships of power' (Erdheim 1992: 308 (author translation)). For this reason, Erdheim sees work ambivalently: it means 'narcissistic mortification', since omnipotence is thereby restricted, 'but at the same time, work is the most important instrument for bringing exactly these fantasies and reality closer together' (Erdheim 1992: 310 (author translation)). Through work, an essential integration into society takes place: 'No other technique of lifestyle connects the individual as closely to reality as enhancement of work, which integrates him or her at least into a part of reality, into the human community securely' (Freud 2000: 212 (author translation)). Loss of gainful employment leads not only to social marginalization that is associated with loss of recognition, but also to crises, since biographically acquired identifications, strongly connected to gainful employment, become fragile.

Referring to role theory, Thomas Kieselbach and Gert Beelmann describe the process of social marginalization that accompanies unemployment as follows: 'Personal and social identity is affected extensively by the adoption of a socially stigmatized role, as for instance unemployment. In work-centered societies, there are just a few occupations that show a lower social prestige than the state of unemployment' (Kieselbach & Beelmann 2006: 19). Loss of workplace, and continuing unemployment are, hence, regarded as independent risk factors 'that can influence health-related behavior negatively as well as cause the development of health-related problems that are either of a psycho-social or a mental nature (causal effect)' (Kieselbach & Beelmann 2006: 13). Through an actual or assumed exclusion from gainful employment, depressing situations are created that may negatively affect well-being and health. Even insecurity about and fear of losing one's job impinge on well-being: 'Employees with a high rate of work insecurity (51 per cent) talk more often about significant or somewhat significant mental pressure than employees who do not suffer from such insecurity (37 per cent). The same applies for employees who receive no help from their colleagues (54 per cent) and those who have not enough time to do their work (59 per cent)' (Krieger & Graf 2009: 45). In addition, there is a known phenomenon in corporations that, in periods of corporate reorganization, the rate of absence increases notably. In such a context, illness always constitutes a reaction to the impending loss of social integration as well. However, this is not to imply that illness represents a form of social disintegration. In fact, what is realized here is an intermediary state of integration based on social state-related boundaries. According to Robert Castel, this can also be described as a 'precarious phase' of social integration (cf. Castel 2000).

Illness is a precarious form of social integration, since it is socially accepted and legitimizes absence from gainful employment (cf. Erdheim 1992). However, illness requires a specific legitimation, which is not inherent to the illness itself but is dependent on external factors, generally on its authentication through experts.[7] On an individual level, illness is connected to loss of autonomy and capacity to act in society. Hence we can assume that a positive effect for the health-related development can be gained through successful reintegration into gainful employment and an increased capacity to act. It has been established by psychosomatic medicine that healing processes, independent from the gravity of the illness, depend heavily on the patient's mental constitution. Therefore, not only curative forms of treatment but also the positive motivations that drive human activity can be beneficial for human health. In this sense, gainful employment represents an essential individual and social resource for good health – for both general and specialized workplace health promotion. Empirical studies state that, compared to interventions, 'reemployment, in particular if stable, [may lead to] a drastic reduction of psychosocial pressure along with depressive disorders, day-to-day mood problems, anxiety and feelings of loneliness' – and this despite new professional requirements (Kieselbach & Beelmann 2006: 28).

Well-being has long been a matter of concern in corporations. It is one of the principal topics of sociopolitical provisions and social security regulations in welfare states established in the course of industrialization (cf. Kraus & Geisen 2001). For a long time, however, questions of social security law, injury/death insurance and the statutory protection of labour through safety measures have been the dominant ones in this domain. Here, Switzerland played a leading role: 'With the manufacturing law of 1877 and the civic liability act of 1881, the federation interfered for the first time in industrial relations' (Wicki 2001: 253). Labour protection in a narrow sense was most notably directed towards hazards that arose from the actual work performed in the company. However, with the transition to a post-industrial or service economy, and the related structural changes in the production process, workplace hazards have been transformed fundamentally. One indication of this is the great increase in forms of psychological stress in recent years. In a Swiss health survey, 'stress, time pressure (62 per cent), tension at the workplace 36 per cent), and nervousness (33 per cent)' are cited as the most frequent health risks; others include excessive pressure to perform (20 per cent), unfair treatment (15 per cent), anxiety (10 per cent), lack of challenge (9 per cent) and bullying (8 per cent) (Krieger & Graf 2009: 15). About 40 per cent of employees indicate 'that they are under significant or somewhat significant mental stress at their workplace; in regard to significant physical stress, [the figure is] about 20 per cent of employees' (Krieger & Graf 2009: 45). Regarding reasons for occupational disability, Switzerland registers, as do many other European countries, a strong increase in the rate of retirement for psychological reasons. 'From 1998 to 2007, the average annual increase in recipients of the invalid insurance system[8] because of psychological illness amounted to roughly 7 per cent. This means that the number of insured individuals requiring a pension because of psychological disorders has risen from 29 per cent in 1998 to 38 per cent in 2007' (Krieger & Graf 2009: 46). Not least of all, the reasons for this are of a social nature and can be traced back to increased competition and pressure to perform at work. Under the conditions of post-industrial societies, these reasons are determined by a growing

---

7   Hence, physicians are allotted a special significance particularly in the context of workplace integration. For instance, it can be gathered from the study Workplace Disability Management in Switzerland that the support of the family doctor, right after support of the family itself, is the most important form of support for the employee (Geisen et al. 2008: 68).

8   The disability insurance system covers the risk of occupational disability in Switzerland (cf. Wicki 2001).

importance of 'psyche as a production capacity (Jouhy 1998: 249 (author translation)). According to this, mental and psychosomatic illnesses also represent a subjective form of processing workplace pressures. For the employee this is a mode of reacting to uncertainty regarding future prospects in order to better deal with that pressure. However, they must also be prepared to deal with their own fears of potential failure This area is of great importance in the modern labour societies, in which gainful employment constitutes the dominant principle of social integration. Yet in the 1980s, a reaction to this change was evident in the debates about well-being in the workplace, and in the extension of the focus of workplace health promotion away from a narrow perspective to a holistic one (cf. Meggeneder et al. 2005; Pelster & Sochert 2005). The workplace is still at the centre, though it is no longer perceived as separate from other aspects of life, but rather as an essential part of the individual's world.

International Developments in Workplace Health Promotion

The paradigm for this reorientation is the World Health Organization's (WHO) Ottawa Charter, a health promotion policy statement ratified in 1986 (WHO 1986). Health promotion is therein aimed at 'enabling people to increase control over, and to improve, their health. To reach a state of complete physical, mental and social well-being' (WHO 1986: 5). Health is regarded here as 'a positive concept emphasizing social and personal resources, as well as physical capacities. Therefore, health promotion is not just the responsibility of the health sector, but goes beyond healthy life-styles to well-being' (WHO 1986: 5). With the Ottawa Charter, a narrowly conceived understanding of health is replaced by a notion of health in everyday life. The focus on specialized institutional and organizational health domains is made redundant and replaced by a demand that modes of life explicitly beneficial to health be established. In this context, the workplace plays a central part, since:

> ... changing patterns of life, work and leisure have a significant impact on health. Work and leisure should be a source of health for people. The way society organizes work should help create a healthy society. Health promotion generates living and working conditions that are safe, stimulating, satisfying and enjoyable. Systematic assessment of the health impact of a rapidly changing environment – particularly in areas of technology, work, energy, production and urbanization – is essential and must be followed by action to ensure positive benefit to the health of the public. (WHO 1986: 6).

Individuals should be enabled 'to learn, throughout life, to prepare themselves for all of its stages and to cope with chronic illness and injuries is essential. This has to be facilitated in school, home, work and community settings' (WHO 1986: 6). Here, the workplace and the company are explicitly identified as places of performance where health promotion needs to be applied.

For this reason, according to Pelster and Sochert (2005: 18f.), the WHO concept of (corporate) health promotion is based on the following three criteria that are crucial for an understanding of health:

- Socio-psycho-somatic understanding of health: Contrary to the classic-medical understanding of health (countering risk factors), health promotion emphasizes the enhancement of individual- and environment-related health-supporting resources in its intervention strategies.
- Concept of work and living modes: The lifestyle of individuals is not the approach and strategic centre of reference for health promotion, but the focus of its conceptual consideration lies on the analytic category of work and living mode, i.e., primarily on the influence of organizational and social relationships.
- Autonomy of action, competence in decision-making, competent management, and social support are central criteria for a health-supporting practice. This only works with the participation of affected persons, as well as through their influence.

Debates about the crisis of the welfare state, which have been occurring since at least the beginning of the 1990s, are also an important influence on the development of workplace health promotion. Increasing financial pressures on social security providers, and falling income due to greater unemployment provide the starting point in this context. Sociopolitical decisions contribute too, for instance, with the cushioning of rationalization and restructuring via increased invalidization of employees and early retirement, implemented in several industrial domains in the 1990s. Health promotion was not easy in this sociopolitical environment; furthermore, there was a sufficient supply of highly qualified workers. For many companies, this meant that the personnel and financial liabilities of workplace health promotion could not be justified. It has been regarded as an important corporate task really only since the end of that decade.

WORKPLACE HEALTH PROMOTION IN SWITZERLAND

Scientific studies of corporate work and health promotion 'have exposed structural, organizational, and qualitative deficits in various domains in the past, Gröben and Bös state, but 'the state of information about the actual distribution of measures of workplace health promotion in particular' is still not sufficient (Gröben & Bös 1999: 9). This assessment is still valid in 2011, particularly for companies in Switzerland. Bauer (2005), for instance, emphasizes that corporate health management (betriebliches Gesundheitsmanagement (BGM)) has been on the agenda in Switzerland since at least 1993. In 1993, the newly founded Health Promotion Switzerland foundation had, among other things, made the topic 'health promotion and work' a key focus. 'Since then, a lot has been done on the supply side in the BGM-domain. On the corporate side, however, there still is significant potential for development (Bauer 2005: 7). On the national level, in 2002, a special department for workplace health promotion was established in the State Secretariat for Economic Affairs (SECO), which is the contact point of the European network for workplace health promotion (Bauer 2005: 7).[9] However, too few companies

---

9   'Since the Network was formally established in 1996, it has been at the leading edge of developments in European workplace health promotion ... [I]t has developed good practice criteria for WHP [workplace health promotion] for many different types of organisation and has established infrastructures for WHP in the Member States ... The European Network for Workplace Health Promotion is an informal network of national occupational health and safety institutes, public health, health promotion and statutory social insurance institutions. In a joint effort, all the members and partners aim to improve workplace health and well-being and to reduce the impact of work-related ill health on the European workforce' (ENWHP 2007: 1).

use the services offered for the application and development of health promotion measures.

> *Despite multifarious actors and services for BGM, still relatively few companies in Switzerland make use of the BGM potential systematically. Yet, there is an urgent need for action from a business point of view: Globalization and pressure for change in corporations demand investments in optimizing work conditions and employees' competences. At the same time, the social demand for improved quality of work and an optimized work–life balance is growing. (Bauer 2005: 9).*

On a practical level, workplace health promotion includes health promotion approaches and measures that aim for behavioural change, including in relation to the use of dependence-creating substances, or which should lead to behavioural change, for example, through increased exercise and healthier food (cf. Gröben & Bös 1999; Ulich & Wülser 2009). While occupational safety measures are established by law, and corporations are obliged to implement them, health promotion is optional. Bauer's study of workplace health promotion by service providers in Switzerland shows that the legally prescribed measures for occupational safety and health protection are evident in four in ten of the companies. 'Concerning the explicit health promotional measures, absence and relationship-oriented measures (that is, ergonomic workplace design) are available more frequently – 16 to 41 per cent – than are behavior-oriented activities such as courses in ergonomics or prevention programs (in 8 to 21 per cent of the companies)' (Bauer 2005: 9). Given these results, Bauer concludes that there is 'still some potential for development' (Bauer 2005: 9).

The Disability Management Approach

The problems outlined here for workplace health promotion apply to disability management as well. Workplace disability management is not common in Switzerland,[10] though some private companies do have in-house disability management, and cities and cantons have begun to implement disability management in recent years, in particular, the city and canton of Zurich, and the cantons Bern, Aargau and Lucerne. In practice, in-house and external disability management can be differentiated. With in-house disability management, the responsibility for the implementation and realization of the approach lies with the companies themselves. In order to implement disability management for employees suffering from an illness or injury, companies establish and develop an internal structure. As well as utilizing organizational connections, such as the human resources department or social counselling (Geisen et al. 2008: 47ff) and other appropriate human resources,[11] companies establish internal operational processes, including continuous

---

10   The study Workplace Disability Management in Switzerland (Geisen et al. 2008) states that the number of companies with in-house disability management (DM) is not very large. Within the framework of the study, '62 companies and public administrations have been identified and contacted, where evidence of DM was available' (Geisen et al. 2008: 13), of which a total of eight companies were singled out on the basis of maximum contrast, diverse locations, different sectors and variable parameters (Geisen et al. 2008: 13).

11   The resources of the companies investigated in the disability management study differ strongly (vgl. Geisen et al. 2008: 49ff). Based on their experience of introducing and implementing disability management projects in Switzerland,

and target-group-specific communication between supervisors and employees. External disability management is provided by corporations as a service. The focus is on casework with ill or injured employees. This latter kind of disability management is comparable structurally to the traditional form of corporate social work, which is primarily about the support of individual employees who have social and health-related problems (cf. Jaeppelt & Görcke 2009; Jente et al. 2001).

The concrete casework in disability management, that is, the counselling and support of employees with an illness or injury, is seen as a professionally guided and structured process with the objective of individual work integration. Disability management thematizes, as a context, the situatedness of the real case in terms of its integration into the corporate functions and the social expectations inherent to a company. Thus, disability management is about taking an organization-related, structured approach that encompasses the following corporate policies and activities: 'Registration and evaluation of employee absences; counselling and support of employees with an illness or injury; coordination of activities and services for re-integration; [and] prevention according to workplace health promotion' (Geisen et al. 2008: 1). The diseased or injured employee is at the centre of disability management. Such employees find themselves in a difficult social situation and constitute the source of professional work in the disability management approach. Within the framework of structured professional work, targeted measures and support activities are implemented, which, individually and on a case-by-case basis, directly contribute to developing and supporting health and rehabilitation processes. Besides medical and therapeutic-rehabilitative treatments, the work activity itself is a central element of this support process. Harder and Scott underline the importance of this aspect:

> The longer the employee is off work the more intense the feelings of not belonging become. It is essential that the workplace remains supportive and for the treatment to focus on restoring the employee to optimal function. In studies going back to the beginning of the DM era it has been found that even casual contact with the employee decreases absence by 30 per cent ... Of course DM has grown in sophistication but the underlying principle of staying in touch has not changed. (Harder & Scott 2005: 18)

New insights are gained through evaluating the full casework, which can affect the corporate organizational and structural processes, as well as work-related facilities and environments as a whole. This is because along with the particulars of the individual case, general aspects relevant to the company and the society are thematized at the same time. For the disability management approach, it is crucial to connect the individual, case-related level with the organizational-structural level. Only when this is done does disability management represent something more than a new term for an old form of methodical action in social work, namely individual case support.

Hans Schmidt and Stefan Kessler state that the ratio of disability managers to employees should be around one to 1,000 (cf. Schmidt & Kessler 2006).

Disability Management as Area-Specific Case Management

The main objective of disability management is to support ill and injured employees on a case-by-case basis. As a rule, this happens with the use of the case management approach (cf. Gursansky, Harvey & Kennedy 2003; Neuffer 2007; Wendt & Löcherbach 2006). The aim is an early and optimal return to gainful employment. The extent to which this is possible depends on the impairments that have been caused by illness or injury. For employees whose capacity is impaired, a return to the same workplace, or to a workplace that has been adapted appropriately, is possible. The crucial matter here is the performance and qualification potential the employee has at his or her disposal, and what adaptations must be carried out in order for this potential to be optimally realized. From the disability management perspective then, the question of the individual employee's resources takes centre stage. But a comprehensive disability management approach goes one step further, conceiving another possibility – that of employment in a different company or supporting a change to self-employment. In the literature in the field, the strategies of disability management are identified as the integration model, the separation model, the increased flexibility model and the outsourcing-insourcing model (Ulich & Wülser 2009: 192). The broadness of these options already indicates an essential aim of disability management: to arrive at a case-specific solution, which responds to each employee's needs, and is realized with corporate and extra-corporate actors, with the aim of work (re)integration.

Disability management also systematically takes an organization-related development approach, shaped by specific knowledge of how illness and injury occur in the workplace, which emerges from the evaluation of cases and casework. If work-related factors become visible in this process, improvements on the organizational level and through adaptations in the workplace are sought. Thus, general measures of workplace health promotion can be integrated into disability management as well, and hence, disability management is an integrated approach that combines different corporate levels. Networking, communication and cooperation within the corporation constitute the central (work) principles of disability management.

Based on its equally case- and system-specific approach in relation to gainful employment, disability management differs fundamentally from workplace health management.[12] Ulich and Wülser highlight that disability management can be 'just one part, even if an essential one, of workplace health management' (Ulich & Wülser 2009: 297). According to them, disability management lacks, for instance, measures that focus on primary and secondary prevention because preventive measures are, here, 'for the most part of a tertiary nature' (Ulich & Wülser 2009: 297). Yet, with its case- and system-specific approach, disability management makes an important contribution to the transformation of the corporation into a learning organization (Arnold & Bloh 2003; cf. Maula 2006). It makes an essential contribution, for example, to the improvement of corporate communication processes.

---

12   Hence, Ulich and Wülser (2009: 297) suggest, correctly, that conflating disability management with workplace health promotion represents a reduction in perspective.

Conclusion

Human resources development has undergone major change in recent years and has developed a broad understanding that combines individual, interpersonal and apersonal (organizational) approaches. In addition, with diversity management a new approach has begun to establish the importance of heterogeneity and equal opportunities in the workplace. Questions about workplace health promotion have gained more importance. The developments and debates of recent years have shown that the health factor has significantly increased in importance in Switzerland, especially in corporations where well-being is increasingly seen as an important factor in relation to productivity. This has, in part, led to corporations taking measures to enhance the well-being of their employees. The systematic promotion and support of ill and injured employees with the aim of actively supporting their reintegration into gainful employment has been made possible primarily through disability management. Resource orientation is the essential principle of disability management. In the concrete implementation of this principle, that is, working at a case as well as at the system level, disability management can be regarded as an important domain of human resources development. This also applies to the relationship between disability management and diversity management, particularly regarding heterogeneity and integration. The increased integration of disability management by corporations could emphasize important and durable features in the domain of human resources development.

Bibliography

Antonovsky, A. (1997). *Salutogenese. Zur Entmystifizierung der Gesundheit*. Tübingen: dgvt Verlag.

Arendt, H. (1996). *Vita activa. Oder vom tätigen Leben*. München: Piper.

Arnold, R. & Bloh, E. (eds). (2003). *Personalentwicklung in lernenden Unternehmen*. Baltmannsweiler: Schneider Verlag Hohengehren.

Badura, B., Ritter, W. & Scherf, M. (1999). *Betriebliches Gesundheitsmanagement. Ein Leitfaden für die Praxis*. Berlin: edition sigma.

Bauer, G. (2005). Gesundheitsmanagement im Betrieb. Entwicklungsstand und Entwicklungspotenzial in der Schweiz. Managed Care – Schweizer Zeitschrift. *Managed Care, Public Health, Gesundheits- und Sozialökonomie* (4), 7–9.

Becker, M. & Seidel, A. (eds). (2006). *Diversity Management. Unternehmens- und Personalpolitik der Vielfalt*. Stuttgart: Schäffer-Poeschel Verlag.

Berthel, J. & Becker, F.G. (2007). *Personal-Management. Grundzüge für die Konzeption betrieblicher Personalarbeit*. Stuttgart: Schäffel-Poeschel Verlag.

Castel, R. (2000). *Die Metamorphosen der sozialen Frage*. Konstanz: UVK Verlagsgesellschaft.

ENWHP. (2007). *European Network for Workplace Health Promotion*. Available at http://www.enwhp.org/index.php?id=5. Accessed 5 December 2007.

Erdheim, M. (1992). *Die gesellschaftliche Produktion von Unbewußtheit*. Frankfurt a. M.: Suhrkamp.

Franke, A. (2008). *Modelle von Gesundheit und Krankheit*. Bern: Verlag Hans Huber.

Freud, S. (2000). Das Unbehagen in der Kultur. In S. Freud (ed.), *Studienausgabe. Fragen der Gesellschaft. Ursprünge der Religion* (Vol. 9, pp. 191–270). Frankfurt am Main: Fischer Taschenbuch Verlag.

Geisen, T., Lichtenauer, A., Roulin, C. & Schielke, G. (2008). *Disability Management in Unternehmen in der Schweiz*. Bern: Bundesamt für Sozialversicherungen.

Giesert, M. (ed.). (2008). *Prävention: Pflicht & Kür. Gesundheitsförderung und Prävention in der betrieblichen Praxis*. Hamburg: VSA-Verlag.

Gröben, F. & Bös, K. (1999). *Praxis betrieblicher Gesundheitsförderung*. Berlin edition sigma.

Gursansky, D., Harvey, J. & Kennedy, R. (2003). *Case Management. Policy, Practice and Professional Business*. New York: Columbia University Press.

Harder, H.G. & Scott, L.R. (2005). *Comprehensive Disability Management*. Toronto: Elsevier.

Jaeppelt, A. & Görcke, M. (2009). *Die neue Generation der betrieblichen Sozialarbeit: Das employee assistance program als innovativer Baustein unternehmerischer Gesundheitsförderung*. Münster: Lit Verlag.

Jente, C., Judis, F., Meier, R., Steinmetz, S. & Wagner, S.F. (eds). (2001). *Betriebliche Sozialarbeit*. Freiburg im Breisgau: Lambertus.

Jouhy, E. (1998). Die Psyche als Produktivkraft. Zum heutigen Verhältnis von entlohnter und nicht entlohnter Arbeit. In T. Geisen, K. Kraus & V. Ziegelmayer (eds.), *Zukunft ohne Arbeit? Beiträge zur Krise der Arbeitsgesellschaft* (pp. 249–86). Frankfurt am Main: IKO-Verlag.

Kieselbach, T. & Beelmann, G. (2006). Arbeitslosigkeit und Gesundheit: Stand der Forschung. In A. Hollederer & H. Brand (eds), *Arbeitslosigkeit, Gesundheit und Krankheit* (pp. 13–34). Bern: Verlag Hans Huber.

Klauk, B. (ed.). (2008). *Alternde Belegschaften – der demografische Wandel als Herausforderung für Unternehmen*. Lengerich: Pabst Science Publishers.

Kraus, K. & Geisen, T. (eds). (2001). *Sozialstaat in Europa. Geschichte – Entwicklung – Perspektiven*. Wiesbaden: Westdeutscher Verlag.

Krieger, R. & Graf, M. (2009). *Arbeit und Gesundheit. Zusammenfassung der Ergebnisse der Schweizerischen Gesundheitsbefragung 2007*. Zürich: Staatssekretariat für Wirtscahft SECO.

Lenhardt, U. & Rosenbrock, R. (2007). Prävention und Gesundheitsförderung in Betrieben und Behörden. In K. Hurrelmann, T. Klotz & J. Haisch (eds), *Lehrbuch Prävention und Gesundheitsförderung* (pp. 295–306). Bern: Verlag Hans Huber.

Maaz, A., Winter, M.H.-J. & Kuhlmey, A. (2007). Der Wandel des Krankheitspanoramas und die Bedeutung chronischer Erkrankungen (Epidemiologie, Kosten). In B. Badura, H. Schellschmidt & C. Vetter (eds), *Fehlzeiten-Report 2006. Chronische Krankhreiten* (pp. 5–24). Heidelberg: Springer Medizin Verlag.

Maula, M. (2006). *Organizatioins as Learning Systems. 'Living Composition' as an Enabling Infrastructure*. Oxford/Amsterdam: Elsevier.

Meggeneder, O., Pelster, K. & Sochert, R. (eds). (2005). *Betriebliche Gesundheitsförderung in kleinen und mittleren Unternehmen*. Bern: Verlag Hans Huber.

Neuffer, M. (2007). *Case Management. Soziale Arbeit mit Einzelnen und Familien*. Weinheim/München: Juventa.

Pelster, K. & Sochert, R. (2005). Die Entwicklung der Betrieblichen Gesundheitsförderung in Deutschland. In O. Meggeneder, K. Pelster & R. Sochert (eds), *Betriebliche Gesundheitsförderung in kleinen und mittleren Unternehmen* (pp. 18–28). Bern: Verlag Hans Huber.

Schmidt, H., & Kessler, S. (2006). 'Ability Management' – Erfahrungen in der Schweiz. In P. Löcherbach & W.R. Wendt (eds), *Case Management in der Entwicklung. Stand und Perspektiven in der Praxis* (pp. 192–208). Heidelberg: Economica.

Ulich, E., & Wülser, M. (eds). (2009). *Gesundheitsmanagement in Unternehmen. Arbeitspsychologische Perspektiven*. Wiesbaden: Gabler.

Veen, S. (2008). *Demographischer Wandel, alternde Belegschaften und Betriebsproduktivität*. München: Hampp.

Wendt, W.R. & Löcherbach, P. (eds). (2006). *Case Management in der Entwicklung. Stand und Perspektiven in der Praxis*. Heidelberg: Economica/MedizinRecht.de.

WHO. (1986). The Ottawa Charter for Health Promotion. First International Conference on Health Promotion, Ottawa, 21 November 1986. Available at http://www.who.int/healthpromotion/conferences/previous/ottawa/en/print.html. Accessed 24 September 2010.

Wicki, M. (2001). Soziale Sicherheit in der Schweiz: Ein europäischer Sonderfall? In K. Kraus & T. Geisen (eds), *Sozialstaat in Europa. Geschichte – Entwicklung – Perspektiven* (pp. 249–72). Wiesbaden: Westdeutscher Verlag.

3

Using Action Research to Develop Effective Disability Management Programs

CHRISTINE RANDALL AND NICHOLAS BUYS

Introduction

It is estimated that globally there are 650 million people with disabilities and each year there are 270 million work accidents in which two million people die from work-related injuries and 60 million people suffer permanent work-related disabilities. The cost of these injuries is estimated to be 1.25 trillion US dollars, which represents 4 per cent of world gross domestic product (GDP) (Zimmerman, 2006). Disability management is internationally accepted as an effective occupational rehabilitation model utilized within large organizations to address these costs (Harder & Scott 2005; Shrey 1996; Westmorland & Buys 2002).

Perhaps the most enduring definition of disability management is that of Akabas, Gates and Galvin (1992: 2), describing it as a 'workplace prevention and remediation strategy that seeks to prevent disability from occurring or, lacking that, to intervene early following the onset of disability, using coordinated, cost-conscious, quality rehabilitation service that reflects an organizational commitment to continued employment of those experiencing functional work limitations'. This definition highlights the integration of prevention and intervention within an organizational culture of commitment to employees. However, not all systems match this disability management ideal. According to Armsworth-Maw (2002) the success of an injury management[1] system depends on consultation with employees, unions and other stakeholders, as well as implementation with clear policies, plans of action and roles.

Introducing disability management into organizations can involve significant changes to management and work practices, generating resistance to change from employees. In this context organizational climate is a critical factor that cannot be ignored, particularly in efforts to manage occupational stress. Improving the climate, and eventually the

---

1   Whilst injury management and disability management are traditionally different models of occupational rehabilitation, they share common features. In Australia, current injury management models, as described by the occupational rehabilitation industry, are becoming increasingly difficult to distinguish from disability management.

culture, of an organization requires supportive leadership and a shared understanding of goals (Cotton 2004).

Unsuccessful implementation of organizational management strategies to improve the overall health of organizations is attributable to the fact that change did not involve the workers and was too focused on the individual rather than the cultural level (Schurman & Israel 1995). Consequently, strategies to improve worker conditions have often been negated by cultural responses designed to restore equilibrium to the system (Kenny 1995). Similarly, lack of worker involvement in integrating occupational health and safety, workers' compensation and rehabilitation can also reduce the potential success of prevention and rehabilitation within an organization (O'Donnell 2000). Indeed some 'post-mortem' research has indicated that rehabilitation programs fail within specific organizational cultures due to the lack of acceptance of programs by workers (Lambropoulou 1995).

These challenges demonstrate that sustainable disability management programs require employees to be fully involved in their development and implementation (Harder & Scott 2005), and that any organizational intervention must be specific to the context rather than 'off-the-shelf'. Employees at all levels of the organization must be engaged in direct learning activities that allow them to understand the process in their organization at a systemic level and be involved in the development of change strategies (Schurman & Israel 1995). Healthy organizations give more control to workers by encouraging their participation in change management, job redesign, open communication, and understanding of the political or economic constraints within which the organization operates (Beer, Eisenstat & Spector 1990; Jaffe 1995). For interventions to succeed it is critical to pay attention to change processes. Organizational systemic change required to implement disability management depends on good communication, a consensus-based approach and support from all areas of the organization (Kendall et al. 2001).

While disability management is now widely accepted in many countries, there remains a lack of evidence about effective processes for implementing programs within specific organizations using more participatory change processes (Westmorland & Buys 2002). The purpose of this chapter is to describe an organizational case study that utilizes action research (AR) as a strategy to promote meaningful employee involvement in the design and introduction of a disability management program. In particular, it outlines how an AR approach can be used by a large public sector organization to identify issues impacting on occupational stress, injuries and return to work, and to develop effective processes to address these issues.

Action Research and Systems Thinking

To promote health in organizations in a sustainable way, changes must be owned, negotiated and accepted by consensus among members of that organization (Harrison 1999). Stakeholder participation in the design, conduct and interpretation of the research, and the development of solutions, is a key feature of AR. In this context AR is defined as:

> *social research carried out by a team that encompasses a professional action researcher and the members of an organisation, community, or network ('stakeholders') who are seeking to improve their local situation. AR promotes broad participation in the research process and*

supports action leading to a more just, sustainable, or satisfying situation for the stakeholders.
(Greenwood & Levin 2007: 3)

AR provided the methodological basis for working with stakeholders involved with rehabilitation in this case study organization. Specifically, it promoted the developing partnership with the research team based on joint negotiation and decision-making processes. It put researchers and participants on an equal level by involving representatives from the organization in every stage of the research process from initial conceptualization to data collection, data analysis and dissemination of research findings. This level of involvement in decision-making increases the relevance of the research to the participants, as well as the organization's ownership of the findings and solutions. This commitment in turn is expected to facilitate the implementation of solutions because they have been generated from within the organization.

When AR is used within an organizational change context it is important to adopt a systems approach as this can assist with addressing the complexity of large organizations (Emmanuelides 1997; Marion 1999). Systems-thinking is defined as a holistic perspective recognizing the 'whole' as consisting of more than the sum of its parts. Systems consist of multiple factors with complex relationships, which change over time (Checkland 1995; Marion 1999; Senge et al. 1994). Systems-thinking is therefore an ideal framework to support AR in promoting the organizational change required to introduce disability management, a strategy that pervades all aspects of a large organization.

The use of a systems approach in occupational rehabilitation practice and research is not new. There are several examples of large-scale studies that have been conducted in a range of countries that have adopted a systems approach (e.g., Kompier & Cooper 1999; Thornton & Lunt 1997; Wynne & McAnaney 2004). For example, in the area of occupational stress, Kompier and Cooper adopted a systemic approach to study 11 participating European countries, focusing on issues such as policy, legal frameworks and national monitoring systems. Indeed there has been a shift in occupational rehabilitation in recent years to an increasing focus on more systemic interventions that focus on 'whole of organization' responses to injury and disability rather than solutions focused just on the individual (Harder & Scott 2005; Kompier & Cooper 1999; Westmorland & Buys 2002; Wynne & McAnaney 2004).

Within a systems context AR can be employed in two ways. First, by including members of the organization in the research design, data collection and data analysis, a unique insight is developed from a range of perspectives from within the organization, providing a more holistic picture than if the researcher's direct contact was with only one member or one group within the organization. Secondly, the repeated consultation–research–action cycles, which constitute the AR process, promote insight into the organization across the research stages, further developing an understanding of the 'whole' rather than just the point-in-time perspective. The AR cycles allow for research stages that have different goals, such as determining what the issues are, exploring the potential solutions and analyzing the processes.

Case Study

OVERVIEW

The case study involved a large public sector organization involved in delivering an area of emergency services in one Australian state. The organization employs over 10,000 staff in service, administration and leadership roles in a variety of metropolitan, regional and rural areas. Staff experienced high levels of occupational stress and management was concerned that its prevention and occupational rehabilitation processes were not adequately addressing this issue. The organization approached Griffith University to undertake research with the aim of improving its occupational rehabilitation programs. An AR process was implemented in consultation with the organization. Figure 3.1 provides an overview of this process.

As a starting point, the organization and researchers reviewed organizational background data, including workers' compensation statistics, organizational policies, existing reports and survey results. Furthermore, numerous consultation meetings were held with members of the research team and the organization. The background data and consultations were used to develop an understanding of the organizational context and issues concerning stress, injury prevention and rehabilitation. This data also provided the basis for interviews conducted with injured workers, rehabilitation and support providers and decision-makers from across the organization. The goal of the interview stage was to develop an understanding of the organizational issues impacting on injury prevention and rehabilitation. The 65 individual interviews, with injured workers and direct support providers, were thematically analyzed to develop in-depth understanding of the views of participants regarding stress and rehabilitation issues within the organization. Issues identified from the interviews were reported back to the organization in the form of themes with recommendations. The organization then implemented the recommended changes over a period of two years, including a redesign of its rehabilitation systems.

Subsequent meetings established the need to continue with the AR process and it was agreed that the researchers should conduct a series of focus groups in metropolitan, regional and rural remote areas with a range of staff, including injured workers, rehabilitation and support providers and managers. Previously analyzed data was used to

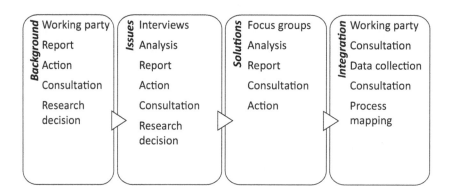

Figure 3.1   Overview of the AR process (background – issues – solutions – integration) used with the case study organization

facilitate the focus groups and to encourage an emphasis on solutions within focus group discussions.

All qualitative data from the individual interviews and the focus groups was transcribed verbatim to ensure an accurate account of the conversations. Thematic analysis, based on the constant comparative method (Babbie 2001), was used to determine the common themes relevant to the organization's occupational stress issues, injury prevention, and occupational rehabilitation systems and practices. This method involves identifying themes from the data by reading and rereading the material. In this study, all transcripts were read and substantive 'segments' (phrases, sentences or paragraphs) were marked. Initially, substantive statements included anything that was relevant to the aims of the research. The transcripts were reread and the theme of each segment noted. As concepts began to emerge, the transcripts were reread to find evidence of the same concept. Substantive segments were organized and reorganized into themes until all thematic areas were defined without significant overlap between themes. Emerging relationships among concepts were noted and the themes were reorganized until these themes and their relationships took shape from the words of all participants. On further rereading, some concepts became irrelevant or merged with others to form more inclusive themes. Systems-thinking provided a conceptual framework for this thematic analysis by maintaining a focus on all factors impacting on occupational stress and occupational rehabilitation within the organization. Formal participant checks were used to corroborate all thematic data analysis.

The results of the six focus groups were summarized and fed back to a project working party, which met on a monthly basis over a period of one year. As part of this process, the working party devised a series of questions and sent them to the management of each area of the organization. The responses returned to the working party were then collated for the purpose of reviewing prevention and rehabilitation processes across the entire organization.

The responses to the questions from the working party were further discussed over several meetings and, in consultation with the organization, these documents were utilized by the researcher to provide the basis for process maps. Process maps focus on the interface between processes and people, showing the steps an organization takes to provide outputs for internal or external 'customers' (Damelio 1996), in this case injured workers. The process maps were used to visually represent the rehabilitation processes affected members go through as reported by leaders from all areas of the organization.

Process-mapping follows a sequence of steps to determine the processes to be mapped, the stakeholders to include, goals, objectives, work steps, roles and responsibilities, timeframes, issues and potential solutions (Dickens 2007). The project working party documents with responses from all nine regions collated under the seven question categories were reviewed using the first seven of Dickens's nine steps for process-mapping. These steps include:

1. determining the level of the map;
2. identifying the stakeholders to provide the data;
3. outlining the major goals and objectives of the process;
4. breaking down the subsets from the big goals and objectives and most important work steps for each subset;

5. exploring the details of each work step, including responsibilities, timeframes and outcomes;
6. identifying the issues and potential reasons for these issues for each work step; and
7. considering potential solutions for the issues identified in Step 6.

These steps were applied to the first three sets of questions from the working party. Question 1 about injury and absence management reporting processes with relevant sections from Questions 4, 5 and 7 determined the level for the first map (Step 1). The issues, potential reasons (Step 6) and potential solutions (Step 7) were determined by the responses to the seven project working party questions and supplemented with additional understanding developed from the focus group data and the background and interview data. Similarly, Question 2 about case management processes determined the level for the second map, and Question 3 about the Early Intervention and Treatment Program determined the level of the third map. Information provided in response to Questions 4 to 7 was used in support of the three maps developed. Steps 8 and 9 of Dickens's process were not completed for any of the questions as these steps were focused on implementing changes, which is outside of the confines of the current study.

The understanding of the common and divergent steps in the injury prevention and intervention processes across the nine regions were then discussed with a process-mapping expert to develop early drafts of the final maps. These maps combined steps across the three sets of questions originally analyzed and evolved into three different maps capturing the injury management processes from initial absence and/or injury and ending with return to work maintenance. The collated project working party documents, as well as the original responses from each of the nine regions (not collated), were continuously revisited by the researcher as the final maps were refined to adequately capture the required details about processes while remaining visually accessible to facilitate further change within the organization.

Themes from the focus group data were linked to these process maps, demonstrating how the discussed issues and solutions related to aspects of the injury/absence process. This approach to data collection is ideal in a large organization where many areas are impacted by prevention and rehabilitation procedures and where the organization is seeking to understand the issues and develop more effective systems. It is the systemic integration of new initiatives and the acknowledgement that processes are interconnected with other components of the organization that makes innovations significant (Senge, cited in Yeung et al. 1999).

SUMMARY OF FINDINGS

A range of findings was obtained from the data sources using the AR process. The background data indicated a high rate of occupational stress, a range of unsuccessful organizational initiatives designed to improve rehabilitation processes and low levels of service knowledge and usage among injured workers, as well as highly variable levels of satisfaction with the services used. As a consequence of these early findings, the organization and the researchers agreed to explore the issues further.

Interviews Exploring the Issues

In 2004, 65 individual interviews were conducted with injured workers and rehabilitation coordinators to explore the issues associated with occupational stress and occupational rehabilitation from the perspective of members across the organization. The interviews were thematically analyzed and the findings included issues associated with job characteristics, rehabilitation procedures, stress management, training and knowledge, organizational culture and policy-practice gaps.

Some job characteristics were found to impede rehabilitation. Participants described their work as overwhelming and stressful due to lack of resources and job conditions. Organizational factors were reported to be at least partially causing injuries and impacting on return to work processes. In addition, participants in rehabilitation coordinator roles described a chronic lack of time and resources to meet system requirements and to facilitate rehabilitation and return to work processes.

In terms of rehabilitation procedures, participants described a lack of contact between injured/absent workers and the organization. This led to withdrawal from the job and reduced motivation to return to work. Poor contact between external service providers (psychologists and doctors) and the organization also impacted on rehabilitation outcomes. Participants who had experienced a mental health issue reported bullying and threats from direct supervisors, lack of support from the workplace, stigma, lack of confidentiality and disempowerment. Middle managers in turn reported a lack of support from higher management levels, which made them feel caught between assisting injured workers and the demands of the organization.

Participants described poor stress management practices within the organization. The organization tended to seek the cause of stress within the affected individual instead of within the organization. Stressed or injured workers feared that claiming for psychological injury would be detrimental to their career prospects, but limited support was available unless a claim was lodged. This conflict meant that opportunities for early intervention were lost.

Participants reported inadequate knowledge of available services, thus limiting access to these supports. Human Service Officers[2] were described as lacking understanding of the substantive job roles of workers. Participants also felt that peer support officers[3] required more skills to enable them to deal with complex conditions. Similarly, it was reported that rehabilitation coordinators received insufficient training to provide effective assistance to injured workers. The rehabilitation process within the organization was described as being 'quick-fix focused'. Staff in support roles had a high turnover rate, resulting in a lack of consistency and accountability as well as unfavourable rehabilitation coordination.

Fear of stigmatization was cited as a barrier to claim lodgement and seeking rehabilitation assistance. Some support providers within the organization advised injured workers to seek help outside of the organization to avoid damage to the career of the affected individual. Opportunities for early intervention were jeopardized as a consequence of extended periods away from the workplace due to fear of stigmatization.

---

2   Human service officers are psychologists or social workers working for the organization, who provide support to employees with complex and psychological problems. The human service officer role is a substantive position.

3   Peer support officers are employees who provide initial and informal support to colleagues. They receive minimal training and perform this role in addition to their substantive position.

All participants reported a significant discrepancy between policy and practice. They described as 'empty policies' the many apparent policies in theory, which were absent from practice. There was also a lack of consistency described between services across different geographical areas of the organization, especially those outside of the metropolitan areas.

Focus Groups Suggesting Solutions

Six different focus groups representing workers from across all levels and areas of the organization were facilitated utilizing previously gained understanding about issues from the individual interviews. These focus groups generated seven major themes grouped into two meta-themes: relationships-focused and process-focused themes. Communication was mentioned within all of the thematic contexts, but was most strongly raised in the four relationship themes that included culture, trust and ownership, information and understanding, and external relationships. Although less emphasized, communication was also a significant aspect of the three process themes that included resources, selection processes and prevention and rehabilitation systems. Figure 3.2 provides an overview of the themes.

The first meta-theme focused on relationships. The *culture* theme included suggestions about the general communication style of the organization and communication issues between different parts and levels of the organization. *Trust and ownership* raised similar communication issues, but at a more specific and individual level. This included communication between superiors and subordinates in specific contexts. The *information and understanding* theme related to information provision, including training, and the need for more information about the prevention and rehabilitation of physical and psychological injury and illness for different types of employees. Finally, *external relationships* emphasized communication with organizations, communities and individuals outside of the organization, particularly with regard to prevention and rehabilitation.

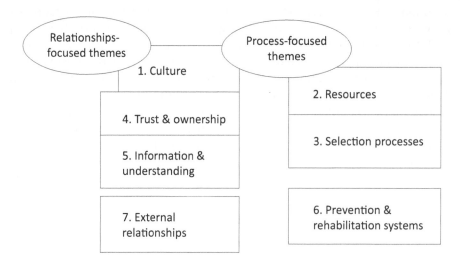

Figure 3.2   Relationships-focused themes and process-focused theme

The second meta-theme focused on processes. The *resources* theme, whilst focused on the availability and provision of resources and the resulting impact on prevention and rehabilitation, included communication in making decisions, about resource acquisition, transparent to employees. Similarly, *selection processes* was focused on the systems and processes for recruiting people into the organization, as well as recruiting existing employees into support roles and promoting employees to leadership roles. Within these systems and processes, communication played a significant role in creating transparency about selection and promotion processes. Finally, *prevention and rehabilitation systems* focused on systems and processes, but depended on communication about those processes to gain support from members.

Process Maps Facilitating Data Integration

Themes generated by the focus groups were included in working party discussions conducted by the organization. The working party developed seven sets of questions about injury and absence reporting, case management, the early intervention treatment program, injury management data collection, absence management, rehabilitation and return to work coordinators, and sent them to the nine major areas of the organization. In line with the AR approach, the researcher utilized process-mapping to present the written responses to these questions provided by management in a practically useful way that facilitated knowledge transfer of the findings into the workplace. The collated descriptive responses were analyzed using the sequence of steps described by Dickens (2007) and developed into process maps commencing with the initial absence and/or injury and ending with return-to-work maintenance.

Pre-injury/absence data could not be presented in the form of a process map. This was partly because the questions asked by the working party were more focused on injury management processes than prevention processes. However, there was useful information about injury and illness prevention and about contextual factors affecting rehabilitation and return-to-work processes. For example, the written responses to the questions asked by the working party and the focus group themes provided information about selection and training of people for key support roles, such as human service officers, peer support officers, rehabilitation coordinators,[4] and injury management coordinators.[5] These findings indicated that most areas provided no rehabilitation coordinator training other than the initial training.

The pre-injury/absence data provided the contextual background to the process maps and was linked with relevant quotes from the focus groups. For example, all of the focus groups raised the impact of general staffing on pre-injury/absence processes, especially on workload and injury/stress prevention measures. One participant stated:

> *Staffing at number one. Big ascent for stress levels because you're doing double workload and you're not getting lunch breaks, you're starting … I'm an administrator, I'll be in there at 7.30 and my first and only break will be lunch at 2.15, if I'm lucky, without a break. I mean I have*

---

4   Rehabilitation coordinators are registered by the workers' compensation authority to manage compensable injuries from within the workplace. Many rehabilitation coordinators perform this role in addition to their substantive position.

5   Injury management coordinators are responsible for injury management across a major area of the organization. They supervise rehabilitation coordinators and take responsibility for complex injury cases.

to stop in the middle of serving someone if I'm on the counter to go, to go to the toilet. Like, I'm 'excuse me', run to the toilet, you know. … we just seem to always make do with bloody, lack of public resource for staffing as we're trying to do two or three jobs at once and if you fail or stuff up, the [Organization] give you dirt because you stuffed up and they don't care about you're trying to handle three things at once.

Within the same sub-theme about general staffing issues, focus groups also suggested solutions, such as the following example about reducing staff turn over:

When a person leaves they have to go through a process of unloading. … there doesn't seem to be any mechanism to review that and to come up with any solutions to any problems that are consistent to the hundreds of people that are leaving. So, you need to look at it from within.

The overall process of managing an injury or other absence once it occurred was presented in a sequence of three maps: reporting, responding and intervening. The reporting process commenced with the absence and/or injury event and ended with a decision about making initial contact with the affected worker. The responding process commenced with the seeking of relevant information about the needs of the affected worker and ended in referral processes initiating interventions. The intervention process commenced with relevant intervention options, such as rehabilitation case management, and ended with return-to-work maintenance and resolution of the issues.

The maps show that there are divergent and parallel paths and that the affected worker can exit from the rehabilitation process with or without resolution at five points in the process. The solid lines indicate clear links from one step to the next, whereas the broken lines indicate unclear links based on the responses from the nine major areas of the organization. It was noted that the most clearly defined components of the process were associated with workers' compensation eligibility determination (Map 2) through to return to work (Map 3). Whilst services were available to workers not claiming or eligible for compensation, the processes were much less clearly defined. Regardless of the worker's compensation status, the process became poorly defined after the initial return-to-work, with significant questions raised around return to work maintenance and final resolution of the injury, illness and related issues.

Each of the five identified steps on Map 1, the reporting process, were linked with themes from the focus groups. For example, *information and understanding*, which related to understanding stress, injury, prevention and rehabilitation, impacted on the injury/absence experience of affected workers and played a role in the recognition of early signs of stress. One focus group participant suggested the need for broader awareness of the causes of stress than just critical incidents:

The other thing is, too, … which also needs to be looked at in the big picture is that stress may not just come from the workplace. But that it can be from home, it can be anything and work or combined and not just say one trigger, and of them the trigger is not a major event. … human beings are designed to handle major catastrophes, we can handle earthquakes and plane crashes and all that sort of thing, but then if you drop the soap twice in the shower you come apart.

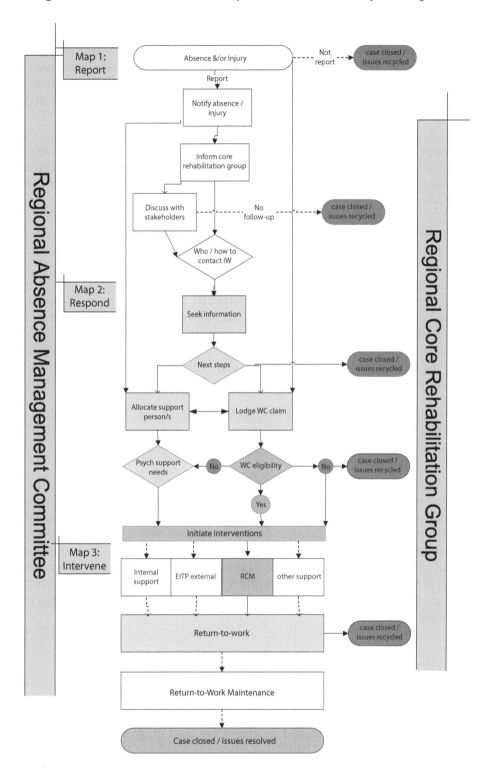

Figure 3.3   Combined process maps developed from the working party documents

Map 2, the responding process, provided an example of a theme from the focus group data demonstrating issues and potential solutions. People in support roles working directly with injured workers reported documentation requirements and unclear role boundaries as limiting factors in initiating interventions. For example, the following quote from the sub-theme, support role staffing and resources, emphasized the need for more dedicated rehabilitation coordinators to manage workers' compensation cases:

> *You cannot tell me that anybody that has another job can do the rehab properly because I'm telling it now, I cannot do it myself and I'm doing it full time. There lies the problem because somewhere along the line, somebody's butt's going to get kicked through the Court for not doing up the case notes or for not getting the document signed in order.*

The three steps on Map 3, the intervention process, were also linked with quotes from the focus group data. For example, delayed responses from specialists, doctors who are too busy to have contact with the rehabilitation coordinators, and doctors' lack of understanding of work factors were discussed as issues impacting on return to work processes. Participants from rural areas in particular suggested the use of doctors who understand the organizational context, and questioned the impact of long-term injured worker relationships with local doctors and short-term transience of doctors in some areas. It was suggested that a local single point of contact within the organization might promote the working relationship with doctors. This quote, for example, is from the *external stakeholder relationships* sub-theme, service providers:

> *There's been an actual case where the GP [doctor] actually gave the worker two months off. When that worker saw a psychiatrist, the psychiatrist actually said the best thing for this person is to remain at work, not to be given complete removal from the workplace.*

This visual presentation of the process maps linked with themes from the focus groups was designed to facilitate the organization's capacity to implement change in manageable pieces, directly responding to suggestions from focus group participants who represented members of the organization across all areas and levels. The findings from the four stages of the AR process used with the case study organization were integrated to develop a picture of the 'whole' across a period of several years. It effectively identified issues and potential solutions relating to injury and illness prevention and rehabilitation and represented these in an easily understandable format to facilitate knowledge transfer back into the organization.

Conclusion

AR is an ideal approach to developing a disability management strategy in a large organization through promoting employee involvement in the identification of issues impacting on injury prevention and rehabilitation, and progressing relevant solutions that can be embedded in organizational practices. In doing so, AR addresses some of the challenges associated with garnering employee commitment to change through valuing their contributions to the research process and the transfer of findings to the workplace to promote change. The AR process therefore also promotes the shared understanding required to improve organizational climate as suggested by Cotton (2004).

Organizations that engage in this type of research are likely to have recognized a need for change and probably experience a level of dissatisfaction among employees. The interviews and focus group stages in this case study demonstrate that people are more willing to be open and honest with external researchers who are bound by university codes of research ethics than they would be if the research were conducted by their own organization. An example of this can be seen in the focus group theme *trust and ownership*, which supports the notion that workers need to own and accept changes to achieve sustainable improvements in organizational health and successful disability management programs (Harder & Scott 2005; Harrison 1999). The independent research process allowed interviewees to be open about issues, including organizational factors reported to be causing injury, stress and return to work barriers. The research process also allowed focus group participants to discuss suggested solutions to identified issues more freely, promoting more active involvement in generating change.

Researchers are often criticized because their findings are not transferrable or accessible to the wider community. For knowledge transfer to occur there needs to be a strong link between the knowledge producers and the knowledge users (Williams et al. 2008). Through engagement of organizational stakeholders AR maximizes the opportunities for change by implementing strategies to identify and address key issues facing the organization (de Lancer Julnes & Holzer 2001). The AR research process used in this case study confirmed this view as the organization adopted most of the changes recommended by the researchers.

It is important to recognize that effective knowledge transfer is not merely dissemination of findings. Instead, it involves integration of these findings into practice through collaboration between the knowledge producers and knowledge users (Williams et al. 2008). In this context it involves prolonged engagement between the parties in an iterative process (Choi 2005) of mutual learning and solution finding (Williams et al. 2008). This case study affirms this process as researchers and organizational representatives worked closely together through four stages of data collection, negotiation and change in relation to disability management practice.

The AR process therefore adds to the body of knowledge about how disability management systems can be developed and implemented within organizations, addressing the gap between disability management research and its application. This benefits research in translating the ideals and theory associated with disability management into practice within a specific organizational context and also highlights areas where further theory-building is required. The process maps, for example, were a response to the question of how to make the themes derived from interviews and focus groups practically useful to the organization. These maps may also be beneficial to research conducted within other organizations that are grappling with questions about the embedding of knowledge derived from employees into practice.

By combining internal organizational knowledge with external analysis of the organizational context AR promotes teamwork. This type of research has been found to promote inter-institutional and inter-organizational collaboration and foster organizational learning and innovation, especially when the interaction is long term (Ortiz et al. 2008). This process has generated solutions that the case study organization might not have seen from within, thereby providing a broader and more accurate picture of the required changes. The depth and breadth of issues and potential solutions identified through the interviews and the focus groups provided the organization with practically relevant data linked with the existing evidence base in published literature and translated into specific suggestions for organizational change.

The integration of internal organizational knowledge with external analysis of the organizational context also gave the researcher an insight they would not have had from outside. Two key principles of participatory research include the utilization of local understanding and participation (Genat 2009; van der Riet 2008). The researcher was a participant in the organization's project working party, allowing an intimate insight into the deliberations of the organization with regard to its injury and illness prevention and rehabilitation issues.

Communication is often a key problem in large organizations, which impacts their capacity for change (Kendall et al. 2001). The case study organization was no exception, with communication identified as a significant issue at each stage of data collection, especially in the themes derived from the interviews and the focus groups. Communication between parties is a central part of the AR approach. It therefore provided a vehicle for stakeholders within and external to the organization to work closely together to develop solutions, thereby promoting the translation of research into practice.

Organizations will continue to be confronted with the challenge of managing illness, injury and disability, particularly with the aging of the workforce and the increasing demands on organizations to address employee health issues. It is incumbent on legislators and policymakers not to impose a one-size-fits-all approach to managing these issues. Localized solutions to these challenges will be required, necessitating organizations to develop strategies to accurately identify the issues and develop responses that are effective, contextually appropriate and accepted by workers. AR is one approach to helping organizations to respond to these challenges.

Bibliography

Akabas, S., Gates, L. & Galvin, D. (1992). *Disability Management*. New York: AMACOM.

Armsworth-Maw, D. (2002). Getting Back to Business. (Rehabilitation). *The Safety & Health Practitioner* 20(9), 28–30.

Babbie, E. (2001). *The Practice of Social Research*. Belmont CA: Wadsworth.

Beer, M., Eisenstat, R.A. & Spector, B. (1990). *The Critical Path for Corporate Renewal*. Harvard: Harvard Business School Press.

Checkland, P. (1995). Systems Theory and Management Thinking. In K. Ellis, A. Gregory, B. Mears-Young & G. Ragsdell (eds), *Critical Issues in Systems Theory and Practice*. New York: Plenum Press.

Choi, B. (2005). Understanding the Basic Principles of Knowledge Translation. *Journal of Epistemology and Community Health* 59(2), 93.

Cotton, P. (2004). *Developing an Optimal Organisational Climate*. Paper delivered at Towards Safest Workplaces II ComCare Conference, Canberra, March 2004.

Damelio, R. (1996). *The Basics of Process Mapping*. Productivity Press: USA.

de Lancer Julnes, P. & Holzer, M. (2001). Promoting the Utilization of Performance Measures in Public Organizations: An Empirical Study of Factors Affecting Adoption and Implementation. *Public Administration Review* 61(6), 693–708.

Dickens, M. (2007). Process Mapping. *Giants* 3(3), 38.

Emmanuelides, P. (1997). Corporate Transformation in Large Industrial Enterprises: Common Emerging Themes. In A. Bhambri & A. Sinatra (eds), *Corporate Transformation*. Massachusetts: Kluwer Academic Publishers.

Genat, B. (2009). Building Emergent Situated Knowledges in Participatory Action Research. *Action Research* 7(1), 101–15.

Greenwood, D. & Levin, M. (2007). *Introduction to Action Research*. (2nd ed). Sage: California.

Harder, H. & Scott, L. (2005). *Comprehensive Disability Management*. Edinburgh: Elsevier Science Limited.

Harrison, D. (1999). Social System Intervention. In E. Perkins, I. Simnett & L. Wright (eds), *Evidence-Based Health Promotion*. Chichester: John Wiley & Sons.

Jaffe, D. (1995). The Healthy Company: Research Paradigms for Personal and Organizational Health. In S. Sauter & L. Murphy (eds), *Organizational Risk Factors for Job Stress*. Washington DC: American Psychological Association.

Kendall, E., Murphy, P., Bursnall, S. & O'Neill, V. (2001). *Containing the Costs of Occupational Stress: A New Approach to Identifying, Defining, Preventing and Managing Stress in the Workplace*. Perth: Workcover WA.

Kenny, D.I. (1995). Stressed Organizations and Organizational Stressors: A Systemic Analysis of Workplace Injury. *International Journal of Stress Management* 2(4), 181–96.

Kompier, M. & Cooper, C. (1999). Stress Prevention: European Countries and European Cases Compared. In M. Kompier & C. Cooper (eds), *Preventing Stress, Improving Productivity*. New York, Routledge.

Lambropoulou, E. (1995). The Autopoietic View of Prison Organization and of Correctional Reforms. In K. Ellis, A. Gregory, B. Mears-Young & G. Ragsdell (eds), *Critical Issues in Systems Theory and Practice*. New York: Plenum Press.

Marion, R. (1999). *The Edge of Organization: Chaos and Complexity Theories of Formal Social Systems*. London: Sage Publications.

O'Donnell, C. (2000). Motor Accident and Workers' Compensation Insurance Design for High-Quality Health Outcomes and Cost Containment. *Disability and Rehabilitation* 22, 88–96.

Ortiz, O., Frias, G., Ho, R., Cisneros, H., Nelson, R., Castillo, R., Orrego, R., Pradel, W., Alcazar, J. & Bazan, M. (2008). Organizational Learning through Participatory Research: CIP and CARE in Peru. *Agriculture and Human Values* 25(3), 419–31.

Schurman, S. & Israel, B. (1995). Redesigning Work Systems to Reduce Stress: A Participatory Action Research Approach to Creating Change. In L. Murphy, J. Hurrell, S. Sauter & G. Keita (eds), *Job Stress Interventions*. Washington DC: American Psychological Association.

Senge, P., Ross, R., Smith, B., Roberts, C. & Kleiner, A. (1994). *The 5th Discipline Fieldbook: Strategies and Tools for Building a Learning Organization*. London: Nicholas Brealey Publishing.

Shrey, D. (1996). Disability Management in Industry: The New Paradigm in Injured Worker Rehabilitation. *Disability and Rehabilitation* 18(8), 408–14.

Thornton, P. & Lunt, N. (1997). *Employment Policies for Disabled People in Eighteen Countries: A Review*. York: Social Policy Research Unit, University of York.

van der Riet, M. (2008). Participatory Research and the Philosophy of Social Science: Beyond the Moral Imperative. *Qualitative Inquiry* 14(4), 546–65.

Westmorland, M. & Buys, N. (2002). Disability Management in a Sample of Australian Self-Insured Companies. *Disability and Rehabilitation* 24(14), 746–54.

Williams, A., Holden, B., Krebs, P., Muhajarine, N., Waygood, K., Randall, J. & Spence, C. (2008). Knowledge Translation Strategies in a Community-University Partnership: Examining Local Quality of Life (QOL). *Social Indicators Research* 85, 111–25.

Wynne, R. & McAnaney, D. (2004). *Employment and Disability: Back to Work Strategies*. Dublin: European Foundation for the Improvement of Living and Working Conditions.

Yeung, A., Ulrich, D., Nason, S. & Von Glinow, M. (1999). *Organizational Learning Capability*. New York: Oxford University Press.

Zimmerman, W. (2006). Disability Management in a Global Context. *Proceedings of the Getting Better Sooner Conference*, WorkCover SA, Adelaide, 27 September.

4 *The Role of Workplace Social Support in Disability Management*

GREGORY C. MURPHY AND MARY A. O'HARE

Introduction

The disability management approach to the prevention of injury and the delivery of effective, workplace-focused rehabilitation services aims, *inter alia*, to re-establish a positive, trusting worker-workplace relationship, both prior to and subsequent to, any work injury. Employer-led rehabilitation interventions, based on positive worker-employer relationships, were a fundamental principle for the creation of effective return-to-work programs for those with ill-health conditions, both work-related and non-work-related.

As a term, disability management (or more specifically workplace disability management) emerged in publications in the 1980s. An early reference to the term by Jarvikoski and Lahelma (1980) in a World Rehabilitation Fund monograph entitled *Early Rehabilitation in the Workplace* was followed in key publications in the mid-1980s, such as Galvin's (1986) review in the *Annual Review of Rehabilitation*, entitled 'Employer-Based Disability Management and Rehabilitation Programs' and the publication of a special issue of the *Journal of Applied Rehabilitation Counselling* (1986, vol. 17) entitled 'Disability Management and Rehabilitation in the Workplace'.

By the start of the 1990s the concept had consolidated its position as confirmed by the special issue of *Rehabilitation Counselling Bulletin* (1991, vol. 34), entitled 'Disability Management and Industrial Rehabilitation', and the publication in 1995 of Shrey and Lacerte's edited volume *Principles and Practices of Disability Management in Industry*. This volume was important not just because it provided a comprehensive overview of optimal disability management services for injured employees, but because it also promoted the concept of the 'occupational bond' (i.e., employer-led rehabilitation interventions based on positive worker-employer relationships) as a fundamental principle for the creation of effective return-to-work programs for those with ill-health conditions.

One reason for the emergence of the employer-driven disability management approach in the mid-1980s was the desire of employers to 'reclaim control over injury' and its sequelae (see Murphy & Foreman 1993). An important (negative) feature of traditional occupational rehabilitation services was that, with services being overwhelmingly delivered by external parties such as health professionals and case managers from approved providers or workers' compensation authorities, injured workers too often found themselves 'bonded to, or dependent upon, treatment providers, attorneys and disability benefits' (Shrey & Lacertes 1995: 7).

This chapter reviews literature on a topic – social support – that has been relatively neglected in the disability management literature and presents findings from studies investigating the relationship between social support and post-injury return to work. Because work behaviour is heavily influenced by social factors, disability management researchers and practitioners need to be well informed about the way that social contacts can influence (both positively and negatively) post-injury work behaviours, including return to work. While it is acknowledged that disability management aims to enhance many indices of organizational performance, and not just return to work (RTW), high RTW rates following injury are important because salary replacement costs are the single most expensive component of any occupational injury scheme – hence, poor RTW rates lower not just productivity within a particular enterprise, but, if widespread, threaten the viability of employer-funded injury compensation schemes, as detailed in Murphy & Foreman (2008).

Benefits of the Disability Management Approach

Since the early presentation of examples of the disability management approach in practice (e.g., Beaudway 1986) a series of research investigations (principally by Habeck and colleagues and by Amick and colleagues) have been conducted, which aimed to illustrate the practically significant effect-size benefits that can accrue to employing organizations that adopt a disability management approach. In one of the first multivariate studies of the correlation of disability management practices with workers' compensation performance indices, Habeck et al. (1991) demonstrated, by use of discriminant function analysis, that certain employer approaches with respect to injury prevention, early intervention and rehabilitation (as assessed by the Michigan Disability Prevention survey) were reliably associated with lower workers' compensation claims rates that were a tenth of those of similar industry organizations that used fewer of various DM elements analyzed. Amick and colleagues (Amick et al. 2000) went further in demonstrating the effect size of particular disability management policies and practices by using logistic regression to estimate the improvements to return-to-work rates that occurred when employers adopted DM policies and practices: for employees whose workplaces had adopted a DM approach, the odds of being back at work six months after surgery for carpel tunnel were increased by more than 120 per cent.

Initially, authors writing about workplace disability management sought to explain the rationale for the approach and to demonstrate its potential contribution to improved injury management performance by the presentation of organizational case study material (e.g., Munrowd & Beecher 1986; Shrey & Hursh 1999). While impressive results were reported from the introduction of the DM approach in various organizational settings, the required research findings from well-controlled studies aimed at demonstrating the effect sizes associated with the introduction of various aspects of DM policy and practice were slow to emerge. The influential pioneering multivariate study of Habeck and colleagues (Habeck et al. 1991), which demonstrated the association between higher rates of DM practice and lower rates of workplace injury claims, was a cross-sectional survey study with obvious limitations in terms of the study's capacity to demonstrate the effects to be expected from the introduction of DM practices. Since the start of the 2000s, however, DM research studies with stronger designs have emerged. A prominent high-quality DM research program has been led by Amick and colleagues (see, for example, Amick et al. 2000; and Williams et al. 2007). Amick's research program has had two foci: first, the development of a psychometrically sound measure (the occupational personality questionnaire (OPP questionnaire)) that comprehensively covered the organizational policies and practices that embodied the DM approach; second, the use of study designs that went beyond point-in-time correlational studies by incorporating at least two measurement points (baseline measures of organizational policies and practices; and post-surgery measures of social role functioning, for example). These two features contribute to the internal validity of Amick's findings in respect of the independent contribution of organizational (disability management) factors to improved employee work role functioning. A comprehensive listing of recent disability management studies is reported in Wallis (2010).

Disability Management and the Occupational Bond

However, while researchers have attempted to establish a more clear definition of the components of the DM approach (see Currier et al. 2001), and to develop better measures of that approach (see Amick et al. 2000), there has been almost no research into the specific nature of the occupational bond and the pathways by which certain salient interpersonal features of the work environment may contribute (positively or negatively) to key rehabilitation outcomes such as return to work. This chapter aims to partly fill this gap by reviewing the literature on workplace social support for those suffering disabling injury and that support's contribution to improved return-to-work rates. Prior to the presentation of the literature review, however, we briefly present a summary of the social support construct and its role generally in influencing health and rehabilitation outcomes, and the theoretical and methodological shortcomings that have impeded progress in this field.

Social Support: A Central Construct for Understanding the Relationship between Health and Rehabilitation Outcomes

During the past three decades the concept of social support has become popular with health and rehabilitation researchers. Veiel and Baumann (1992) concluded that, measured by the sheer volume of publications, social support had joined stress and coping as one of the three most important constructs in current health psychology research. Cobb's (1976) Presidential Address to the American Psychosomatic Society seems to have aroused much initial interest by health and rehabilitation researchers in the topic of social support. Cobb's main conclusion from his peer review of the social support literature was that social support may reduce the amount of medication required, accelerate recovery and facilitate compliance with prescribed medical regimens (Cobb 1976: 300). The wide-spanning set of benefits posited to flow from social support made it particularly attractive to rehabilitation researchers seeking to explain such post-injury outcomes as quality of life, rehabilitation progress and even vocational status.

Much of the impetus for the popularity of social support as a construct central to a comprehensive understanding of many phenomena of interest to public health researchers has derived from its putative role in mediating the impact of stress (see Cohen & Wills 1985 for a landmark review of this topic). Stress theory in its original form (see Selye 1950) regarded the individual as a (relatively) passive organism reacting to adverse environmental conditions. The introduction of a construct such as social support seemed to extend our understanding of individual differences in response to certain environmental stressors by postulating a beneficial environmental (social) condition that could modulate and perhaps even compensate for the effects of environmental stress. Major reviews of the social support and stress literature which appeared in the 1980s (for example Cohen & Wills 1985; Gottlieb 1983) indicated that people who have socially supportive relationships are less likely to experience a wide range of negative physical and psychological consequences, and also that social support can play a buffering role in protecting persons from the pathogenic influence of stressful events. Suls, in 1982, confidently summarized the 1970s social support literature as arguing that:

> ... persons who are part of a social network are less negatively affected by stressful life problems and are less likely to fall ill. It is also widely maintained that naturally existing support systems facilitate coping and recovery if the person should succumb to some form of illness. (Suls 1982: 255)

Suls concluded his summary of the early social support literature by asserting that there was 'broad consensus about the benefits of social support' (Suls 1982: 255), although he did acknowledge that there was considerable diversity of opinion about how it should be defined or operationalized.

Factors Influencing the Relationship between Social Support and Health Outcomes

Subsequent to the encouraging tone of the early writings about social support as a moderator of life stress (for example, Cobb 1976) and the basic conclusions of the mid-1980s reviews of the positive health benefits of social support (Cohen & Wills 1985), authors since the 1990s, however, have been more restricted in their claims about the health benefits of social support. Thus, Schwarzer and Leppin (1992: 435) argue that 'social relationships might have rather inconsistent effects on health'. The reasons for the inconsistent findings alluded to by Schwarzer and Leppin are, of course, many, including both theoretical and measurement matters.

> One of the main reasons for such inconsistent findings might be due to the considerable heterogeneity of existing theoretical formulations, including a lack of clarity as well as deficits in measurement. Instruments which are psychometrically unsound or which have evolved from different concepts of social support produce diverse results. (Schwarzen & Leppin 1992: 435).

Much of the more recent social support literature has attempted to explain the inconsistent health correlates of social support by examining the psychometric adequacy of the various measures of social support used in particular studies (see for example,

Veiel & Baumann 1992; Pierce, Sarason & Sarason 1991). One of the most important measurement issues raised, and one particularly of concern to the more sociologically oriented researchers such as House (see House, Umberson & Landis 1988), has been the importance of distinguishing between objective as opposed to subjective measures of social support. That is to say, the importance of measuring not just functional social support (that is, the perceived function and quality of social relationships) but also structural support (that is, measures of social support network size and density). The importance of separately measuring these aspects of the social environment is based on the contention that these are independent constructs with very little intercorrelation in particular situations (see Schwarzer & Leppin 1992 for a more detailed discussion of this point).

Complementary to the larger literature devoted to the psychometric adequacy of various measures of social support, a relatively small number of papers (for example, Kaplan & Toshima 1990; Rook 1984) have addressed theoretical matters in an attempt to explain why certain social interactions might lead to negative outcomes in particular situations. Rook (1984) used social-exchange theory (Homans 1974) to guide her research into the negative impact of social interaction. Rook was one of the first to strongly criticize social support researchers for tending to equate social interaction with social support. Based on social-exchange theory, Rook argued that because social relations entail costs as well as rewards, positive and negative social outcomes should be examined for their relative effects on individual well-being:

> *Frequent interaction with friends and neighbours is interpreted as a high level of social support. The possibility that social interaction might occasionally involve disputes, embarrassment, envy, invasion of privacy or other negative outcomes is not addressed. An overlooked risk that lies in asking respondents only to tell us how many friends they have, or how often they socialize with others, is that we miss a potentially important dimension of their social lives: the troublesome aspects of relating to others. (Rook 1984: 1097)*

Consistent with her theoretical orientation, Rook distinguished between positive and negative outcomes and thus, when studying the experience of widowhood, she measured both supportive ties and problematic social ties. She found: (a) that positive and negative interpersonal experiences were relatively independent of each other in her sample of 120 widowed women; and (b) that the number of social problems reported was significantly related to lower well-being, whereas the number of social supports reported was unrelated to well-being.

In a later paper, Rook (1992: 157) described as 'an emerging literature' the relatively small body of research that reported on the problematic as well as the supportive aspects of social bonds. From a research perspective, Rook's papers are important because they emphasize that social interactions, even when measured solely from the affected individual's point of view, need to be measured more comprehensively, and that, in the case of an individual with a chronic condition, some recurring interactions relating to health might be negative as opposed to positive in their impact on indices of individual well-being.

Kaplan and Toshima (1990) proposed that social relationships might have different functions for the chronically ill than they do for other members of the population, and described a 'functional effects' model of social support. According to their model, social support can be confidently expected to enhance only mental health outcomes and it cannot be assumed that a patient's social interactions will produce correlated, positive improvements in functional outcomes, that is, in those self-care behaviours relevant to the chronic conditions at hand. One of the model's potentially most useful contributions to the conceptualization of social support effects is its premise that general self-report measures (such as perceived well-being) are inadequate as dependent measures in health-related social support research, because, argue Kaplan and Toshima, a social environment can have negative health-behaviour influences even while providing emotional satisfaction. While the present authors do not accept Kaplan and Toshima's proposition that social support has distinctive effects for the chronically ill, we do agree with their argument that negative functional outcomes can occur when a patient's social environment supports behaviour which is detrimental to health or rehabilitation, or discourages behaviour which may be health-promoting such as return to work behaviour (see McKee-Ryan et al. 2005).

During the last decade (2000 to 2010), research has continued to investigate the link between social support and diverse health outcomes, such as recovery from medical procedures (Petrie 2004), exposure to traumatic stressors (Borja, Callahan & Rambo 2009) and cardiovascular and immune functioning (Uchino 2006). Uchino (2006) has suggested that future social support research should investigate the physiological processes and biological pathways that underlie the relationship between social support and health outcomes. For example, Eisenberger et al. (2007) report that greater social support diminishes cortisol reactivity following exposure to a stressor. However, from an applied perspective, little research has focused on the role of social support in workplace rehabilitation programs, despite the established association between social support and reduced rates of morbidity and mortality.

Work-Related Social Support: Literature Search Findings

An extensive electronic search for studies of work-related social support following injury was undertaken. In order to identify studies with more robust findings, the search terms deliberately excluded studies of employees with mild psychological injuries, including those with pain conditions, and concentrated on studies of workers with disabling traumatic injuries. The following databases were searched: Pubmed; PsychINFO; AMI (Australian Medical Index); Humanities and Social Sciences Collection Informit e-library; and Journals at Ovid Full Text. Databases were searched using the following keywords: rehabilitation outcome; vocational outcome; employment (status); return to work (RTW); quality of life; social integration; social support; social network; severe injury; traumatic brain injury; spinal injury; multiple injuries; orthopaedic injury; lower extremity (injury); upper extremity (injury); amputation, (Level 1) Trauma Centre; and prospective. Spelling derivatives of the search terms were also used. Initially, the search was confined to prospective-design studies, but was later widened to include all study designs. Initially, also, the search was restricted to articles published from 1990 to 2009. This 20-year catchment period was selected to ensure comprehensive coverage of research in the emerging field of disability management. However, due to the scarcity of studies that assessed the influence of social and workplace support on rehabilitation outcomes, the timeframe was widened to include research from 1980 onwards.

The electronic search located 2,230 entries from Pubmed, 530 entries from PsychINFO, 41 entries from AMI, 23 entries from Humanities and Social Sciences Collection and 790 entries from Journals at Ovid Full Text. Study titles and abstracts were scanned for relevance. Of the 3,614 entries, 3,533 were discarded and 81 were retained. The reference lists of retained articles were also examined to identify missed articles. In addition, individual journals, e.g., *Archives of Physical Medicine and Rehabilitation*, were searched for relevant missed articles. A total of 155 articles were assessed as relevant. A further cull, in which RTW was used as the sole criterion variable, resulted in the retention of 52 articles for the present analysis. All but three of these articles were published from 1990 to 2008.

Frequency of Peer-Reviewed Studies that Assessed Variables Associated with RTW Following Traumatic Injury

Table 4.1 presents the frequency of peer-reviewed studies included in the present literature review that examined the relationship between five classes of variables and the outcome measure 'return to work'. Only empirical studies are listed in the table (reviews and dissertations were excluded). When presenting the tabular results, predictors of RTW were given precedence over correlates. Some studies investigated multiple categories of variables and are, therefore, listed in more than one category. (Please contact the authors for details of references relevant to each class of variable.)

Table 4.1   Frequency of peer-reviewed studies[a] that assessed the variables associated with RTW following injury

Variables	Total	Predictors	Correlates	Descriptive
Demographic	22	12	9	1
Injury and Functional Independence	34	19	14	1
Psychosocial (excluding Social Support)	16	8	8	0
Non-Workplace Social Support	2	2	0	0
Workplace Social Support	8	4	1	3
Grand Total	82[b]	45	32	5

[a] Only empirical studies are listed in this table.

[b] The Grand Total figure exceeds 52 (the total number of identified relevant studies) due to the inclusion of variables from more than one category in some studies.

The outcome measure – return to work – was interpreted broadly to include the following terms: return to work, days lost, and work absence at various post-injury follow-up times (such as 6 months or longer). Predictors and correlates of return to work were classified into five main groups of variables as follows:

- *Demographic variables* included: age, gender, marital status, educational level and geographical place of residence (i.e., rural versus urban).

- *Injury and functional independence variables* included: injury severity, functional independence, impairment, disability, motor index score, neuropsychological impairment, length of treatment, length of hospitalization and cognitive functioning.
- *Psychosocial variables (excluding social support)* included the following variables: personality traits, sense of coherence, social abilities, social functioning, coping, self-efficacy, self-blame, attributions, instrumental mastery, fear avoidance, mental health state and psychological distress.
- *Non-workplace social support variables* included: perceived general social support, social network size, social integration and family support.
- *Workplace social support variables* included: supervisor support, co-worker support, peer support, job satisfaction and management-worker relationships (this variable includes pre-injury employer contact or involvement because, if an employer initiates contact with an injured worker who is away from work, this is taken as evidence of implicit social support).

The data in Table 4.1 suggests a clear preference for researchers to use demographic or injury variables as predictors of return to work. This traditional focus may be due, in part, to measurement issues and ease of access to injury and demographic data. Although evidence from allied fields indicates that social support can (in certain situations) facilitate recovery from illness (Sarason et al. 1997), very little research has been conducted on the role of social support on the later (re-)employment of traumatic injury survivors. The relative neglect of social support as a predictor of post-injury vocational achievement may be primarily due to measurement impediments. If social support is a multifaceted construct that, when measured, needs to include both the objective and subjective components (see Sarason et al. 1997), this makes data collection more difficult. Of more direct relevance to this chapter on disability management is the role of workplace social support in facilitating positive rehabilitation outcomes such as timely return to work. This is the focus of the following section.

Summary of Peer-Reviewed Studies that Assessed the Association between Workplace Social Support and Return to Work

Few studies have rigorously investigated the relationship between workplace social support and return to work. Of those that have, workplace social support has been operationalized in several, non-standard ways. For example, Katz et al. (2005) assessed workplace social support at the macro-level of organizational climate, that is, the effect of supportive policies and practices on return to work. In contrast, Esselman et al. (2007) measured workplace support at the micro-level, that is, supervisor and co-worker contact during hospitalization. Furthermore, due to the scarcity of studies that have analyzed workplace social support, the present literature review included implicit indices of this construct. For example, job satisfaction was used as a proxy for a supportive work environment, and a return to pre-injury employers was taken as implying ongoing workplace support. A total of eight studies that reported the effects of workplace social support on return to work were identified. These studies are reviewed below.

PREDICTION STUDIES

Esselman et al. (2007) examined the effect of workplace social support on burn injury survivors. High levels of employer and co-worker support were reported. A total of 71 per cent of patients stated that employers had contacted them during hospitalization, while 81 per cent reported that co-workers had called to offer support. However, employer support did not predict return to work. Esselman et al. (2007) speculated that the lack of a demonstrated association between employer support and RTW may have been due to a poor definition and description of 'employer contact' (i.e., duration and nature of contact was not assessed in detail).

Katz et al. (2005) assessed the predictors of return to work among carpal tunnel syndrome patients. In bivariate analyses, social support both of co-workers and of supervisors was positively associated with post-operative work status at six months. Less supportive organizational policies and practices independently predicted work absence at 12 months. Less supportive occupational health and rehabilitation policy and practice was associated with almost three times the rate of work absence at 12 months post-surgery. Overall, Katz et al. (2005) commented that clinical factors (such as worker self-efficacy or reported pain) were more salient predictors of RTW at six months but organizational factors featured more prominently in RTW at twelve months.

CORRELATION STUDIES

Fabiano et al. (1995) found that traumatic brain injury (TBI) survivors who returned to their pre-injury employer were more likely to remain employed compared with TBI survivors who commenced work with a new employer. Furthermore, workers who returned to their pre-injury employer received higher remuneration than those who began with a new employer. However, Fabiano et al. (1995) also reported that TBI survivors with better neuropsychological performance were also more likely to return to their pre-injury employer. Therefore, level of impairment may moderate the relationship between RTW and workplace social support.

DESCRIPTIVE STUDIES

Descriptive studies comprise those that reported the proportions of injured workers who returned to their previous employers or the proportion of employers who were prepared to accommodate injured workers. These studies provide a crude measure of workplace social support only. Among small enterprises, a return to pre-injury employers was attributed to the close social and workplace relations between employers and employees that exist in such settings (Anderson et al. 2007).

Franulic et al. (2004) reported that a high proportion of TBI patients were hired post-injury by their previous employers. The proportion of hires varied as a function of injury evolution. The highest proportion of TBI patients (88 per cent) who returned to their previous employer were injured 10 years previously and reported the highest level of job satisfaction (90 per cent). This group also comprised the highest rate of rehires to the same or similar position. The lowest proportion of TBI patients (76 per cent) who returned to their previous employer were those whose injury occurred two years previously. This group also reported the lowest levels of job satisfaction (66 per cent).

Similarly, Millstein et al. (1985) found that 65 per cent of pre-injury employers offered work to amputees. However, only 21 per cent returned to their previous job while 42 per cent settled into modified jobs. Other workplace injury-related repercussions included limited scope for career advancement and salary increases.

Review of Interventions that Target Return to Work

Of the 52 references identified for this literature review, 11 (21 per cent) evaluated intervention programs designed to enhance return to work (Anema et al. 2007; Armengol 1999; Cullen et al. 2007; Groswasser et al. 1999; Karrholm et al. 2008; Klonoff et al. 2008; Loisel et al. 1997; Mayer et al. 1998; Vanderploeg et al. 2008; West et al. 1990). Of these eleven intervention studies, only two assessed the role of workplace social support in return to work (Anema et al. 2007; Loisel et al. 1997). Loisel et al. (1997) evaluated a workplace intervention in Canada, and Anema et al. (2007) replicated the study in the Netherlands.

A Comparison of the Efficacy of Workplace versus Clinical Interventions on RTW

Loisel et al. (1997) undertook an empirically rigorous evaluation of four different types of intervention on RTW among back-injured employees. The aim of the interventions was to minimize long-term disability and facilitate return to work. Using a population-based, randomized, clinical trial Loisel et al. (1997) evaluated the efficacy of four approaches: an occupational intervention, a clinical intervention, a full intervention and a usual care intervention. A total of 130 participants were recruited from 31 study-eligible workplaces in the Sherbrooke area of Québec, Canada. Inclusion criteria for participants were absence from work due to occupational back pain that exceeded four weeks, aged between 18 and 65 years and a recipient of back pain compensation. Participants were randomized into one of the following four interventions.

> *Occupational Intervention.* The occupational intervention was implemented after six weeks' absence from work and comprised recommendations based on consultation with an occupational physician and a worksite evaluation team. The worksite evaluation team included an ergonomist, the injured worker, the injured worker's supervisor and union and management representatives. Specific ergonomic recommendations based on a diagnostic analysis of the injured worker's tasks were forwarded to the employer for implementation.

> *Clinical Intervention.* The clinical intervention commenced after 8 weeks' absence from work and comprised a consultation with a back pain specialist and attendance at a school for back-care education. Participants who were still unable to return to work underwent further functional rehabilitation in the form of a physical fitness and work hardening program, which ended with a progressive return to work.

Full Intervention. The full intervention comprised a combination of the occupational and clinical intervention.

Usual Care Intervention. This intervention comprised the usual care prescribed by the workers' physician.

The effect of each of the interventions on two RTW variables, 'duration of absence from regular work' and 'duration of absence from any work', was assessed. *Regular work* was defined as 'work identical to that performed before the onset of the work-related back pain' (Loisel et al. 1997: 2913). *Any work* included regular work or light duties.

Return to Regular Work. The following differences (p=0.04) in the median duration of absence from regular work were observed for each of the interventions: full intervention (60 days); occupational intervention (67 days); clinical intervention (131 days); and usual care intervention (120.5 days). Cox regression analysis revealed that only the full intervention significantly accelerated return to work. Specifically, full-intervention participants returned to work 2.4 times faster than usual-care participants (95% CI: 1.19 to 4.89; p = 0.01). The occupational intervention component of the full intervention program accounted for the largest part of this result. A Kaplan-Meyer analysis also revealed that the two groups that received the occupational intervention required significantly fewer days off work compared with the two groups that did not (67 days versus 131 days (p = 0.01). This result was also confirmed after adjustments were made for age, gender co-morbidity and body-mass index – return to work among the two groups with the occupational intervention was 1.91 times faster (95% CI: 1.18 to 3.1; p < 0.01).

Return to Any Work. None of the interventions conferred a significant benefit on the outcome variable of return to any work (which includes a return to light work duties). This result was deemed to be important because light duties are 'increasingly used in industrial settings' (Loisel 1997: 2916).

Overall, these results clearly demonstrate that an integrated occupational-clinical model of occupational back pain management accelerates return to work. Compared with usual care, an intervention that incorporates workplace support and medical care can more than double the rate of return to work.

The above study was replicated in the Netherlands by Anema et al. (2007). Workers who had been absent from work for two to six weeks with lower back pain were randomly assigned to the workplace intervention (n =196) or the graded activity intervention (n=112). The workplace intervention comprised workplace assessment and workplace adjustments. A participatory approach was adopted in which all major stakeholders – worker, supervisor and relevant others – met to brainstorm and discuss feasible solutions to return to work problems. The graded activity intervention comprised an individually tailored exercise program. An operant-conditioning behavioural approach was adopted with bi-weekly exercise sessions which lasted for 1 hour each.

Workplace Intervention. Participation in the workplace-based intervention accelerated return to full-time, lasting work. The median number of days' absence for the intervention group was significantly lower than that of the group receiving usual care (77 versus 104 days). Furthermore, the intervention group required significantly fewer sick leave days during the 12-month follow-up period compared with the non-intervention group (84 days versus 105). Overall, compared with the control group, the workplace-based intervention resulted in a 70 per cent increase in RTW.

Graded Activity. Participation in the graded activity intervention hindered return to full-time, lasting work. The graded activity group required significantly more days off work than the control group (median = 144 versus 111 days). In addition, graded activity participants incurred a greater number of work absences during the 12-month follow-up period (145 versus 111 days). Overall, compared with the control group, the graded activity intervention resulted in a 60 per cent decrease in RTW.

Based on these results, Anema et al (2007) recommend the use of workplace-based interventions, not graded exercise programs, to facilitate a return to lasting and full-time employment. These results generally replicate those of Loisel et al. (2005) suggesting that the workplace-based intervention is applicable in different socio-economic and cultural environments. In addition, the results are generalizable because a wide variety of occupational groups were sampled and a high proportion of eligible workers (81 per cent) were included. Anema et al (2007: 296) note that 'the intervention [works] because it involves a mediation process in the perception of both workers and supervisors about the workplace's capabilities and the workplace's opportunities for RTW'. Although coordination of social support from the workforce was not assessed, it was implicit in this coordinated workplace-based intervention.

The studies reviewed in Section 2 included non-standardized indices of workplace social support, such as informal practices and organizational policy. This methodological shortcoming may have masked the effect of this crucial form of social support on RTW. In contrast, the two intervention studies (Anema et al. 2007; Loisel et al. 1997) reviewed in Section 3 included formalized and structured programs which enabled a comprehensive and empirically sound evaluation of the effect of workplace social support on the duration of work absence. The results of these two studies clearly demonstrate the features of a successful workplace social support program, that is, the inclusion of personnel who represent the interests both of the organization and the injured worker, as well as enlisting specialist advice to provide impartial, diagnostic ergonomic solutions. Inclusion of the worker in the decision-making process fosters acceptance of workplace changes, as well as increased productivity and satisfaction (Miller & Monge 1986). In addition to strengthening the organizational bond, workplace social support intervention programs can (potentially) improve an organization's financial performance in terms of reduced work absence, thus resulting in increased productivity. Non-tangible benefits may also accrue from workplace social support programs. Intangibles include positive worker-employer relationships, and improved job satisfaction, morale and perceptions of fairness. Ultimately, these intangibles impact on organizational performance and, thus, the bottom line (Babin & Boles,1996; Miller & Monge 1986).

The efficacy of a structured workplace social support program in facilitating successful RTW appears to generalize across countries, cultures and occupations. The Canadian study demonstrated the advantage of an occupational intervention over a clinical intervention while the Dutch study showed that a combination approach was the most successful. It is noteworthy that, in the latter study, the occupational component of the combined intervention contributed the most to RTW. Participants in these two studies suffered debilitating occupational back pain that necessitated in excess of four weeks' absence from work. Further research is required to determine whether the beneficial effect of workplace social support programs on RTW generalize to other clinical populations, such as severe traumatic spinal cord injury patients (see Murphy & Foreman 2008).

Conclusion

Following the presentation of an overview of the social support literature as it pertains to health and rehabilitation, this chapter presented results from a review of studies into the relationship of workplace social support to return to work. Workplace social support (while implicit in Shrey's concept of the occupational bond that underpins disability management approaches to the prevention and management of work injury) has been relatively neglected by RTW researchers who have overwhelmingly preferred to study demographic and injury-related correlates of RTW. The small number of social support studies investigating RTW outcomes following injury produced some initial encouraging results for the use of social support (a) as a predictor variable in RTW research investigations, and (b) as a complement that is well worth including in workplace interventions aimed at improving RTW rates post-injury.

Consistent with the wider literature on social support and health and rehabilitation outcomes (see Murphy and Jackson 2009), the well-designed study of Katz et al. (2005) obtained results that illustrated the importance of measuring social support by more than one method. Katz's results support one clear recommendation for disability management researchers: when assessing workplace social support, use more than one measure of social support. Ideally, disability management researchers would include not just measures of supervisor support and co-worker support, but also measures of non-work social support (e.g., intimate-partner support) so that a more comprehensive understanding is obtained of the positive (or negative) impact of social support on the key rehabilitation outcome of return to work.

Bibliography

Amick, B., Habeck, R., Hunt, A., Fossel, A., Chapin, A., Keller, R. et al. (2000). Measuring the Impact of Organizational Behaviors on Work Disability Prevention and Management. *Journal of Occupational Rehabilitation* 10, 21–38.

Anderson, L.P., Kines, P. & Hassle, P. (2007). Owner Attitudes and Self–Reported Behaviour towards Modified Work after Occupational Injury Absence in Small Enterprises: A Qualitative Study. *Journal of Occupational Rehabilitation* 17, 107–21.

Anema, J.R., Steenstra, I.A., Bongers, H.C.W., de Vet, H.C., Knol, D.R., Loisel, P. et al. (2007). Multidisciplinary Rehabilitation for Subacute Low Back Pain: Graded Activity or Workplace Intervention or Both? A Randomized Controlled Trial. *Spine* 32, 291–98.

Armengol, C.G. (1999). A Multimodal Support Group with Hispanic Traumatic Brain Injury Survivors. *Journal of Head Trauma Rehabilitation* 14, 233–46.

Babin, B.J. & Boles, J.S. (1996). The Effects of Perceived Co-worker Involvement and Supervisor Support on Service Provider Role Stress, Performance and Job Satisfaction. *Journal of Retailing* 72, 57–75.

Beaudway, D. (1986). 3M: A Disability Management Approach. *Journal of Applied Rehabilitation Counselling* 17, 20–22.

Borja, S.E., Callahan, J.L. & Rambo, P.L. (2009). Understanding Negative Outcomes Following Traumatic Exposure: The Roles of Neuroticism and Social Support. *Psychological Trauma: Theory, Research, Practice, and Policy* 1, 118–29.

Cobb, S. (1976). Social Support as a Moderator of Life Stress. *Psychosomatic Medicine* 38, 300–14.

Cohen, S. & Wills, T. (1985). Stress, Social Support and the Buffering Hypothesis. *Psychological Bulletin* 98, 310–57.

Cullen, N., Chundamala, J., Bayley, M. & Jutai, J. (2007). The Efficacy of Acquired Brain Injury Rehabilitation. *Brain Injury* 21, 113–32.

Currier, K., Chan, F., Berven, N., Habeck, R. & Taylor, D. (2001). Functions and Knowledge Domains for Disability Management Practice. *Rehabilitation Counselling Bulletin* 44, 133–43.

Eisenberger, N.I., Taylor, S.E., Gable, S.L., Hilmert, C.J. & Lieberman, M.D. (2007). Neural Pathways Link Social Support to Attenuated Neuroendocrine Stress Response. *NeuroImage* 35, 1601–612.

Esselman, P.C., Askay, S.W., Carrougher, G.J., Lezotte, D.C., Holavanahalli, R.K., Magyar-Russell, G. et al. (2007). Barriers to Return to Work After Burn Injuries. *Archives of Physical Medicine Rehabilitation* 88(Suppl 2), S50–S56.

Fabiano, R.J., Crewe, N. & Goran, D.A. (1995). Differences between Elapsed Time to Employment and Employer Selection in Vocational Outcome Following Severe Traumatic Brain Injury. *Journal of Applied Rehabilitation Counselling* 26, 17–20.

Franulic, A., Carbonell, C.G., Pinto, P. & Sepulveda, I. (2004). Psychosocial Adjustment and Employment Outcome 2, 5 and 10 years after TBI. *Brain Injury* 18, 119–29.

Galvin, D. (1986). Employer-Based Disability Management and Rehabilitation Programs. In E.L. Pan et al. (eds) *Annual Review of Rehabilitation*. New York: Springer.

Gottlieb, B. (1983). *Social Support Strategies: Guidelines for Mental health Practice*. London: Sage.

Groswasser, Z., Melamed, S., Agranov, E. & Keren, O. (1999). Return to Work as an Integrative Outcome Measure Following Traumatic Brain Injury. *Neuropsychological Rehabilitation* 9, 493–504.

Habeck, R., Leahy, M., Hunt, H., Chan, F. & Welch, E. (1991). Employer Factors Related to Workers' Compensation Claims and Disability Management. *Rehabilitation Counselling Bulletin* 34, 211–26.

Homans, G. (1974). *Social Behaviour*. New York: Harcourt, Brace, Jovanovich.

House, J., Umberson, D. & Landis, K. (1988). Structures and Processes of Social Support. In W. Scott & J. Blake (eds), *Annual Review of Sociology* (293–318). Pao Alto CA: Annual Reviews.

Jarvikoski, A. and Lahelma, E (1980). *Early Rehabilitation in the Workplace*. New York: World Rehabilitation Fund.

Kaplan, R. & Toshima, M. (1990). The Functional Effects of Social Relationships on Chronic Illness and Disability. In B.R. Sarason, I.G. Sarason & G.R. Pierce (eds), *Social Support: An Interactional View* (427–53). NewYork: Wiley.

Karrholm, J., Ekholm, K., Ekholm, J., Bergroth, A. & Ekholm, K.S. (2008). Systematic Co-operation between Employer, Occupational Health Service and Social Insurance Office: A 6-year Follow-up of Vocational Rehabilitation for People on Sick Leave, including Economic Bbenefits. *Journal Rehabilitation Medicine* 40, 628–36.

Katz, N., Amick, B.C., Keller, R., Fossell, A.H., Ossman, J., Soucie, V. et al. (2005). Determinants of Work Absence following Surgery for Carpal Tunnel Syndrome. *American Journal of Industrial Medicine* 47, 120–30.

Klonoff, P.S., Talley, M.C., Dawson, L.K., Myles, S.M., Gehrels, J. & Henderson, S.W. (2007). The Relationship of Cognitive Retraining to Neurological Patients' Work and School Status. *Brain Injury* 21, 1097–107.

Kuoppala, J. & Lamminpaa, A. (2008). Rehabilitation and Work Ability: A Systematic Literature Review. *Journal of Rehabilitation Medicine* 40, 796–804.

Loisel, P., Abenhaim, L., Durand, P., Esdaile, J., Suissa, S., Gosselin, L. et al. (1997). A Population-Based, Randomized Clinical Trial on Back Pain Management. *Spine* 22, 2911–918.

Loisel, P., Buchbinder, R., Hazard, R., Keller, R., Scheel, I., van Tulder, M. & Webster, B. (2005). Prevention of Work Disability Due to Muskuloskeletal Disorders: The Challenge of Implementing Evidence. *Journal of Occupational Rehabilitation* 15, 507–24.

Mayer, T., McMahion, M., Gatchel, R.J., Sparks, B., Wright, A. & Pegues, P. (1998). Socioeconomic Outcomes of Combined Spine Surgery and Functional Restoration in Workers' Compensation Spinal Disorders with Matched Controls. *Spine* 23, 598–605.

McKee-Ryan, F., Song, Z., Wanberg, C. & Kinicki, A. (2005). Psychological and Physical Well-being during Unemployment. *Journal of Applied Psychology* 90, 53–76.

Miller, K.I. & Monge, P.R. (1986). Participation, Satisfaction, and Productivity: A Meta-Analytic Review. *The Academy of Management Review* 29, 727–53.

Millstein, S., Bain, D. & Hunter, G.A. (1985). A Review of Employment Patterns of Industrial Amputees – Factors Influencing Rehabilitation. *Prosthetics and Orthotics International* 9, 69–78.

Munrowd, D. & Beecher, P. (1986). Rehabilitation in an Industrial Setting: The General Motors B-O-C Group Lansing. *Journal of Applied Rehabilitation Counselling* 17, 23–27.

Murphy, G.C. & Foreman, P. (1993). General Patterns of Managerial Approaches to Work Motivation: Implications for Rehabilitation Professionals Involved in Occupational Rehabilitation. *Journal of Occupational Rehabilitation* 3, 51–62.

Murphy, G.C. & Foreman, P. (2008). Implementing Post-Injury Rehabilitation Policy. In S. Barraclough and H. Gardner (eds). *Analysing Health Policy* (250–61). Sydney: Churchill Livingstone.

Murphy G.C., & Jackson, M. (2009) *Social Support in Rehabilitation: Theory, Measures and Contribution to Outcomes*. Conference Proceedings of the Australian Psychological Society Annual Conference. Darwin. October 2009.

Oddy, M. & Humphrey, M. (1980). Social Recovery During the Wear Following Severe Head Injury. *Journal of Neurology, Neurosurgery, and Psychiatry* 43, 798–802.

Petrie, K.J. (2004). Social Support and Recovery from Disease and Medical Procedures. *International Encyclopedia of the Social and Behavioral Sciences*, 14458–4461.

Pierce, G., Sarason, I. & Sarason, B. (1991). General and Relationship-Based Perceptions of Social Support: Are Two Constructs Better than One? *Journal of Personality and Social Psychology* 61, 1028–039.

Pransky, G.S., Benjamin, K.L., Savageau, J.A., Currivan, D. & Fletcher, K. (2005). Outcomes in Work-Related Injuries: A Comparison of Older and Younger Workers. *American Journal of Industrial Medicine* 47, 104–12.

Rook, K. (1984). The Negative Side of Social Interaction: Impact on Psychological Well-being. *Journal of Personality and Social Psychology* 46, 1097–108.

Rook, K.S. (1992). Detrimental Aspects of Social Relationships: Taking Stock of an Emerging Literature. In H.O.F. Veiel and U. Baumann (eds), *The Meaning and Measurement of Social Support* (157–170). New York: Hemisphere.

Sarason I.G., Sarason, B.R., Shearin, E.N. & Pierce, G.R. (1997). A Brief Measure of Social Support: Practical and Theoretical Implications. *Journal of Social and Personal Relations* 4, 497–610.

Schwarzer, R. & Leppin, A. (1992). Social Support and Mental Health: A Conceptual and Empirical Overview. In L. Montada, S. Fillip, & M. Lerner (eds), *Life Crisis and Experiences of Loss in Adulthood* (435–58). New Jersey: Lawrence Erlbaum Associates, Publishers.

Selye, H. (1950). *Stress*. Montreal: Acta.

Shrey, D. & Hursh, N. (1999). Workplace Disability Management: International Trends and Perspectives. *Journal of Occupational Rehabilitation* 9, 45–59.

Shrey, D. & Lacertes, M. (1995). Principles and Practices of Disability Management in Industry. Winter Park FL: GR Press.

Shrey, D. & Mital, A. (1994). Disability Management and the Cardiac Rehabilitation Patient. *Journal of Occupational Rehabilitation* 4, 39–53.

Suls, J. (1982). Social Support, Interpersonal Relations and Health: Benefits and Liabilities. In G. Sanders & J. Suls (eds). *Social Psychology of Health and Illness* (255–77). Hillside: Erlbaum.

Uchino, B. (2006). Social Support and Health: A Review of Physiological Processes Potentially Underlying Links to Disease Outcomes. *Journal of Behavioral Medicine* 29, 377–87.

Vanderploeg, R.D., Schwah, K., Walker, W.C., Fraser, J.A., Sigford, B.J., Date, E.S. et al. (2008). Rehabilitation of Traumatic Brain Injury in Active Duty Military Personnel and Veterans: Defense and Veterans Brain Injury Center Randomized Controlled Trial of Two Rehabilitation Approaches. *Archives of Physical Medicine Rehabilitation* 89, 2227–238.

Veiel, H. & Baumann, U. (1992). *The Meaning and Measurement of Social Support.* New York: Hemisphere Publishing Corporation.

Wallis, L. (2010). Disability Prevention and Effective Disability Management Practices in the Australian Red-Meat-Processing Industry. PhD thesis, School of Public Health, La Trobe University, Melbourne.

West, M., Fry, R., Pastor, J., Moore, G., Killam, S., Wheman, P. et al. (1990). Helping Postacute Traumatically Brain Injured Clients Return to Work: Three Case Studies. *International Journal of Rehabilitation* Research 13, 291–98.

Williams, R., Westmoreland, M., Shannon, H. & Amick, B. (2007). Disability Management Practices in Ontario Healthcare Workplaces. *Journal of Occupational Rehabilitation* 17, 153–65.

5 Changes in Managing Disability in the Workplace in Germany: Chances of Professionalization?

DÖRTE BERNHARD, MATHILDE NIEHAUS AND
BRITTA MARFELS

Introduction

Managing disability aims to secure the participation of people with illnesses and disabilities in the labour market, and thereby meets a fundamental political and societal duty (United Nations 2007). In Germany, the Social Code Book 9, Rehabilitation and Participation of Disabled Persons, serves as a legal framework as it stipulates and consolidates measures and benefits of rehabilitation. It underlines the necessity for self-advocacy and empowerment of persons with disabilities and their participation in society, particularly in light of the history of managing disability in Germany. Traditionally, persons with disabilities were excluded from working in highly specialized and complex institutions. Today, the focus is on inclusion, and thus no longer exclusively on caring and helping people who are disabled or at risk of becoming disabled. Instead, services ought to provide for the self-determined participation of persons with disabilities in society and empowerment as citizens by offering equal opportunities (Schian 2006).

The participation of sick or disabled employees at the workplace is internationally discussed and known as disability management. About two decades ago companies realized that employee absenteeism caused by illness and disability can be rather costly. Therefore new solutions were needed, emphasizing company-based rehabilitation measures. This means that a disability management program is applied within corporations and therefore requires the collaboration of the different actors. Furthermore, the program calls for early intervention and return to work (Akabas & Gates 1995; Dyck 2000).

This chapter focuses on the developments following the implementation of the German legislation for preventing and managing disability that was amended in 2004. It shows what tasks and duties occur when managing disability. It leads to a discussion as to how this affects the process of professionalization of disability management practice.

Increased Need to Manage Disability in Workplaces

The increased need to manage disability in workplaces can be noticed when observing developments at different levels. A priority in the legislation, as stated in clause 3, is the prevention of disability (Federal Ministry of Labour and Social Affairs 2006). Regardless of the cause of the incapacity to work, rehabilitation aims to keep the physical or mental condition from deteriorating. Further regulations regarding managing disability at the workplace are to be found in part II of the Social Code Book.

According to clause 84.2 of the Social Code Book, Part II, rehabilitation measures with regard to integration management should start when an employee absent from work six weeks or longer due to an accident, illness or disability. A procedure for an integration management can be based on so-called integration agreements (clause 83), i.e., contracts that are signed between the different actors and interest groups within a company and that entail details regarding timeframe, organization and responsibilities of the rehabilitation measures on processes regarding return to work (RTW) and managing disability at the workplace (see Niehaus & Bernhard 2006).

The legislation that came into force in 2001–04 can be seen as an answer to the rising employment age of the workforce due to the demographic changes. Older employees are sick less frequently, but nevertheless away from work for longer periods; in the event of illness or injury, they require more time to return to work (OECD 2009). Employees aged 50 or older are the largest workforce cohort. The US Bureau of Labour Statistics estimates that the number of employees aged 55 and older rise by about 50 per cent from 2002 to 2012 (Bruyère 2006; Reynolds, Ridley & Van Horn 2005). Not only fewer employees, but also a considerably aged workforce will meet the requirements of the working world in the near future. Therefore companies will be forced to incorporate the needs of an ageing workforce and increase their efforts with respect to maintaining the health and employability of the workers. In this way, health promotion and disability prevention are of particular interest and, in consideration of this, in-house solutions become inevitable (International Labour Organization (ILO) 2002; OECD 2009).

The necessary tasks in managing disability are not only determined by the change of legislation and the new framework of disability allowing for empowerment and participation, but also by a change of workers within the group of persons with health problems and disabilities. While 30–40 years ago managing disability at German workplaces was mainly addressed at physically disabled persons whose disability had been caused during the war, by exposure to harmful substances in the workplace or by work accidents, now persons with disabilities in companies often have histories of a chronic disease leading in the long term to an acquired disability, often with a mental illness component (Huber & Ochs 2004).

This means that the focus is on those individuals who are in danger of acquiring a disability during their working career. In consequence, those charged with managing disability in the workplace have to be prepared to address the needs of various vulnerable groups within the workplace (Bernhard 2008). Furthermore, individual case management and counselling also ought to meet the need for empowerment and participation of the disabled employees as outlined in the legislation. It can be summarized that responsible actors and their organizations have to allow for these changes and ought to incorporate the new frameworks into their daily practice.

Franche et al. (2006) show that effective RTW interventions in the workplace require the support of a professional disability manager or RTW counsellor. In Germany, the new clause 84.2, which focuses on preventing disability, has led to the creation and implementation of a new actor: the disability manager. This new professional provides support before the person with the disability returns to work, thus enabling them to return to work. Furthermore, these professionals should have the potential to help to prevent illness and injury (early intervention/risk management) and to recognize health risks within the company setting. Their specific role, the interaction with the other players in the company, the necessary skills regarding their training needs, become a matter of concern, both in practice and for academic discussions. While internationally the role, tasks and competencies of disability management professionals have increasingly become a focus of research in the last decade, Germany has had little research in this area.

The professional group of disability managers is in addition to the well-established representatives who have different yet similar tasks and responsibilities, as outlined according to the German legislation in the Social Code Book 9, clauses 93ff. The work by Bernhard (2008) provides a comprehensive description on the players in the workplace. First, there are different actors who all are responsible for managing disability in the workplace: representatives of the severely disabled employees, works councils who advocate the employees' rights and employers' representatives who ensure that the employer meets his/her legal requirements regarding the employment of (severely) disabled employees.

Second, these players represent different stakes, i.e., different interests within companies. Therefore their duties and tasks differ. Third, according to German legislation, clause 99 of the Social Code Book 9, the responsible representatives ought to collaborate to support both prevention as well as management of disability. But who are all the actors?

The representative of the severely disabled employees provides guidance and assistance to the severely disabled persons. He/she advocates their interests in the RTW process as laid out in clause 94ff. They provide support by planning and applying measures of workplace adjustments and rehabilitation (workplace adjustments), by individual one-to-one counselling, as well as by representing severely disabled employees as a group and by monitoring the employer's completion of legal obligations. The function of the representative of the severely disabled employees has a long tradition and dates back to the 1920s. When considered internationally, he/she is a unique actor; only in Austria does a similar position representing the interests of severely disabled workers exist (BMSK 2003). Empirical data has shown that, for example, these representatives take on an active role by initiating discussions about integration agreements as outlined in clause 83 of the Social Code Book 9 (Niehaus & Bernhard 2006).

Another player representing the employee perspective is the works council that is elected as outlined in the Works Constitution Act (BetrVG) and supports all employees in a company. Clause 93 in the Social Code Book 9 underlines and emphasizes the obligations of works councils towards workers with disabilities, such as the need to implement measures of prevention and rehabilitation. Furthermore, the works council monitors the employer's compliance with and fulfilment of duties. The tasks of the work council are similar to those of the representatives of the severely disabled employees: the works council is in charge of all employees, as well as those who need support due to their health conditions, whereas the representatives of the severely disabled employees are responsible for employees who have a legally recognized disability.

The interests of the employer are met by an employers' representative who is appointed to support the employer supplying the work accommodation, according to the severely disabled person's needs. He/she support the employment, retention and recruitment of employees with severe disabilities. In order to find suitable RTW solutions, the employers' representative joins committees and cooperates with the other representatives. This position is often held by someone from the human resource department, thus enabling ease of access and insight into relevant employee information (Bernhard 2008).

In addition to the above mentioned players, and outlined in legislation other than the Social Code Book 9, there are also physicians/company doctors who are in charge of diagnosing work incapacities, certifying health-related abilities and accommodating health-impaired and disabled employees.

Given that there are different representatives with specific tasks supporting the RTW process, and that each of these actors mainly deals with one specific aspect of managing disability, one person is needed to coordinate all tasks and to collaborate with all the above-mentioned actors (ILO 2002). This person is internationally referred to as a disability manager or disability management professional.

It can be summarized that by the clauses on self-determined participation of disabled persons as well as those on disability prevention, the Social Code Book 9 provides the actors, including the above-mentioned disability managers in the workplace, with a new conceptual framework within which to work. This shift of paradigm in disability policy and practice leads to the assumption of a change of the self-perception of people with disabilities, as well as a change conception of disability by their professionals. On the one hand, people with disabilities postulate the need for professional support, and on the other hand, they demand participation as well as the ability to take an active role in their rehabilitation process. Moreover, interaction and collaboration between the actors and how that impacts their professional understanding become an issue of concern. Consequently, the actors, both the professionals in corporations and those working in the social security system, need to adapt their professional actions and they require training.

Disability Managers – A New Group Managing Disability in the Workplace

The introduction of disability management practices within companies goes along with the evolution of rehabilitation counselling services. Internationally, the rehabilitation counselling is seen as a fast changing profession. While in the 1970s, rehabilitation counselling was primarily performed in rehabilitation agencies far away from the workplace, since the 1990s the workplace as means of rehabilitation has gained importance. Havranek (1997: 357) calls the development a 'shift toward a multidisciplinary model of rehabilitation at the workplace'. It was in the 1990s that rehabilitation counsellors began to coordinate the reintegration process which entailed a broader range of duties, such as providing mentoring, negotiating as well as program development services (Calkins, Lui & Wood 2000).

With these new tasks and fields of responsibility, there is the need to engage this professional group in educational programs. In the 1990s, the National Institute of

Disability Management Research (NIDMAR), Canada, began to develop occupational standards for professionals. This organization offers an internationally known qualification system for those who manage disability in the workplace, and it leads to a certified disability management professional qualification (CDMP). This qualification follows a consensus-based approach in managing disability, and accordingly a CDMP should work together with all representatives to find solutions to retain the position of the injured or ill worker and to enable disabled workers to return to work (disability management).

Today, international discussions that refer to those who manage disability at workplaces refer to disability management professionals, such as disability management or return to work coordinators and rehabilitation counsellors, who guide the health-impaired person and facilitate their social integration and labour market participation. Their particular roles vary with reference to the particular sociopolitical context and the organizational setting they work in. They might be employed by a company, or might work for themselves or for a consultancy that provides services to a variety of different companies. They also might work in a clinical setting or be employed at a social insurance organization such as a workers compensation board (Shaw et al. 2008).

The qualifications the actors who manage disability has become a special issue for German companies in connection with rehabilitation providers/insurances. The current situation of professionals managing disability in German workplaces can be characterized by a large variation in educational and professional backgrounds. Moreover, every insurance fund (accident insurance, pension fund, labour office) offers system-specific and, therefore, specialized training. The situation thus shows a 'considerable heterogeneity in the training and background of their members', quoting Hudson and Sullivan (2002: 295). Correspondingly, disability managers increasingly emerge as a new group of professionals because international solutions, which were established in Canada in the early 1990s, provide a suitable framework for the different players light of the sociopolitical context in Germany. Following international efforts regarding the standardization and quality management of training programs for vocational rehabilitation counsellors, the German Statutory Accident Insurance (*Deutsche Gesetzliche Unfallversicherung* (DGUV)) has initiated training for certified disability management professionals (CDMP) and has started off this new era by introducing a new professional group.

The first initiatives were taken at the time the Social Code Book 9 came into force in 2001 and were intensified when it was amended in 2004. From then on, a growing market for the training and qualification of disability managers has been noticed. And, growing numbers of these professionals (CDMPs) are to be found in German companies. The recent developments have led to a tremendous rise of the numbers of certified disability managers in Germany. By 2010, about 900 disability management professionals and return-to-work coordinators (CRTWC) had been certified in Germany (Niehaus & Marfels 2010).

German literature in this field is rare and mostly of descriptive character, published by its promoters and without any empirical base (Mehrhoff 2004; Mehrhoff & Schönle 2005). While there is, for example, research that refer to the educational needs and necessary professionalization with respect to a changing labour market (Minssen & Riese 2007), as well as studies outlining the role and responsibilities of the established representatives and their tasks and educational needs (Bernhard 2008; Niehaus & Bernhard 2006; Bernhard & Niehaus 2005), precise and detailed information regarding the use of disability managers in Germany is lacking. Taking into consideration the fields of activity, skills and competencies described in studies in the United States, Australia, New Zealand and Canada (Leahy, Chan & Saunders 2003; Matthews et al. 2007; Rosenthal et al. 2007; Shaw et al. 2008), there is documentation about the international training programmes for disability management professionals; however, there is little information available as to how or if this knowledge has been incorporated in Germany.

Applying a sociological and social science perspective to these developments leads to the question of to what extent the implementation of a certification system in managing disability (CDMP) in Germany can be regarded as part of the professionalization process. In sum, a necessary academic discussion evolves around the question of whether or not training for actors who are managing disability is a 'flash in the pan' or an imperative necessity. Or, in other words, should certified disability managers be a new profession, or are other professional developments needed? The following discussion is mainly embedded in the conceptual framework of professionalization.

Is Disability Management Developing as a New Profession?

In order to meet quality management criteria, standardized education and training programmes, which call for professionalization of staff, are required for rehabilitation and disability management professionals. Professionalization is initiated whenever a field has to be developed and when new solutions are needed. This is particularly the case with the evolution of company-based integration measures that are in addition to independent vocational training centres. Along with these changes, which can be regarded as an answer to challenges society faces, the creation of a new type of professional actor is required (Stichweh 1999).

The concept of professionalization was developed five decades ago and has been widely discussed internationally as well as in Germany ever since, especially in the 1970s and 1980s, but also now (Brandt 2009; Evetts 2003). The discussion is particularly prevalent among occupations such as social work (Reeser & Epstein 1990) and education for the following reason: 'profession' as a construct refers to occupations that hold as central values or goods such as justice, health or education. The concept applies when specialized knowledge, as a result of university education, has led to expertise enabling, in particular, professionals like lawyers, medical doctors and teachers to establish a professional relationship with their clients, patients or students. This client-expert relationship serves as a trustworthy base for providing personal support to individuals and to finding solutions for their concerns. Operating as a problem-solving scheme, along with professionals' 'obligation for service to society' (Abbott 1983: 855), leads to their great importance to society. The question whether an occupation is a profession or not has led to agreement on a continuum as to what constitutes non-professional, a semi-professional and a professional (Reeser & Epstein 1990).

A framework of four common elements has been defined (Brandt 2009; Hudson & Sullivan 2002):

1. a body of knowledge and its standardization (i.e., training or courses);
2. the formation of an organization;

3. the development of a certification process (mandate that workers in the profession are licensed or certified); and
4. a code of ethics.

However, when societies' knowledge production happens outside of universities and virtual learning opportunities flourish, the end of the era of professionalization is being seen. Although the complexity of our knowledge-based societies requires expertise and professionalism, the traditional professions' systems are diminishing. Nowadays, one can observe the growing importance of professionalism for all experts in a particular field (Kurtz 2004). One answer to these developments is, for example, seen in the concept of communities of practice (Lave & Wenger 1991), which, in short, describes relations among people and their surroundings and creates 'a basis for learning and identity construction' (Guldberg & Mackness 2009). This concept leads to questions such as whether certified disability managers create their 'own profession', whether managing disability in German workplaces is in a phase of professionalization, or whether the different representatives who have disability management tasks and responsibilities form communities of practices. The four professional attributes mentioned above aim to find out whether or not CDMPs in Germany create their own profession.

STANDARDIZING THE BODY OF KNOWLEDGE

The abstract and specialized knowledge that a professional group of CDMPs masters derives from university education and further training programs, combined with knowledge transfer in professional networks. Since 2004–05, disability management training has been offered by German Statutory Accident Insurance in cooperation with other rehabilitation-supporting organizations. In this way, training in disability management is also available to professionals working in contexts other than Accident Insurance (Mehrhoff 2004). Another organization/corporation offering disability management training, with a focus on employers, is the *Fortbildungsakademie der Wirtschaft* (FAW) gGmbH.[1] The interest of employee representatives and their need for a qualification is supported by the union-oriented organization *Arbeit und Leben* (Work and Life) of the Confederation of German Trade Union (DGB) that, in cooperation with Accident Insurance, provides training modules for all responsible actors.[2]

Course follow the curriculum developed by NIDMAR in Victoria, Canada, and which was bought by the German Accident Insurance and adapted in light of the German legislation. In this way, the training offered to professionals providing support in the return to work process follows the standard/guideline of the International Disability Management Standards Council (IDMSC). The NIDMAR training leads to two different internationally accepted qualifications and certifications: the Certified Return to Work Coordinator (CRTWC) and the Certified Disability Management Professional (CDMP). So far, Germany has focused primarily on the CDMP certification, which provides for

---

1   See FAW website. Available at: http://www.faw.de/standorte/hamburg/ausbildung-zum-disability-manager/, accessed 7 February 2010.

2   See Arbeit und Leben NRW website. Available at: http://www.aulnrw.de/interessenvertretung/betriebsraete-und-personalraete/seminarkalender-2009/, accessed 7 February 2010.

an organization-based and joint labour-management approach regarding managing disability.

FORMING AN ORGANIZATION

Following the example of the Canadian Society of Professionals in Disability Management (CSPDM) as well as the International Association of Professionals in Disability Management (IAPDM), the German CDMPs have also established their professional organization. To become a member in the association of certified professionals, *Verein der zertifizierten Disability-Manager Deutschlands* (VDiMa), gives one the potential to further develop one's body of knowledge as part of professional culture, and also allows one to become a member of a national network of experts. At the end of 2008, there were 73 members.[3] In addition, there is also a website especially dedicated to disability managers, which linked with the Accident Insurance's website and which provides information.[4] Membership helps to establishment a professional culture with norms and values.

DEVELOPING A CERTIFICATION PROCESS

Because it is an internationally standardized qualification, the NIDMAR training was adapted to the German jurisdiction and is now offered all over Germany. This training provides a basis for the CDMP certification process. Hudson and Sullivan (2002: 289) state that 'professions require licensing by the state. Because the NIDMAR licensing procedure derives from a private company, it has a different approach than the licensing procedures of professions such as lawyers and medical doctors. Therefore, it is evident that a disability manager isn't certified in the same way as the other traditional professionals. The DM's actions may depend on their work settings, i.e., there are differences depending on whether a disability manager is placed within a company or within the social insurance structures.

The basis for the certification process is a set of strict rules and regulations. There are costs for training courses, as well as for the examinations. Training is a certification prerequisite which has to be undertaken before registering for and taking the exam. The number of modules to be studied depends upon one's school-leaving certificate and practical work experience. In conclusion, the lower the level of one's education and the less experience that one has, the more courses and modules one has to attend. In order to maintain the certification, one has to undertake 20 hours of further training every year. This can be achieved by attending conferences or workshops that are offered by rehabilitation centres or other organizations.

CODE OF ETHICS

CDMPs may have certain autonomy in applying their knowledge and in acting on the professionals' own account for the common good. Yet, they are led by ethical and professional standards, and by codes and policies. A code of ethics is incorporated under

---

3   See VDiMa website. Available at: http://www.vdima.de/index.php, accessed 7 February 2010.

4   See the Accident Insurance website. Available at: http://www.disability-manager.de/d/pages/index.html, accessed 1 July 2009.

the headline 'social and ethical behaviour' as part of the CDMP guidelines[5] which has been applied in Germany. Considering that CDMPs have to make decisions regarding clients' lives, ethical behaviour, as stated in a code, is necessary. Furthermore, autonomy in decision-making and in planning actions for the client is seen as characteristic for professions. Autonomy in a CDMPs' practice refers to decision-making regarding the reintegration of the individual into the workplace and entails the best solution for the individual, but at the same time the CDMP always has to act within a given organizational setting. Linked with autonomy in decision-making is authority. This will be likely to depend on whether or not a CDMP is part of a company setting and part of the integration team, or coming from elsewhere, because it will influence how he or she makes decisions and works together with the injured or sick persons as well as with other representatives. It can be assumed that there could be a conflict of interests if the CDMP position is taken by, for example, the representative of the severely disabled employees who have fewer but also different possibilities regarding decision-making. Another aspect in terms of authority are the issues of gaining the clients' trust and the protection of personal data.

In order to assess the extent of autonomous acting, one needs empirical material taken from interviews and/or observations of the tasks of disability managers and their professional practice. This would require a study to get an insight into the organizational structures of corporations with respect to learning how disability managers intervene and interact with their clients and how the managerial authority is given and dealt with. The analysis of disability management practice would have to focus on how the return-to-work process is supported by the CDMP and how collaboration with other representatives within the company setting is realized.

Conclusion

Political changes as well as innovations in managing disability have created new liaisons, following a discussion of the professionalization process of CDMPs. The analysis with reference to professionalization attributes leads to the conclusion that Germany is in a pro-professionalization phase. The discussion reflects that the role and function of CDMPs take centre stage, in light of the need to provide high-quality and effective counselling measures. Not only is CDMP certification seen as a qualification, popular with promising future perspectives, but also the rising number of certified professionals can be seen as an indication of its importance. Currently, there are more than 700 disability managers certified in Germany; this is the largest professional population of certified DMs worldwide. However, further investigations are needed as to how the other performers, who also manage disability in German workplaces, react to the professionalization of CDMPs and how they handle professionalization in regard to how they form and develop their communities of practice.

Due to the lack of empirical studies on disability managers in Germany, there is little knowledge about the employment situation of these experts, let alone their practice. In other words, there is a blatant need for research in this field in Germany. For years, internationally, research on competencies and professionalization has been

---

5   See Deutsche Gesetzliche Unfallversicherung website. Available at: http://www.disability-manager.de/d/pages/ausbild/pdf_images/cdmp_pruef.pdf, accessed 28 July 2011.

the focus, aiming at the identification and description of skills and fields of activity of disability management experts. In order to get a broader picture of the international professionalization process there is a need to describe the tasks and duties of disability managers in different countries. Bearing in mind different systems and jurisdictions, the DM professionalization process could also help to overcome some of the obstacles the systems face. Nonetheless, one has to question whether or not an internationally applied formal degree and certification program would really meet the needs of the various players within companies. In relation to a potential global professionalization process, it has to be investigated as to why disability management professionals are more prominent in some jurisdictions than in others.

Additionally, research is needed into the extent to which supervision as means of professional support could add to the process of professionalization. Given that participation and empowerment are key elements of the German legislation, further research into professionalization could focus particularly on the counselling setting. Light particularly needs to be shed onto the impact that counselling can have when carried out, on the one hand, by disability professionals, and on the other hand by peer counselling. Lastly, it can be assumed that professionals working in rehabilitation services will have to be certified.

Bibliography

Abbott, A. (1983). Professional Ethics. *American Journal of Sociology* 88(5), 855–85.

Akabas, S.H. & Gates, L.B. (1995). *Planning for Disability Management. An Approach to Controlling Costs while Caring for Employees*. Scottsdale: American Compensation Association.

Bernhard, D. (2008). *Weiterbildung betrieblicher Akteure im Kontext der beruflichen Integration behinderter Menschen. Eine Bildungsbedarfsanalyse*. Aachen: Shaker Verlag.

Bernhard, D. & Niehaus, M. (2005). Integration Agreements as a New Approach on Dealing with Disability in Companies. *International Journal of Disability, Community & Rehabilitation* 4(2). Available at: http://www.ijdcr.ca/VOL04_02_CAN/articles/bernhard.shtml, accessed 7 February 2010.

Brandt, T. (2009). *Evaluation in Deutschland. Professionalisierungsstand und-perspektiven*. Münster: Waxmann Verlag.

Bundesministerium für soziale Sicherheit, Generationen und Konsumentenschutz in Zusammenarbeit mit anderen Bundesministerien (BMSK) (ed.). (2003). *Bericht der Bundesregierung über die Lage der behinderten Menschen in Österreich*. Vienna: Austrian Association for Rehabilitation.

Bruyère, S.M. (2006). Disability Management and the Enterprise. Paper presented at the Korea Employment Promotion Agency for the Disabled [KEPAD], Seoul.

Calkins, J., Lui, J.W. & Wood, Ch. (2000). Recent Developments in Integrated Disability Management. Implications for Professional and Organizational Development. *Journal of Vocational Rehabilitation* 15, 31–37.

Dyck, D. (2000). *Disability Management: Theory, Strategy and Industry practice*. Toronto and Vancouver: Butterworths.

Evetts, J. (2003). *International Sociology* 18(2), 395–415.

Federal Ministry of Labour and Social Affairs (2006). *Social Security at a Glance*. Federal Ministry of Labour and Social Affairs: Bonn.

Franche, R.L., Cullen, K., Clarke, J., MacEachen, E., Frank, J., Sinclair, S. & Reardon, R. (2006). *Workplace-based Return-to-Work Interventions: A Systematic Review of the Quantitative and Qualitative Literature* (Summary). Toronto: Institute for Work & Health.

Guldberg, K. & Mackness, J. (2009). Foundations of Communities of Practice: Enablers and Barriers to Participation. *Journal of Computer Assisted Learning* 25, 528–38.

Havranek, J.E. (1997). Historical Perspectives on the Rehabilitation Counseling Profession and Disability Management. In D. Shrey & M. Lacerte (eds), *Principles and Practices of Disability Management in Industry* (355–70). Boca Raton: CRC Press LLC.

Huber, A. & Ochs, P. (2004). *Die Vertretung schwerbehinderter Menschen im Betrieb.* (3rd ed.) Frankfurt am Main: Bund.

Hudson, R. & Sullivan, T. (2002). *The Social Organization of Work.* (3rd ed.). Belmont CA: Wadsworth/ Thomas Learning.

International Labour Organization (ILO) (2002). *Managing Disability in the Workplace. ILO Code of Practice.* Geneva: International Labour Organization.

Jackson, J.A. (1970) (ed.). *Professions and Professionalization.* Cambridge: Cambridge University Press.

Kurtz, T. (2004). Organisation und Profession im Erziehungssystem. In W. Böttcher & E. Terhart (eds), *Organisationstheorie in pädagogischen Feldern* (43–68). Wiesbaden: VS Verlag für Sozialwissenschaften.

Leahy, M.J., Chan, F. & Saunders J.L. (2003). Job Functions and Knowledge Requirements of Certified Rehabilitation Counselors in the 21st Century. *Rehabilitation Counseling Bulletin* 46(2), 66–81.

Lave, J. & Wenger, E. (1991). *Situated Learning: Legitimate Peripheral Participation in Communities of Practice.* New York: Cambridge University Press.

Matthews, L.R., Buys, N.J., Crocker, R. & Degeneffe, C.E. (2007). Overview of Disability Employment Policy and Rehabilitation Practice in Australia: Implications for Rehabilitation Counselor Education. *Rehabilitation Education* 21(4), 241–50.

Mehrhoff, Friedrich (ed.), *Disability Management. Strategien zur Integration von behinderten Menschen in das Arbeitsleben. Ein Kursbuch für Unternehmer, Behinderte, Versicherer und Leistungserbringer* (9– 19). Stuttgart: Gentner Verlag.

Mehrhoff, F. & Schönle, P.W. (2005) (eds). *Betriebliches Eingliederungsmanagement. Leistungsfähigkeit von Mitarbeitern sichern.* Stuttgart: Gentner Verlag.

Minssen, H. & Riese, C. (2007). *Professionalität der Interessenvertretung. Arbeitsbedingungen und Organisationspraxis von Betriebsräten.* Berlin: Edition sigma.

Niehaus, M. & Bernhard, D. (2006). Corporate Integration Agreements and Their Function in Disability Management. *International Journal of Disability Management Research,*1(1), 42–51.

(OECD) (2009). *Sickness, Disability and Work. Keeping on Track in the Economic Downturn.* Background Paper. Organisation for Economic Co-operation and Development Directorate for Employment, Labour and Social Affairs. Available at: http://www.oecd.org/dataoecd/42/15/42699911.pdf, accessed 7 February 2010.

Niehaus, M. & Marfels, B. (2010). Competencies and Tasks of Disability Management Professionals in Germany. *International Journal of Disability Management*, 5(2), 67–72. DOI 10.1375/jdmr.5.2.67.

Reser, L.C. & Epstein, I. (1990). *Professionalization and Activism in Social Work: The Sixties, the Eighties, and the Future.* New York: Columbia University Press.

Reynolds, S., Ridley, N. & Van Horn, C.E. (2005). *A Work-filled Retirement: Workers' Changing Views on Employment and Leisure.* New Brunswick NJ: Rutgers, the State University of New Jersey, John J. Heldrich Center for Workforce Development.

Rosenthal, D.A., Hursh, N., Lui, J., Isom, R. & Sasson, J. (2007). A Survey of Current Disability Management Practice. Emerging Trends and Implications for Certification. *Rehabilitation Counseling Bulletin* 50(2), 76–86.

Schian, H.M. (2006). Vocational Rehabilitation and Participation in Working Life: The German Model. C. Gobelet & F. Franchignoni (eds). *Vocational Rehabilitation* (309–27). Paris: Springer-Verlag France.

Shaw, W., Hong, Q.-N., Pransky, G. & Loisel, P. (2008). A Literature Review Describing the Role of Return-to-Work Coordinators in Trial Programs and Interventions Designed to Prevent Workplace Disability. *Journal Occupational Rehabilitation*, 18, 2–15.

Stichweh, R. (1999). Professionen in einer funktional differenzierten Gesellschaft. In A. Combe & W. Helsper (eds). *Pädagogische Professionalität. Untersuchungen zum Typus pädagogischen Handelns* (49–690. (3rd ed.). Frankfurt a. M.: Suhrkamp.

United Nations (2007). Convention on the Rights of Persons with Disabilities. Available at: http://www.un.org/disabilities/convention/conventionfull.shtml, accessed 8 May 2009.

6 Human Rights and Duty to Accommodate in Employment: Perspectives from Canada

DANIEL HUANG, SHANNON L. WAGNER AND HENRY G. HARDER

Introduction

Since the Second World War, human rights and the duty to accommodate in employment have become increasingly prominent, particularly as legislation has developed to protect the rights of those belonging to a protected group. The definition of protected group varies from one jurisdiction to another. However, a generally protected group is defined as those who have membership in the following groups: race, national or ethnic origin, colour, marital status, religion, age, family status, sex, sexual orientation, disability and conviction for which a pardon has been granted.

In light of these developments, disability management has emerged to facilitate the ongoing needs of the various stakeholders in this area. Disability management focuses on the integration and participation of people in the protected group in competitive employment through proactive involvement and accountability of key stakeholders (Dyck 2002). The key stakeholders include employees, employers, unions, healthcare/ rehabilitation professionals, insurance/other service providers and government/other public officials. To achieve this objective, stakeholders must not only be proactive, involved and accountable for their actions (Dyck 2002), they must also possess adequate knowledge of human rights and their duty to accommodate. In addition, stakeholders' attitudes toward human rights and the duty to accommodate also play an important role in accomplishing this end.

This chapter will provide an overview of the development of human rights legislation and the duty to accommodate provision in Canada as it pertains to employment.

Acts and Regulations

Human rights legislation in Canada began as early as 1944 when the Racial Discrimination Act in Ontario was passed (Howe & Johnson 2000). In 1960, the Canadian Bill of

Rights was passed in parliament followed by the Canadian Human Rights Act (CHRA) in 1977 (CHRA, 1985). In 1982, the Canadian Charter of Rights and Freedoms (CCRF) was incorporated into the Constitution Act of 1982 (Peters & Montgomerie 1998). Furthermore, the rights and protection of Canadians in the area of employment, housing and access to government and public goods and services are also provided under human rights legislations at the various federal, provincial and territorial levels. These statutes have been established to provide protection against discrimination and to advance equality of rights for all Canadians (Howe & Johnson 2000), particularly for those in the protected groups. Table 6.1 lists the Acts and Regulations governing human rights in their respective jurisdiction.

Table 6.1   Acts and Regulations

Jurisdiction	Acts and Regulation
Canada	Canada Labour Code (1985) Canada Labour Standards Regulations (2006) Canadian Charter of Rights and Freedoms (1982) Canadian Human Rights Act (1977) Canadian Human Rights Benefit Regulations (1980) Constitution Act, 1867 Criminal Records Act (1970) Federal Courts Act (1985) Income Tax Act (1952) Indian Act (1867) Parliament Employment and Staff Relations Act (1985) Unemployment Insurance Act (1940)
Alberta	Human Rights, Citizenship and Multiculturalism Act (2000) Individual's Rights Protection Act (1972) (Human Rights Act 1966)
British Columbia	Civil Rights Protection Act (1981) Family Relations Act (1978) Human Rights Code (1969)
Manitoba	Age of Majority Act (1988) Employment Standards Act (2004) Human Rights Code (1970) Manitoba Evidence Act (1988)
New Brunswick	Age of Majority Act (1972) Employment Standards Act (1982) Human Rights Code (1967) Industrial Relations Act (1982)
Newfoundland and Labrador	Human Rights Code (1969)
Northwest Territories	Human Rights Act (2002)
Nova Scotia	Boards of Inquiry Regulations (1991) Human Rights Act (1963) Public Inquiries Act (1989)
Nunavut	Human Rights Act (2003)

Table 6.1   *Concluded*

Jurisdiction	Acts and Regulation
Ontario	Accessibility for Ontarians with Disabilities Act (2005) Change of Name Act (1990) Co-operative Corporations Act (1990) Education Act (1871) Human Rights Code (1962) Limitations Act (2002) Statutory Powers Procedure Act (1990) Workplace Safety and Insurance Act (1997)
Prince Edward Island	Human Rights Act (1968)
Quebec	Act to secure the handicapped in the exercise of their rights with a view to achieving social, school, and workplace integration (2004) Charter of Human Rights and Freedoms (1975)
Saskatchewan	Saskatchewan Human Rights Code (1979)
Yukon	Human Rights Act (1987) Human Rights Regulations (2009)

Purpose of Human Rights

The 'overriding purpose of human rights legislation is the elimination of discrimination' (MacNeill 2003: 2-2) where the principles of equality, inherent dignity and worth of the person (MacNeill 2003) are found to be within all federal, provincial and territorial human rights legislations. The spirit of these legislations are enacted and enforced in support of section 15(1) of the Charter of Rights and Freedoms which specifically states:

> *Every individual is equal before and under the law and has the right to the equal protection and equal benefit of the law without discrimination and, in particular, without discrimination based on race, national or ethnic origin, colour, religion, sex, age, or mental or physical disability.*

Although human rights legislation varies from one jurisdiction to another and from provincial to federal levels, they all generally share the following purposes:

1. Human rights legislation is regarded as quasi-constitutional, granting power and status of this legislation to supersede nearly all other private contracts, laws and statutes. Other laws and contracts must be interpreted and applied in accordance with each of the federal, provincial or territorial human rights legislation (D'Andrea, Corry & Forester 2004; MacNeill 2003). In the *O'Malley* case to be discussed below, Mr Justice McIntyre of the Supreme Court of Canada states 'legislation of this type is of special nature, not quite constitutional but certainly more than the ordinary – and it is for the court to seek out its purpose and give it effect' (Zinn 2009: 1–2).
2. Human rights legislation cannot be contracted out. For example, in a unionized environment where a collective agreement sets out the relationship (contract) between employer and employee, this collective agreement cannot be used to waive,

modify or overwrite human rights legislation (D'Andrea, Corry & Forester 2004; MacNeill 2003).

3. Human rights legislation is remedial and not punitive in nature. Therefore, violators of human rights legislation are not brought to justice by being punished. Instead, human rights legislation seeks to 'prevent discrimination or provide relief against the effects of discrimination' (MacNeill 2003: 2–4). Remedies for human rights violations may be monetary, non-monetary and/or by mitigation of the effects of discrimination. Monetary remedies may include lost wages, lost opportunity of employment, monetary awards, general, exemplary and punitive damages. Non-monetary remedies may include apology, reinstatement, staff training and posting, amending the collective agreement, recruitment and advertising, cease and desist and the adoption of a non-discrimination action plan. Mitigation remedies may include pension benefits, interest, costs, treatment of unemployment and social assistance benefits (Zinn 2009).

4. Human rights legislation is to be interpreted broadly and purposefully. In the interpretation of human rights, Mr Justice McIntyre of the Supreme Court of Canada states that the court is to 'give to it an interpretation which will advance its broad purposes' (Zinn 2009: 1–2). For example, proof of intent to discriminate is not necessary to make out a human rights complaint' (MacNeill 2003: 2–6). Discrimination can exist even if it's not overt. This is referred to as adverse effect discrimination.

5. Human rights legislation prohibits discrimination based upon membership in a protected group which includes all of the following: race, national or ethnic origin, colour, marital status, religion, age, family status, sex, sexual orientation, disability, conviction for which a pardon has been granted (D'Andrea, Corry & Forester 2004; MacNeill 2003). Some of the categories listed may vary slightly from one jurisdiction to another. However, these are the primary categories of protected groups under human rights legislation.

Interpretation and Application of Human Rights

In Canada, human rights legislation is applied and interpreted by a human rights tribunal, human rights panel or board of inquiry (Zinn 2009; MacNeill 2003). However, as outlined in MacNeill (2003), human rights adjudicators may include any and/or all of the following: human rights commissions/tribunals/boards of inquiry, labour arbitrators, employment standard adjudicators, occupational health and safety adjudicators, labour relations boards and police service boards. Generally, human rights legislation is governed by each of the federal, provincial and territorial acts. Depending on the matter at hand, in which violations may or may not have occurred, the human rights legislation of the appropriate act within each of the jurisdiction will be in effect when adjudicating the matter. However, interpretation and decisions can rely on other jurisdictions' decisions to help make the case of discrimination (D'Andrea, Corry & Forester 2004; MacNeill 2003). Although there are different and distinct human rights legislations for different jurisdictions, it is important to note that there are considerable similarities in language and approach taken in each jurisdiction when applying, interpreting and adjudicating these legislations. In fact, one human rights arbitrator clearly articulated that given the requirements set out in section 15(1) of the CCRF and the fact that most case precedents, be they provincial, territorial or federal, were established by the Supreme Court of Canada, and that human rights tribunals, boards of inquiry, and other adjudicators should not find distinction between the various legislations, but should come to a decision in a fair and consistent manner (MacNeill 2003).

The process by which human rights complaints are filed and resolved varies from one jurisdiction to another. However, Zinn (2009) and MacNeill (2003) generally outline the process of human rights complaints and its ultimate resolution in the following steps.

First, a complaint of a human rights violation is filed with the human rights commission of the jurisdiction in which the alleged violation occurred. In most jurisdictions, any individual or group of individuals may initiate the complaints, including the human rights commission itself. Depending on the jurisdiction, the statute of limitation to file a complaint ranges from six months to two years from the last date of the alleged infraction.

Second, the complaint is investigated by the director of the human rights commission, the human rights commission or parties involved. The complaint is mediated and/ or settled by the director, human rights commission, the respective parties and/or the adjudicators outlined above. The complaint can also be dismissed by the director or the human rights commission. In some jurisdictions, the settlement may require the approval of a human rights commission to make it binding on the parties.

Third, if the complaint is not settled, the complaint is referred to the human rights tribunal, human rights panel or board of inquiry for follow-up investigation, adjudication and an ultimate decision on the case at hand.

Fourth, if the complaint is still not satisfactorily settled or there has been an error in law, an appeal may be filed in jurisdiction that allows for appeal of the human rights commission/tribunal decision. Consequently, if an appeal is not an available option, the only other redress is to request a judicial review of the decision. This may be ultimately decided by the highest court in Canada, which is the Supreme Court of Canada.

Human Rights and Employment

Human rights legislation applies to employment, housing and public services. With respect to employment specifically, human rights legislation applies to employer-employee relationships, unions, employer organizations, employment agencies and vocational/professional associations (D'Andrea, Corry & Forester 2004). However, human rights legislation does not have jurisdiction in an employment relationship that is within a private residence. As an example, an employment relationship between a homeowner and someone the homeowner employs to clean their house, babysit their children, etc., is considered to be an employment relationship within a private residence. The employer (homeowner) in this case is exempt from the provisions under human rights legislation.

With respect to the employment relationship, provincial or territorial legislation has jurisdiction in their respective province or territory with the exception of matters that fall under the constitutional jurisdiction of the federal parliament (Zinn 2009; MacNeill 2003). These may be employment relationships regulated by federal legislation such as the regulation of trade and commerce, employment insurance, the postal service, the military, shipping, telecommunication, federal public service, etc. (Zinn 2009; MacNeill 2003).

There has been an increased sensitivity to and interest in human rights in many parts of the developed world (Peters & Montgomerie 1998). A literature review conducted for the period of 1991 to 2010 found that in the 1990s, several countries enacted legislation specifically to protect the rights of persons with disabilities in the areas of employment, housing and access to government and public goods and services. Although specific to persons with disabilities, legislations are being enacted around the world with respect to human rights and the duty to accommodate in employment.

In brief, one of the first legislated acts was the Americans with Disabilities Act (1990) in the United States (Wehman 1993), providing the most comprehensive civil rights law protecting persons with disabilities in the area of employment, state and federal government services, private and public accommodations and services, and telecommunication (Hernandez, Keys & Balcazar 2004; Hernandez et al. 1998). This act followed the earlier Civil Rights Act of 1964 (Hernandez et al. 1998) and Rehabilitation Act of 1973 (Hernandez, Keys & Balcazar 2004) providing protection for persons with disabilities against workplace discrimination.

The Americans with Disabilities Act (ADA) was followed by the enactment of the Disability Discrimination Act (DDA) in 1992 in Australia. Similar to the ADA, the DDA provides persons with disabilities protection from discrimination in the areas of employment and access to public goods and services (Handley 2001). Then in 1995, the United Kingdom enacted its own Disability Discrimination Act providing similar protection for persons with disabilities (Jackson, Furnham & Willen 2000). The most recent country to pass legislation was Israel in 1998 with the Equal Rights for People With Disabilities (ERPWD) law (Vilchinsky & Findler 2004).

Although Canada, as a whole, does not have a specific legislated act for persons with disability, the rights and protection of persons with disabilities in employment, housing and access to government and public goods and services is provided under law in the acts and regulations listed in Table 6.1. However, in 2001, the province of Ontario passed the Ontarians with Disabilities Act, which was later amended to the Accessibility for Ontarians with Disabilities Act in 2005 (Ministry of Community and Social Services 2005). The legislation is similar, in spirit, to the ADA. In fact, Canada is currently reviewing the Accessibility for Ontarians with Disabilities Act to move towards developing an act that would be legislated federally for all jurisdictions.

It is important to note and most certainly be aware and have an understanding of other international acts and legislations in the area of human rights and the duty to accommodate as it is common, and sometimes necessary, to refer to international sources of law to provide guidance with respect to human rights and the duty to accommodate in employment. Specifically, American statutes contained in the ADA, Civil Rights and Rehabilitation Acts have been influential sources of statutes bearing on human rights adjudication in Canada (MacNeill 2003).

CASE SETTING PRECEDENTS

As stated above, human rights legislation in Canada dates back as far as 1944 and has developed and evolved over a number of years. Several cases have set precedents that have had a significant impact on human rights in Canada with respect to the interpretation and application of the legislation. In addition, the implications of human rights legislation established from these cases have far-reaching effects in the field of disability management, particularly as disability management professionals must be knowledgeable about the legislation and its effect on employers, employees and unions. The *Huck*, *O'Malley* and *Robichaud* cases are discussed in detail below.

The Huck Case

Canadian Odeon Theatres Ltd v Huck (Canadian Human Rights Reporter 1985) was of particular importance in establishing the principle of 'equality of outcome' for people in the protected groups and supporting section 15(1) of the CCRF. Michael Huck relies on a motorized wheelchair for mobility. In 1980, Mr Huck entered a movie theatre where he was advised that he could transfer to a chair or sit in the area in the front row of the theatre with his wheelchair. Consequently, Mr Huck was seated at the front of the movie theatre because the nature of his disability did not allow him to transfer into a regular seat.

Mr Huck grieved that because of his disability he did not receive the 'equality of outcome' of others who attended the movie theatre. Although the theatre provided the same treatment for Mr Huck as for other patrons of the theatre (i.e., had room to accommodate Mr Huck and his wheelchair in the theatre), Mr Huck was seated at the front of the movie theatre, which made it difficult to enjoy the movie due to the proximity to the screen. The Saskatchewan Court of Appeal concluded that it was not enough to provide equal treatment to all, but that all persons, regardless of the fact that they belong to a protected group, should have the equality of outcome. In this case, equality of outcome would be the same enjoyment of the movie as everyone else in that theatre.

The O'Malley Case

Ont. Human Rights Comm. v Simpsons-Sears (Supreme Court of Canada 1985) established that discrimination does not have to be intentional to be discriminatory. Theresa O'Malley was employed with Simpsons-Sears. After a few years of employment with Simpsons-Sears, Ms O'Malley joined the Seventh-Day Adventist Church, which required a strict observance of the Sabbath from sundown Friday to sundown Saturday. The employment condition was that employees are required to work on Friday evenings and two out of every three Saturdays. The employer fired Ms O'Malley because she could not work her rotation during this period. Ms O'Malley filed a complaint stating that while the employment rule requiring employees to work Saturdays was made for sound business reasons and applied equally to all employees, it was in its effect discriminatory because it required that she act against her religious belief while this rule did not have the same effect on other employees. The Supreme Court of Canada recognized this and held that while this was not intentional, it was still discriminatory.

In essence, the court writes:

> *an employment rule honestly made for sound economic and business reasons and equally applicable to all to whom it is intended to apply, may nevertheless be discriminatory if it affects a person or persons differently from others to whom it is intended to apply. The intent to discriminate is not a governing factor in construing human rights legislation aimed at eliminating discrimination. Rather, it is the result or effect of the alleged discriminatory action*

that is significant. The aim of the Ontario Human Rights Code is to remove discrimination – its main approach is not to punish the discriminator but to provide relief to the victim of discrimination. (Supreme Court of Canada 1985).

The Robichaud Case

Robichaud v Canada (Treasury Board) (Supreme Court of Canada 1987) established that employers are liable for the discriminatory act of their employee(s). Bonnie Robichaud was employed with the Department of National Defence. She filed a complaint with the Canadian Human Rights Commission that she was sexually harassed and discriminated against by her employer and her supervisor. The Supreme Court of Canada found that the Department of National Defence was liable for the action of its supervisory personnel. In short, the court states that 'a discriminatory practice by the employee is to be considered a discriminatory practice by the employer as well, whether or not authorized or intended by the latter' (Supreme Court of Canada 1987).

The Duty to Accommodate

These three cases clearly outlined the development and progression of human rights in Canada since 1944 when the Racial Discrimination Act was adopted in Ontario. The fundamental human rights principles established in the cases presented have important implications for disability management professionals. It is imperative that in the process of developing programs and policies for integration and participation of persons belonging to a protected group in competitive employment, that professionals in the field have the knowledge and clearly understand the fundamental principles established in these cases in order to not contravene human rights legislation. They must be responsible and held accountable for ensuring programs and policies are implemented in accordance with human rights legislation. Specifically, the fundamental principles established in the cases have direct impact on the roles and responsibilities of disability management professionals.

The duty to accommodate is defined as a legal obligation of employers to facilitate the inclusion of persons in a protected group (MacNeill 2003). In other words, an employer may have a responsibility to adapt or adjust employment requirements, such as making a facility accessible or scheduling flexibility to meet the needs of someone who belongs to a protected group (Zinn 2009). In doing so, the primary source of the duty to accommodate in employment in Canada can be found in the Canadian Charter of Rights and Freedoms, provincial and federal human rights legislation, the Employment Equity Act (Harder & Scott 2005), and other acts and regulations as outlined in Table 6.1 (Zinn 2009). The CCRF is part of the Constitution and human rights legislation is considered to be quasi-constitutional, which overrides nearly all other laws and private contracts. The duty to accommodate is borne from human rights legislation and case law precedents (Humphrey 2002). Since the primary source of the duty to accommodate is within the CCRF and human rights legislation, the responsibility lies heavily on employers. Therefore, any law or private contract must be interpreted and applied in accordance with provisions set out in human rights legislation. Additionally, other statutory sources with the duty to accommodate provision in employment includes workers' compensation legislation in some Canadian jurisdictions, the Ontario Police Service Act (MacNeill 2003), the Accessibility for Ontarians with Disabilities Act 2005 (AODA), among others outlined in Table 6.1.

In Canada, section 15(1) of the CCRF provides a broad and general definition of anti-discrimination protection for persons in the protected groups. Specific laws and legislation protecting persons in these groups are contained in case law precedents in the court, provincial and federal human rights legislation, provisions set out in collective agreements and workers' compensation board legislation. It is a legal obligation of employers to facilitate inclusion of persons in a protected group outlined in the CCRF (Humphrey 2002).

Interpretation and Application of the Duty to Accommodate

In order for the duty to accommodate in employment to come into effect under human rights legislation, a *prima facie* case of prohibited discrimination must be established (MacNeill 2003). To establish a *prima facie* case of discrimination, three criteria must be met as follows: (a) there must be an adverse and differential treatment; (b) it must be within the public arena, such as employment, housing and public services; and (c) it must be the result of a membership in a protected group (MacNeill 2003).

Once a *prima facie* case of discrimination is established against an employer by the employee, responsibility shifts to the employer to prove that there was no violation of human rights and duty to accommodate. Before the *Meiorin* case (discussed below), there were two approaches, also known as the two-pronged approach (Zinn 2009), to dealing with a *prima facie* case of discrimination based on two categories of discrimination. These are direct discrimination and adverse effect discrimination.

MacNeill (2003) defined direct discrimination as obvious, blatant or expressed discrimination. In the simplest term, an employment policy stating that the employer will not employ persons who are black or Catholic is considered direct discrimination (Zinn 2009). In the case of direct discrimination, when an employee has established a *prima facie* case of discrimination, the onus is on the employer to prove that the discriminatory act was based on a *bona fide* occupational requirement (BFOR), that is to say, that the standard imposed on the employee was imposed honestly and in good faith and was not designed to contravene human rights legislation and that the standard was imposed because it was necessary for the safe and efficient performance of the work and does not place an unreasonable burden on the employee. If an employer is able to establish BFOR, then there would be no discrimination.

MacNeill (2003) defined adverse effect discrimination as subtle, less obvious or implicit, but still discriminatory in its effect. In the simplest terms, an employer may establish an employment policy that all employees must work on Saturday. Although, this policy may apply equally to all employees, it may be discriminatory in its effect on those whose religion does not permit working on Saturday. Therefore, the policy is considered as adverse effect discrimination. In this case, the employer would have to show a rational connection between the employee's employment and the standard established and that the employer could not accommodate the employee without undue hardship to the employer.

The problem with these separate approaches was that employers can manipulate the outcome of a discriminatory effect at the workplace simply by characterizing the discrimination as direct or adverse effect, depending on what the employer feels would be most defensible (MacNeill 2003). To avoid this problem, the 'unified approach' or 'unified test' was established in the *Meiorin* case.

The unified approach to discrimination has three distinct steps. First, the standard must be rationally connected to the duties of the job. Second, the standard was established in honest and good faith. Third, the standard was reasonably necessary to carry out the duties of the job and that the employer cannot accommodate the employee without experiencing undue hardship (D'Andrea, Corry & Forester 2004; MacNeill 2003). All three steps must be met before a discrimination claim can be dismissed after a *prima facie* case of discrimination has been established.

CASE SETTING PRECEDENTS

The following four cases, all of which were decided in the highest court (Supreme Court of Canada) in the country, were significant in establishing the duty to accommodate standards, including the law regarding the defences of *bona fide* occupational requirement (BFOR) and *bona fide* justification (BFJ) and the duty to accommodate to the point of 'undue hardship' for employers as well as unions. The *Meiorin*, *Grismer*, *Christie* and *Renaud* cases are discussed in detail below to provide the context of the fundamental principles that establish the duty to accommodate. However, it is important for disability management professionals to understand the fundamental principles and not the details of the cases themselves when contemplating accommodation of employees.

The Meiorin Case

British Columbia (Public Service Employee Relations Commission) v BCGSEU (Supreme Court of Canada 1999) established the 'unified approach' for a three-step test for a *bona fide* occupational requirement, including the duty to accommodation to the point of undue hardship. Tawney Meiorin, a female forest firefighter, had been working successfully as a firefighter for three years when she was fired from her job one day because she failed one part of the minimum fitness standard that was introduced by the Government of British Columbia for all forest firefighters in the province. These standards were established and adopted by the government, and included a running test designed to measure aerobic fitness, which was the test Ms Meiorin failed. Ms Meiorin complained that this was discriminatory and violated the British Columbia Human Rights Code based on the fact that women generally have lower aerobic capacity than men. Secondly, Ms Meiorin had sufficiently demonstrated that she could do the job of a forest firefighter in a safe and effective manner. The Government of British Columbia, however, argued that the aerobic standard established was a BFOR for the firefighter position and that all firefighters, be they male or female, must meet this requirement in order to perform the job safely and effectively.

In reaching a decision for the case on appeal, the Supreme Court of Canada considered the traditional two-pronged approached which looked at whether the discrimination was direct or adverse effect. In the Court's analysis, they concluded that the two-pronged approach in the distinction between direct and adverse effect discrimination and the separate defences for each were artificial, difficult to characterize accurately and inconsistent with the purpose of human rights legislation. Therefore, it was determined that the aerobic standard established by the Government of British Columbia was, in fact, not a valid BFOR. The significance of this case was that court rejected the traditional two-pronged approach that had been in effect up to this point and established the unified test, as outlined above, in all cases of discrimination, be they direct or adverse effect.

It is important to note that the last step, 'the standard was reasonably necessary to carry out the duties of the job and that the employer cannot accommodate the employee without experiencing undue hardship', is the most difficult test to meet to successfully defend a discrimination based on a BFOR. Not only will the employer be required to establish that the standard was reasonably necessary to carry out the duties of the job, but they must also demonstrate that they cannot accommodate the employee without experiencing undue hardship. This requirement was clearly demonstrated in the *Grismer* case below in which the Supreme Court, relying on the *Meiorin* decision, struck down the British Columbia Superintendent of Motor Vehicles' standard because it failed the final element of the unified test.

The Grismer Case

British Columbia (Superintendent of Motor Vehicles) v British Columbia (Council of Human Rights) (Supreme Court of Canada 1999) defined individual testing to the point of undue hardship as a part of the duty to accommodate. Terry Grismer had an eye condition known as *homonymous hermianopia* (HH), which eliminated his left-side peripheral vision in both eyes. Mr Grismer's driver's licence was cancelled by the British Columbia Superintendent of Motor Vehicles on the basis of Mr Grismer's eye condition as he did not meet the minimum field of vision of 120-degree standard established by the British Columbia Superintendent of Motor Vehicles.

Mr Grismer reapplied several times for his driver's licence, each time passing all of the requisite tests except the field of vision test. Mr Grismer then filed a complaint with the British Columbia Council of Human Rights claiming that his human rights were violated because of his eye condition. The Supreme Court of Canada agreed and struck down the standard of 120-degree field of vision in Mr Grismer's case and quashed the Superintendent of Motor Vehicles' BFJ defence because it failed the third step of the *Meiorin* unified test.

The significance of the *Grismer* case was its definition of individual testing to the point of undue hardship as a part of the duty to accommodate. The goal here was not absolute safety but reasonable safety. Undue hardship was also defined in the *Christie* case below.

The Christie Case

Central Alberta Dairy Pool v Alberta (Human Rights Commission) (Supreme Court of Canada 1990) defined 'undue hardship' in terms of safety, excessive financial costs, effect on the collective agreement, employee morale, adaptability or interchangeability of work force and facilities, and the size of the employer's operations. Jim Christie was an employee of Central Alberta Dairy Pool. He started employment in 1980 and joined the Worldwide Church of God in 1983. The religion required that Mr Christie observe his faith on certain days and take those days off work. Initially, Mr Christie was granted the days off work until he requested a Monday after Easter to observe his faith and was told that if he did not show up for work, he would be terminated. Mr Christie did not work Monday and when he returned on Tuesday, he found that he had been replaced.

Mr Christie submitted a complaint under the Individual's Right Protection Act that his rights were violated based on the grounds of his religion. The employer argued that Monday was a busy day at the milk plant and that the requirement to work that day was a BFOR. The Supreme Court of Canada agreed with Mr Christie and held that the Monday in question was not a BFOR and that the employer did not accommodate the employee to the point of undue hardship. The Court found that this was a case of adverse effect discrimination and that the Monday in question was an isolated incident and that there was no evidence that this would be a recurring event.

The Court went further and established and defined undue hardship to include safety, excessive financial costs, effect on the collective agreement, employee morale, adaptability or interchangeability of work force and facilities, and the size of the employer's operations.

The Renaud Case

Central Okanagan School District No. 23 v Renaud (Supreme Court of Canada 1992) established that unions also have the duty to accommodate to the point of undue hardship even if it violates the provisions set out in the collective agreement. Larry Renaud was an employee of the Central Okanagan School District No. 23. Mr Renaud was a unionized custodian. He was also a Seventh-Day Adventist. His religion required strict observance of the Sabbath from sundown Friday to sundown Saturday, meaning that he could not work during the Sabbath. However, the employment condition set out in the collective agreement between the employer and employees included shifts on Friday evening. Mr Renaud and the school board tried several times to set the employment condition to a Sunday to Thursday shift, but the union could not agree to this arrangement because it was an exception to the collective agreement. Eventually, the union threatened to launch a policy grievance and in light of other unsuccessful attempts to accommodate Mr Renaud, the employer eventually dismissed Mr Renaud for missing his Friday night shifts.

Mr Renaud submitted a complaint under the British Columbia Human Rights Act against the school board and the union on religious ground. The Supreme Court of Canada agreed with Mr Renaud and held that not only the employer, but the union also has a shared duty to accommodate Mr Renaud to the point of undue hardship. Furthermore, the union cannot contract out of human rights legislation by setting out provision in the collective agreement.

The above four cases established key definitions of the extent of the duty to accommodate in the context of human rights legislation. It is not the details of the cases that disability management professionals must understand, but the fundament principles of the duty to accommodate established from the cases that are vitally important. For example, the *Christie* and *Renaud* cases were based on the principle of the duty to accommodate a person, based on religious beliefs and customs. However, the fundamental principle established in the *Christie* case is that employers have the duty to accommodate to the point of undue hardship, which was defined by the Supreme Court of Canada to include safety, excessive financial costs, effect on the collective agreement, employee morale, adaptability or interchangeability of work force and facilities, and the size of the employer's operations. The fundamental principle established in the *Renaud* case was that unions also have the duty to accommodate to the point of undue hardship. Therefore, disability management professionals must understand these fundamental principles established in case law in their duty to manage, facilitate and accommodate employees in the workplace. Additionally, the accommodee (the person being accommodated) also has the duty and responsibility to provide information and participate in the process of accommodation without demands or expectations of a perfect solution (Humphrey 2002).

Conclusion

As has been shown in this chapter, Canada is moving to codify the rights of persons with disabilities with respect to being accommodated in society and especially in the work world. Employers can no longer use the excuse that it is too difficult or too costly to accommodate a worker with a disability unless there is a *bona fide* reason to do so.

Disability management professionals can make use of this legislation and the emerging jurisprudence in two ways. First, they can use their own knowledge in this field to educate employers, unions and workers with respect to human rights and the duty to accommodate. Such education will have the impact of easing a culture of accommodations into workplaces and paving the way for future accommodations. Second, the disability management professionals can use this legislation, and in particular examples from case law and the remedies awarded, to encourage recalcitrant employers to engage in providing accommodations for persons with disabilities.

Canada is by no means alone in moving in this direction. In the US the Americans with Disabilities Act has been a model for some years now. It is also encouraging to see the World Health Organization and the International Labour Organization providing leadership in Europe and worldwide. While it has taken a long time to move in this direction it is gratifying to see the momentum that is building in the industrialized world with respect to the basic human right of persons with disabilities to be accommodated while they engage in that very elemental and so critical societal function of work.

Bibliography

Accessibility for Ontarians with Disabilities Act 2005 (AODA). Available at: http://www.e-laws.gov. on.ca/html/statutes/english/elaws_statutes_05a11_e.htm, accessed 27 December 2009.

Canadian Charter of Rights and Freedoms (1982) (CCRF). Available at: http://laws.justice.gc.ca/en/ charter/, accessed 3 February 2008.

Canadian Human Rights Act (1985) (CHRA). Available at: http://laws.justice.gc.ca/en/showdoc/ cs/H-6/bo-ga:l_I/20090915/en#anchorbo-ga:l_I, accessed 10 January 2010.

Canadian Human Rights Reporter (1985). *Michael Huck* case. Available at: http://www.cdn-hr-reporter.ca/index.cfm?fuseaction=hrp.disabilityRights, accessed 27 January 2008.

D'Andrea, J.A., Corry, D.J., & Forester, H.I. (2004). *Illness and Disability in the Workplace: How to Navigate through the Legal Minefield*. Aurora, Ontario: Canada Law Book Inc.

Dyck, D.E.G. (2002). *Disability Management: Theory, Strategy, and Industry Practice*. (2nd ed.). Markham, Ontario: Butterworths Canada Ltd.

Handley, P. (2001). 'Caught between a Rock and a Hard Place': Anti-Discrimination Legislation in the Liberal State and the Fate of the Australian Disability Discrimination Act. *Australian Journal of Political Science* 36(3), 515–28.

Harder, H.G., & Scott, L.R. (2005). *Comprehensive Disability Management*. Toronto, Ontario: Elsevier Churchill Livingstone.

Hernandez, B., Keys, C. & Balcazar, F. (2004). Disability Rights: Attitudes of Private and Public Sector Representatives. *Journal of Rehabilitation* 70(1), 28–37.

Hernandez, B., Keys, C., Balcazar, F. & Drum, C. (1998). Construction and Validation of the Disability Rights Attitude Scale: Assessing Attitudes toward the Americans with Disabilities Act (ADA). *Rehabilitation Psychology*, 43(3), 203–18.

Howe, R.B., & Johnson, D. (2000). *Restraining Equality: Human Rights Commissions in Canada*. Toronto, Ontario: University of Toronto Press Incorporated.

Humphrey, B.G. (2002). *Human Resources Guide to the Duty to Accommodate*. Aurora, Ontario: Canada Law Book Inc.

Jackson, C. J., Furnham, A. & Willen, K. (2000). Employer Willingness to Comply with the Disability Discrimination Act regarding Staff Selection in the UK. *Journal of Occupational and Organizational Psychology* 73, 119–29.

MacNeill, K.D. (2003). *The Duty to Accommodate in Employment*. Aurora, Ontario: Canada Law Book Inc.

Ministry of Community and Social Services (2005). Available at: http://www.e-laws.gov.on.ca/html/statutes/english/elaws_statutes_05a11_e.htm, 11 February 2008.

Peters, F. & Montgomerie, C. (1998). Educators' Knowledge of Rights. *Canadian Journal of Education* 23(1), 29–46.

Supreme Court of Canada (1985). *O'Malley* case. Available at: http://scc.lexum.umontreal.ca/en/1985/1985rcs2-536/1985rcs2-536.html, accessed 27 January 2008.

Supreme Court of Canada (1987). *Robichaud* case. Available at: http://scc.lexum.umontreal.ca/en/1987/1987scr2-84/1987scr2-84.html, accessed 27 January 2008.

Supreme Court of Canada (1990). *Christie* case. Available at: http://scc.lexum.umontreal.ca/en/1990/1990rcs2-489/1990rcs2-489.html, accessed 27 January 2008.

Supreme Court of Canada (1992). *Renaud* case. Available at: http://scc.lexum.umontreal.ca/en/1992/1992rcs2-970/1992rcs2-970.html, accessed 27 January 2008.

Supreme Court of Canada (1999). *Meiorin* case. Available at: http://scc.lexum.umontreal.ca/en/1999/1999rcs3-3/1999rcs3-3.html, accessed 27 January 2008.

Supreme Court of Canada (1999). *Grismer* case. Available at: http://scc.lexum.umontreal.ca/en/1999/1999rcs3-868/1999rcs3-868.html, accessed 27 January 2008.

Vilchinsky, N. & Findler, L. (2004). Attitudes toward Israel's Equal Rights for People With Disabilities Law: A Multiperspective Approach. *Rehabilitation Psychology* 49(4), 309–16.

Wehman, P. (1993). *The ADA Mandate for Social Change*. Baltimore, ML: Paul H. Brookes Publishing Co.

Zinn, R.W. (2009). *The Law of Human Rights in Canada: Practice and Procedure*. Aurora, Ontario: Canada Law Book.

7 How to Deal with Disability-Related Diversity: Opportunities and Pitfalls

STEPHAN A. BÖHM, DAVID J.G. DWERTMANN AND
MIRIAM K. BAUMGÄRTNER

Introduction

Classic disability management (DM) constitutes a continuum dealing with several issues, namely prevention, claim initiation, claim management and return to work (Akabas, Gates & Galvin 1992; Harder & Scott, 2005). Among these fields, return-to-work is viewed as a 'primary goal of any disability management program' (Harder & Scott 2005: 20). The return-to-work process not only includes the initial return to work, but also deals with long-term issues concerning the remaining in employment of the respective employee (Harder & Scott 2005).

Apart from health-related issues and the need for accommodation, interaction processes with co-workers, supervisors and subordinates become even more critical aspects for a successful long-term (re-)integration. In their conceptual model for disability management, Harder and Scott (2003; 2005) emphasized the influence of the organization's management during the return-to-work process. Moreover, interaction processes and their influencing factors, such as social support, expectations and culture, were explicitly discussed.

The field of disability management provides little information about social interaction processes and how they can be influenced. This aspect is instead addressed within diversity research. According to Van Knippenberg and Schippers (2007: 517), '... how differences between work group members affect group process and performance, as well as group member attitudes and subjective well-being [is] the key question in diversity research'. Thus, the aim of this chapter is to make a contribution to the literature by introducing conceptual knowledge from the diversity research and relating it to disability management. We pay special attention to the relationship between organizational context factors and social interaction processes. By doing so, we strive to improve upon the understanding of psychological processes at the team level, which may contribute to a successful long-term integration of returning workers, as well as newly hired employees with disabilities, into the workforce. This chapter consists of three sections that emphasize different aspects of the topic.

In the first part of this chapter, we review the differences and similarities between disability and diversity management, illustrating why knowledge from the field of diversity can contribute to disability management programs. The second part of this chapter introduces psychological interaction theories that explain how disability-related diversity influences group processes. Part three focuses on the practical implications of the presented theoretical reasoning and also provides recommendations for a successful disability management process.

The Relationship between Disability and Diversity

To examine the relationship between disability management and diversity management, we first need to define the concepts of disability and diversity. The Americans with Disabilities Act of 1990 states that a disability is: 'An impairment that restricts the ability to perform normal daily activities'. Having a legal definition is important, due to insurance, pension and other regulations.

Diversity does not have a legal definition, but instead has several scientific definitions. Diversity is a relatively new field of research (Ashkanasy, Härtel & Daus 2002), which emerged from the anti-discrimination movement in the United States of America during the 1960s (Ivancevich & Gilbert 2000). In the scientific literature, diversity began receiving attention in the 1990s (e.g., Cox 1993). Definitions substantially differ in terms of content and broadness (for further details see Ashkanasy, Härtel & Daus 2002). However, there is agreement that the original aspects of diversity, namely race and gender, should be extended (Kulik & Bainbridge 2006).

One definition for diversity, which includes various forms of diversity, stems from Harrison and Klein (2007). They '... use "diversity" to describe the distribution of differences among the members of a unit with respect to a common attribute, X, such as tenure, ethnicity, conscientiousness, task attitude, or pay' (Harrison & Klein 2007: 1200). Providing a list of further diversity dimensions, Thomas (1992: 10) stated that diversity '... extends to age, personal and corporate background, education, function, and personality. It includes lifestyle, sexual preference, geographic origin, tenure with the organization, exempt or non-exempt status, and management or non-management'. Consequently, disability is also captured as one dimension within the diversity construct (e.g., Shore et al. 2009).

The Relationship between Disability Management and Diversity Management

We will now outline the concepts of disability and diversity management. Shrey and LaCerte (1995: 5) defined disability management as: 'A proactive process that minimizes the impact of an impairment on the individual's capacity to participate competitively in the work environment'. This definition primarily focuses on impairment as a physiological barrier, and therefore, on health-related issues and the individual person. Diversity management is defined as: '... the voluntary organizational actions that are designed to create greater inclusion of the employees from various backgrounds into the formal organizational structures through deliberate policies and programs' (Mor-Barak 2005: 208). Compared to disability management, this particular definition not only focuses on one specific target group (i.e., persons with disabilities), but on a variety of target groups.

As described in the definitions, disability management and diversity management both have their unique thematic aspects. For disability management, on the one hand, these are basically issues related to prevention, accommodations, being injured and the resulting return-to-work process. Thus, disability management primarily deals with actual physical barriers arising from health issues. It focuses on the individual employee (Harder & Scott 2005). Within this context, it is important to note that DM is oriented towards a relative health concept, focusing on the functionality of an individual (Harder & Scott 2005).

Diversity management, on the other hand, focuses more heavily on integrating different groups or units of employees. In addition, it covers various forms of being different from others. Among these aspects of diversity are all the dimensions introduced in the definition of diversity. Consequently, diversity management also includes disability. In addition, since diversity management focuses on various groups (Horwitz & Horwitz 2007), it emphasizes the importance of interaction processes within diverse work groups and companies. Thus, diversity management, compared to DM, deals primarily with psychological barriers arising from stereotypes and social distance instead of physiological barriers arising from impairments. Figure 7.1 displays the relationship between the constructs of DM (circle A) and diversity management (circle B).

However, the fields of DM and diversity management share a common focus (see circle C in Figure 7.1). People with lasting impairments or disabilities have diverse health issues and functionalities (i.e., disabilities). The fact that disability or ability has its own chapter in many of the modern books about diversity management confirms this rationale (e.g., Bell 2007; Stone-Romero, Stone & Lukaszewski 2006).

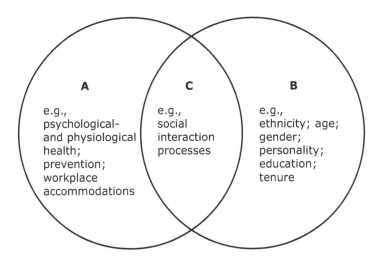

Figure 7.1   The relationship between disability and diversity management

A = DM; B = diversity management

In addition, the aforementioned psychological barriers often play an important role in the return-to-work process. These barriers may arise within the employee who has disabilities, or between the person and his/her supervisors and co-workers. Apart from the previously mentioned physiological barriers, including people with disabilities and people with other diverse demographic attributes in the workforce is challenging in a similar way. Thus, being aware of group processes explained by sociological and psychological theories used in diversity research seems to be equally important for dealing with disability-related diversity.

Introducing Findings from the Field of Diversity Research

As mentioned above, there are some problems within diversity research. One issue concerns the limitations stemming from an unclear definition of diversity. To deal with these issues, researchers have created many classifications to categorize the differences between people (Harrison & Sin 2006). A frequently used classification by Harrison, Price and Bell (1998) proposed surface versus deep level diversity (e.g., gender, age, etc., versus cognitive resources, personal characteristics, etc.). In a similar manner, Jackson, May and Whitney (1995) distinguished detectable and underlying diversity. This classification helped to improve diversity research.

Studies have often led to inconsistent results regarding various outcomes, especially performance (Jehn, Northcraft & Neale 1999; Van Knippenberg & Schippers 2007). Thus, Jackson and colleagues concluded that '... the literature offers few conclusive findings about the effects of diversity in the workplace' (Jackson, Joshi & Erhardt 2003: 807). Even more provocative, Milliken and Martins (1996: 403) called diversity a '... double-edged sword increasing the opportunity for creativity as well as the likelihood that group members will be dissatisfied and fail to identify with the group'.

A recent meta-analytic review by Horwitz and Horwitz (2007) shed some light on the effects of task-related (e.g., cognitive resources, personal characteristics) and demographic (e.g., gender, age) group diversity on performance. They reported a small, but significant, effect (ρ=.13) of the influence of task-related diversity on the quality of team performance (e.g., decision-making, creativity, problem-solving) and the relationship between task-related diversity and the quantity of team performance (ρ=.07). No significant results were found for demographic diversity.

Concerning the findings of disability-related diversity, Shore et al. (2009: 122) concluded in a recent review that '... the literature tends to view disability as negative'. This applies to social interaction processes in groups, leading to discrimination, as well as performance. However, the authors also emphasize that 'a few theories view disability more positively' and that '... work in vocational or rehabilitation journals, while more practical than theoretical, is increasingly taking a positive perspective' (Shore et al. 2009: 122). In summary, research on disability-related diversity revealed the same inconsistent pattern of results as diversity research in general.

In the following sections we will discuss reasons for the inconsistency of findings. Then we will review social interaction theories, explaining why diversity – including disability-diversity – could lead to either positive or negative effects.

SEPARATION, VARIETY AND DISPARITY

Harrison and Klein (2007) stated multiple reasons for the mixed results within the field of diversity research. Besides the already mentioned lack of a clear definition of the diversity construct, they highlighted the fact that diversity is a very broad topic that includes various forms of being diverse (e.g., age, ethnicity, gender). Therefore, results from different facets of diversity are difficult to integrate. All these reasons led to the understanding that diversity is a 'murky' construct (Harrison & Klein 2007: 1201).

To cope with the problems of diversity research, Harrison and Klein (2007) argued for the existence of not one, but three distinctive types of diversity: separation, variety and disparity. Each of these types implies a different form of maximum diversity, leading to varying group processes and therefore, different outcomes.

Separation occurs when team members hold opposing positions on a task- or team-relevant issue (e.g., health status). Regarding disability, a group consisting of three people without, and one with, disabilities could lead to separation if group members focus on disability as a team-relevant issue. Thus, separation could result from the composition of disability-diverse groups. Maximum diversity exists if group members are equally split at opposing endpoints of the continuum (i.e., two people with and two people without disabilities (Harrison & Sin 2006)).

Variety exists if group members have different knowledge (which might be based on demographics, e.g., age), resulting in a fruitful pool of information regarding various tasks. A diverse educational background could lead to variety. People with disabilities, especially over the long term, could have different experiences, as outlined above. Therefore, they could have different information or even skills. For example, a blind person may be more advantaged in hearing voices (Röder, Rösler & Neville 1999) and therefore, may be capable of interpreting the mood of co-workers better than his or her colleagues. Thus, variety is another possible effect arising from disability-diverse work groups. Maximum variety would result if every group member were to come from a unique category and hold unique information or skills (Harrison & Klein 2007).

Finally, disparity captures constellations in which there is a difference in the distribution of social assets (e.g., influence, money) among group members. Differences in the power of group members result from these unequal distributions. Oftentimes, people returning to work after they are injured begin their career again by only working part-time instead of full-time. This may be due to the fact that the employee is physically 'deconditioned', because he or she could not use the muscles necessary to conduct the job (Harder & Scott 2005: 113). As a result, employees might not be as integrated into everyday work life as they were before and, therefore, may not be as respected by their co-workers as they were prior to the disability causing incident. In this case, someone with a disability may not have equal power or influence (social asset) as their co-workers. Thus, disparity can develop within disability-diverse work units. If one unit member outranks all others in regard to the social asset in question, maximum disparity exists (Harrison & Klein 2007).

The outlined classification explains the contrasting effects of diversity. Disability can lead to all three types of diversity. Variety leads to positive outcomes. Separation and disparity cause detrimental group processes and losses in effectiveness (Harrison & Klein 2007). Hence, the main goal of this chapter is to describe the relationship between organizational context factors and social interaction processes aimed at avoiding the negative effects of disability-related diversity.

In the second part of the chapter, we will outline the underlying processes that cause the positive effects of diversity as variety and the negative effects of diversity as separation and disparity.

Sociological and Psychological Processes that Effect Diversity

Most authors have argued for the positive (performance) consequences of diversity in the workplace, which are related to the effects of variety. Some scholars also use the term 'information/decision-making perspective' (Van Knippenberg & Schippers 2007: 518) to describe when a team or workgroup can be understood as an 'information processing instrument for an organization' (Harrison & Klein 2007: 1205; Hinsz, Tindale & Vollrath 1997).

Diverse team members typically possess different knowledge bases, experiences or skills, which might help them to come up with a better solution to a problem than employees with more homogenous characteristics. This larger pool of resources often stems from different backgrounds, including a variety of demographic attributes (e.g., age, education). In addition to their own cognitive resources, diverse members also tend to possess different external and internal networks and have access to information important for the group's performance (Austin 2003).

When dealing with non-routine problems, it seems to be especially beneficial when diverse team members can use this additional 'sociocognitive horsepower' (Carpenter 2002: 280). Moreover, diverse teams seem to be more adaptive to environmental changes and might have a better understanding of their diverse customers. In addition, employees with different experiences and skill sets are likely to be more creative (Burt 2002; Jackson et al. 1995) and less impeded by the effects of groupthink (Janis 1972) through more intense discussions and the prevention of a premature consensus.

In summary, scholars adopting a variety perspective infer a higher performance level of diverse teams and workgroups (Bantel & Jackson 1989). In the case of diversity stemming from the disability status of certain group members, one could expect that employees with an impairment are more likely to help the group to approach problems from completely different angles. This is the case because they might have learned that normal solutions do not work for them. Disability-related knowledge could become especially important in a case where the organization has stakeholders, e.g., customers, with disabilities.

As both research and practice have shown, increasing levels of diversity can also result in negative outcomes, such as higher levels of conflict and withdrawal, as well as lower levels of cohesion and performance (Sacco & Schmitt 2005). Possible explanations for the negative effects of diversity can be derived from the concepts of separation and disparity.

In regard to separation, which focuses on potential differences in employees' demographic attributes, opinions or attitudes, scholars have identified at least two underlying psychological processes to explain the exclusion and potential discrimination of certain groups of employees: the similarity-attraction paradigm (Byrne 1971) and the social identity approach (Tajfel & Turner 1986).

The similarity-attraction paradigm describes the tendency of individuals to prefer contact and collaboration with others who are comparably similar to themselves (Byrne 1971). This actual, or perceived, similarity can comprise demographic characteristics (e.g., age, education), as well as similar opinions, attitudes or beliefs. As to the underlying psychological motivation, scholars have described that consensual validation mitigates uncertainty (Hinds et al. 2000). Individuals seem to receive more affirmative feedback from people they feel are similar to them and tend to trust them more.

Interpersonal heterogeneity may lead to decreased levels of communication, as well as more communication errors, within teams or workgroups (see Barnlund & Harland 1963). From an empirical point of view, the effects of similarity-attraction have been shown in both friendships and voluntary interactions (Blau 1977; McPherson & Smithlovin 1987), as well as in professional environments (see Hinds et al. 2000). In work groups where one or more employees have an impairment, employees, both those with and without disabilities, might (unconsciously) decide to keep to themselves and not form an inclusive community.

The similarity-attraction paradigm is complemented by a second psychological process, which may also lead to the exclusion of employees with disabilities. Theories of social identity (Tajfel & Turner 1986) and self-categorization (Turner 1987) suggest that individuals tend to classify themselves, and others, into certain groups on the basis of dimensions that are relevant to them. These dimensions often include demographic categories, such as race or disability status.

Individuals make use of these group classifications to differentiate between potentially similar in-group members and different out-group members. Such group categorizations are of high importance for individuals, as they derive a large part of their social identity from membership in particular groups. Following a basic human need to maintain and strengthen their self-esteem, individuals strive to perceive their own group as superior to others (Abrams & Hogg 1988). As a consequence, individuals tend to favour members of their own group (in-group) and exhibit higher levels of trust, communication and cooperation with them. Members of other groups (out-groups) may face certain forms of stereotyping and discrimination (Brewer & Brown 1998).

Two concepts explain why certain demographic categories, such as disability status, have a potentially stronger effect on individuals' self-definition and discriminative behaviour: the permeability of the attribute and the salience of the attribute. Permeability is defined as 'the degree to which that attribute can be altered moving a person from one social category to another social category' (Pelled, Eisenhardt, & Xin 1999: 5). Salience refers to the degree of visibility of the attribute. For physical disabilities, the potential for in-group/out-group formation should consequently be fairly high, as those with disabilities are, in most cases, both visible (high salience) and irreversible (low permeability).

It must be noted, however, that the percentage of employees with disabilities is rather small in most organizations (typically below 10 per cent). Therefore, it seems likely that employees with disabilities might experience a so-called token status (Kanter 1977; Young & James 2001) which describes how minorities (typically less than 15 per cent of the total group) in organizations are perceived as symbols of a certain category and less than individuals. Kanter (1977) described the negative outcomes of a token status, including increased levels of stereotyping, unfair performance pressure and the creation of interpersonal boundaries that might, in turn, lead to the formation of in- and out-groups.

In summary, for employees with disabilities, feelings of detachment and exclusion (separation) might arise, no matter if similarity-attraction, social identity or tokenism mechanisms cause them.

Finally, the concept of diversity will be analyzed from a disparity perspective, highlighting the underlying key assumptions. In contrast to both the variety and the separation perspective, scholarly work on the disparity perspective is surprisingly limited (Harrison & Klein 2007: 1206). It has its theoretical source in the sociological literature, in which it is discussed under the term 'inequality' (Blau 1977; Kreckel 2004). In the organizational-psychology-related literature on diversity, the concept of disparity is used in a similar, yet distinct, way. Scholars typically use it to analyze and describe the effects of unevenly distributed, valued or desired resources, such as power, status or prestige (Harrison & Klein 2007). It is assumed that individuals within teams or workgroups tend to differ in the extent to which they possess a share of the relevant resource. As a consequence of the unequal distribution, certain processes might be triggered within the group. For example, individuals with a disadvantaged status within the team (e.g., missing influence) might experience feelings of dissatisfaction and a desire to leave the group.

A potentially negative effect stemming from disparity issues may make intuitive sense regarding people with disabilities within workgroups. Persons with disabilities often hold low-status jobs (Schur et al. 2009) and might typically possess less power and social influence than other members of the organization. If such a lack of power is perceived as being unfair, a drop in commitment, satisfaction and ultimately performance may arise.

Practical Implications

In the third part of the chapter, practical implications and recommendations will be provided. The general goal of every DM program should be the creation and support of conditions that maximize the effects resulting from variety, while minimizing those of separation and disparity (Harrison & Klein 2007). Contextual factors should foster a conflict-free collaboration and the use of diverse knowledge, skills and competencies. To do so, there are different strategies that companies can apply at the supervisor and at the organizational levels (which includes the team), facilitating social interaction processes between persons with and without disabilities.

SUPERVISOR LEVEL

The supervisor and his or her relationship with an employee with disabilities is a critical factor for the integration of an employee with disabilities within a working group (Colella & Varma 2001). Consequently, managers need to be sensitized for a possible homophilic bias and should pay specific attention to their behaviour towards a person with disabilities in order to establish a good relationship with the person, which, in turn, may improve the standing of the person with diabilities within a working group.

For the effective functioning of teams in general, and diverse teams in particular, leadership plays a key role. Transformational leadership is considered to be one of the most effective forms of leadership related to several positive outcomes (Bass & Riggio 2006; Rubin, Munz & Bommer 2005). These outcomes include increased employee satisfaction, motivation, effectiveness of teams and organizational commitment (Bass 1985; Lowe, Kroeck & Sivasubramaniam 1996). 'Transformational leaders inspire, energize, and intellectually stimulate their employees' (Bass 1990: 19).

Transformational leadership behaviours can be classified into four components: role modelling, intellectual stimulation, inspiring motivation and individual consideration (Bass 1985; Avolio et al. 2004). *Role modelling* comprises behaving with integrity, as well as the demonstration of high ethical standards, values and beliefs. Leaders should function as a role model for others in relation to the integration of employees with disabilities and the strengthening of their in-group position. *Intellectual stimulation* relates to the ability of a leader to make employees think creatively and innovatively and motivate them to find solutions, even for complex problems. They enable their subordinates to get over their old ways of thinking. In terms of individualized solutions for a person with disabilities, a team leader can help to think beyond existing procedures or processes.

Inspiring motivation refers to the development and communication of a common vision for the future, which is the demonstration of optimism and enthusiasm concerning the attainment of goals. A transformational leader motivates employees to act beyond their self-interests, stressing the group instead of the individual goals. By creating a common social identity, team member subgroup formation can be reduced by including all the team members into 'one single in-group'. As a consequence, discrimination and exclusion can be diminished, preventing employees with disabilities from becoming the disliked members of an out-group.

Individual consideration describes the individual responsiveness of a leader to employees and their specific needs. This transformational leadership dimension is especially important for responding to the specific needs of persons with disabilities, to take their concerns into account, to motivate them and to make use of their particular strengths and weaknesses. This, in turn, contributes to the overall success of the team.

Recent studies found evidence for the positive effects of transformational leadership on the development of diverse groups (Kearney & Gebert 2009; Kunze & Bruch 2010). Kearney and Gebert (2009) showed that transformational leadership can be a key factor in supporting positive, and preventing negative, effects, i.e., process losses in diverse teams. They conclude that 'both demographic and informational heterogeneity constitute potentially valuable variety – as defined by Harrison and Klein (2007) – and that it depends on contextual conditions such as the type of leadership that is provided whether this variety will have predominantly positive or negative effects' (Kearney & Gebert 2009: 86).

TEAM LEVEL

The starting point for the creation of effective, diverse teams is team composition, which should be conducted purposefully. The following recommendations apply to employees changing their jobs within a company, as well as to those entering a new company. First of all, teams should be goal-oriented. Complementary competencies of employees, with and without disabilities, should be taken into account. The top management and supervisors should clearly communicate their goals and their appreciation of the different team members. As a consequence, prejudices can be reduced and each team member understand that the other team members can make a meaningful contribution. Thus, the effects of variety leading to cognitive diversity can be fostered while stereotyping and effects of separation and disparity are minimized.

Related to considerations concerning team composition is the finding that heterogeneous teams can use their diversity potential best if they work on complex non-routine tasks (Pelled, Eisenhardt & Xin 1999). Hereby, they can fully use their cognitive diversity in areas such as problem-solving skills and creativity. Furthermore, the added value of additional opinions, perspectives and experiences is more obvious and accepted.

ORGANIZATIONAL LEVEL

The design of supportive organizational conditions plays an essential role for all DM activities and represents a first step towards creating a diversity-friendly organizational culture. Organizational culture has a great impact on how people with disabilities are treated, creating the presence, or absence, of attitudinal, behavioural and physical barriers (Schur, Kruse, & Blanck 2005). To reduce barriers for employees with disabilities, it is important to develop and stress organizational norms and values that emphasize appreciation of every employee and respond to individual needs. This individual responsiveness also included the rethinking of some organizational habits and processes.

One key success factor of organizational conditions can be seen in designing appropriate reward and compensation systems. Contrary to recommendations concerning diversity, in general, it is not recommended that team-based compensation systems include persons with disabilities. Research has shown that collective performance systems can lead to disparity and separation between individuals with, and without, disabilities in competitive working environments (Stone & Michaels 1993, 1994). If a disability affects a person's performance, the use of team pay tends to have rather detrimental effects for persons with disabilities. When teams need to compete against each other for scarce resources, the negative social processes of excluding people with disabilities are amplified (Stone & Michaels 1993, 1994). In addition, a company's reward system should be aligned with the integration processes of people with disabilities (Stone & Colella 1996). Thus, incentives for integrating individuals with disabilities should be provided to managers.

Social approval on the part of a company's management can foster more favourable reactions concerning employees with disabilities. Formally recognizing units that have successfully integrated employees with disabilities can also increase acceptance. '[S]ocial approval by top management may alter members' behaviors toward persons with disabilities' (Stone & Colella 1996: 391). Changing behaviours by adjustments of reward systems may also successfully lead to changes in attitudes (Porter, Lawler & Hackman 1975).

Providing suitable accommodations for people with disabilities is a prerequisite for every DM program. As research has shown, perceived fairness when it comes to accommodation grants is a key factor in undermining harmful group processes between employees with, and without, disabilities leading to unproductive interaction processes (Colella 2001; Paetzold et al. 2008). A company must be aware that perceptions of unfairness and favouritism by non-disabled persons may become problematic (Colella 2001).

If non-disabled employees gain the impression that people with disabilities get preferential treatment, stereotypes of and negative attitudes against persons with disabilities are more likely. In many cases, colleagues simply do not know enough about a certain disability and why an accommodation is necessary. Thus, organizations should educate their employees about different types of disabilities. In addition, clear communication of reasons for accommodations may also help to gain acceptance for special treatment. Furthermore, accommodations are often not only helpful for a person with disabilities, but also for his or her non-disabled colleagues.

There are many examples of how initially pure-DM solutions are beneficial for all organizational members. A certain technology, for example, can be provided to every employee making everyone's job easier (Colella, Paetzold & Belliveau 2004). Getting an ergonomic chair, for instance, does not only help employees who suffer from back pain, but also everyone else in terms of pain prevention and a more comfortable sitting position. Furthermore, allowing for a certain flexibility concerning work schedules may also be advantageous for everyone. Moreover, there might be more than just one best way to do a certain job. Organizations should specify the job requirements, but allow the job incumbent to determine how these are accomplished. This autonomy assists employees, with and without disabilities, to work in accordance with their special strengths and weaknesses.

In summary, expanding measures to all employees may decrease the out-group status of persons with disabilities, thus leading to inclusive, rather than exclusive, interaction processes.

A concrete measure used to reduce the impact of prejudices and stereotypes and support a diversity-friendly organizational culture are diversity workshops and training, educating both supervisors and non-supervising employees about the negative effects of discriminatory behaviour (McKay & Avery 2005). Much of the diversity training research focuses on altering stereotype content (Kulik & Bainbridge 2006). Providing effective training conditions refers back to psychological theories.

Demuijnck (2009), for example, described a training program that aims to make employees aware of unconscious stereotypes by which they are manipulated. For this purpose, a company involved a theatre company, which played scenes incorporating common stereotypes, or reversed them. These sequences were followed by an analysis of existing stereotypes.

Conclusion

In this chapter, we sought to close the knowledge gap regarding social interaction processes within the field of DM by introducing knowledge from diversity research. We analyzed the relationship between the disability and diversity concepts and focused on the similarities of the two, including psychological barriers, potential conflicts and discrimination resulting from social interaction. The presented practical implications and recommendations drawn from diversity research focused on designing and influencing interactive processes between employees with, and without, disabilities on the supervisor, team and organizational levels.

The primary goals were found to be fostering an understanding for employees with disabilities, facilitating positive team processes and rethinking organizational structures. Purposefully creating favourable organizational conditions by taking psychological mechanisms and social interactions into account represents a critical success factor in return-to-work and long-term integration processes. The majority of these measures are not only beneficial for employees with disabilities, but also for employees without disabilities and the organization as a whole.

Bibliography

Abrams, D. & Hogg, M.A. (1988). Comments on the Motivational Status of Self-Esteem in Social Identity and Intergroup Discrimination. *European Journal of Social Psychology* 18(4), 317–34.

Americans with Disabilities Act of 1990. P. L. 101–336.

Akabas, S.H., Gates, L.B. & Galvin, D.E. (1992). *Disability Management*. New York: AMACOM.

Ashkanasy, N.M., Härtel, C.E.J. & Daus, C.S. (2002). Diversity and Emotion: The New Frontiers in Organizational Behavior Research. *Journal of Management* 28(3), 307–38.

Austin, J.R. (2003). Transactive Memory in Organizational Groups: The Effects of Content, Consensus, Specialization, and Accuracy on Group Performances. *Journal of Applied Psychology* 88(5), 866–78.

Avolio, B.J., Zhu, W.C., Koh, W. & Bhatia, P. (2004). Transformational Leadership and Organizational Commitment: Mediating Role of Psychological Empowerment and Moderating Role of Structural Distance. *Journal of Organizational Behavior* 25(8), 951–68.

Bantel, K. & Jackson, S. (1989). Top Management and Innovations in Banking: Does the Composition of the Team Make a Difference? *Strategic Management Journal* 10(1), 107–24.

Barnlund, D.C. & Harland, C. (1963). Propinquity and Prestige as Determinants of Communication Networks. *Sociometry 26*(4), 467–79.

Bass, B.M. (1985). *Leadership and Performance Beyond Expectations*. New York: Free Press.

Bass, B.M. (1990). From Transactional to Transformational Leadership: Learning to Share the Vision. *Organizational Dynamics* 18(3), 19–31.

Bass, B.M. & Riggio, R.E. (2006). *Transformational Leadership*. Mahwah NJ: Erlbaum.

Bell, M.P. (2007). *Diversity in Organizations*. Mason OH: South-Western, Cengage Learning.

Blau, P.M. (1977). *Inequality and Heterogeneity*. New York: Free Press.

Brewer, M.B., & Brown, R.J. (1998). Intergroup Relations. In D.T. Gilbert & S.T. Fiske (eds), *Handbook of Social Psychology* (554–94). Boston: McGraw-Hill.

Burt, R.S. (2002). The Social Capital of Structural Holes. In M.F. Guillen, R. Collins, P. England & M. Meyer (eds), *The New Economic Sociology* (148–89). New York: Russell Sage Foundation.

Byrne, D. (1971). *The Attraction Paradigm*. New York: Academic Press.

Carpenter, M.A. (2002). The Implications of Strategy and Social Context for the Relationship between Top Management Team Heterogeneity and Firm Performance. *Strategic Management Journal* 23(3), 275–84.

Colella, A. (2001). Co-worker Distributive Fairness Judgments of the Workplace Accommodation of Employees with Disabilities. *Academy of Management Review* 26(1), 100–16.

Colella, A. & Varma, A. (2001). The Impact of Subordinate Disability on Leader-Member Exchange Relationships. *Academy of Management Journal* 44(2), 304–15.

Colella, A., Paetzold, R.L. & Belliveau, M.A. (2004). Factors Affecting Co-workers' Procedural Justice Inferences of the Workplace Accommodations of Employees with Disabilities. *Personnel Psychology* 57(1), 1–23.

Cox, T. Jr. (1993). *Cultural Diversity in Organizations: Theory, Research, and Practice*. San Francisco: Berrett-Koehler.

Demuijnck, G. (2009). Non-Discrimination in Human Resources Management as a Moral Obligation. *Journal of Business Ethics* 88(1), 83–101.

Harder, H.G. & Scott, L.R. (2003). A Conceptual Model for Comprehensive Disability Management. *Journal of the Ontario Occupational Health Nurses Association* Winter, 20–22.

Harder, H.G. & Scott, L.R. (2005). *Comprehensive Disability Management*. Edinburgh: Elsevier Churchill Livingstone.

Harrison, D.A., Price, K.H. & Bell, M.P. (1998). Beyond Relational Demography: Time and the Effects of Surface- and Deep-Level Diversity on Work Group Cohesion. *Academy of Management Journal* 41(1), 96–107.

Harrison, D.A. & Sin, H.P. (2006). What is Diversity and How Should it be Measured? In A.M. Konrad, P. Prasad & J.K. Pringle (eds), *Handbook of Workplace Diversity* (191–216). London: Sage.

Harrison D.A. & Klein, K.J. (2007). What's the Difference? Diversity Constructs as Separation, Variety, or Disparity in Organizations. *Academy of Management Review* 32(4), 1199–228.

Hinds, P.J., Carley, K.M., Krackhardt, D. & Wholey, D. (2000). Choosing Work Group Members: Balancing Similarity, Competence and Familiarity. *Organizational Behavior and Human Decision Processes* 81(2), 226–51.

Hinsz, V.B., Tindale, R.S. & Vollrath D.A. (1997). The Emerging Conceptualization of Groups as Information Processors. *Psychological Bulletin* 121(1), 43–64.

Horwitz, S.K. & Horwitz, I.B. (2007). The Effects of Team Diversity on Team Outcomes: A Meta-Analytic Review of Team Demography. *Journal of Management* 33(6), 987–1015.

Ivancevich, J.M. & Gilbert, J.A. (2000). Diversity Management. Time for a New Approach. *Public Personnel Management* 29(1), 75–92.

Jackson, S.E., Joshi, A. & Erhardt, N.L. (2003). Recent Research on Team and Organizational Diversity: SWOT Analysis and Implications. *Journal of Management* 29(6), 801–30.

Jackson, S.E., May, K.E. & Whitney, K. (1995). Understanding the Dynamics of Diversity in Decision-Making Teams. In R.A. Guzzo & E. Salas (eds), *Team Decision-Making Effectiveness in Organizations* (204–61). San Francisco: Jossey-Bass.

Janis, I.L. (1972). *Victims of Groupthink: A Psychological Study of Foreign-Policy Decisions and Fiascos*. Boston: Houghton Mifflin.

Jehn, K.A., Northcraft, G.B. & Neale, M.A. (1999). Why Differences Make a Difference: A Field Study of Diversity, Conflict, and Performance in Workgroups. *Administrative Science Quarterly* 44(4), 741–63.

Kanter, R.M. (1977). *Men and Women of the Corporation*. New York: Basic Books.

Kearney, E. & Gebert, D. (2009). Managing Diversity and Enhancing Team Outcomes: The Promise of Transformational Leadership. *Journal of Applied Psychology* 94(1), 77–89.

Kreckel, R. (2004). *Politische Soziologie der sozialen Ungleichheit*. Frankfurt/Main: Campus Verlag.

Kulik, C.T. & Bainbridge, H.T.J. (2006). Psychological Perspectives on Workplace Diversity. In A.M. Konrad, P. Prasad & J.K. Pringle (eds), *Handbook of Workplace Diversity* (25–52). London: Sage.

Kunze, F. & Bruch, H. (2010). Age-Based Faultiness and Perceived Productive Energy: The Moderation of Transformational Leadership. *Small Group Research* 41(4), 1–27.

Lowe, K.B., Kroeck, K.G. & Sivasubramaniam, N. (1996). Effectiveness Correlates of Transformational and Transactional Leadership: A Meta-Analytic Review of the MLQ Literature. *Leadership Quarterly* 7(3), 385–425.

McPherson, J.M. & Smithlovin, L. (1987). Homophily in Voluntary Organizations – Status Distance and the Composition of Face-to-Face Groups. *American Sociological Review* 52(3), 370–79.

McKay, P.F. & Avery, D.R. (2005). Warning! Diversity Recruitment Could Backfire. *Journal of Management Inquiry* 14(4), 330–36.

Milliken, F.J. & Martins, L.L. (1996). Searching for Common Threads: Understanding the Multiple Effects of Diversity in Organizational Groups. *Academy of Management Review* 21(2), 402–33.

Mor-Barak, M. (2005). *Managing Diversity. Towards a Globally Inclusive Workplace*. Thousand Oaks: SAGE.

Paetzold, R.L., García, M.F., Colella, A., Ren, L.R., Triana, M. & Ziebro, M. (2008). Perceptions of People with Disabilities: When is Accommodation Fair? *Basic and Applied Social Psychology* 30(1), 27–35.

Pelled, L.H., Eisenhardt, K.M. & Xin, K.R. (1999). Exploring the Black Box: An Analysis of Work Group Diversity, Conflict, and Performance. *Administrative Science Quarterly* 44(1), 1–28.

Porter. L.W., Lawler, E.E. & Hackman, J.R. (1975). *Behavior in Organizations*. New York: McGraw-Hill.

Röder, B., Rösler, F. & Neville, H.J. (1999). Effects of Interstimulus Interval on Auditory Event-Related Potentials in Congenitally Blind and Normally Sighted Humans. *Neuroscience Letters* 264(1–3), 53–56.

Rubin, R.S., Munz, D.C. & Bommer, W.H. (2005). Leading from Within: The Effects of Emotion Recognition and Personality on Transformational Leadership Behavior. *Academy of Management Journal* 48(5), 845–58.

Sacco, J.M. & Schmitt, N. (2005). A Dynamic Model of Demographic Diversity and Misfit Effects. *Journal of Applied Psychology* 90(2), 203–31.

Schur, L., Kruse, D.L., Blasi, J. & Blanck, P. (2009). Is Disability Disabling in All Workplaces? Workplace Disparities and Corporate Culture. *Industrial Relations* 48(3), 381–410.

Schur, L., Kruse, D. & Blanck, P. (2005). Corporate Culture and the Employment of Persons with Disabilities. *Behavioral Sciences and the Law* 23(1), 3–20.

Shore, L.M., Chung-Herrera, B.G., Dean, M.A., Holcombe Ehrhart, K., Jung, D.I., Randel, A.E. & Singh, G. (2009). Diversity in Organizations: Where are We Now and Where are We Going? *Human Resource Review* 19(2), 117–33.

Shrey, D. & LaCerte, M. (1995). *Principles and Practices of Disability Management in Industry*. Winter Park FL: GR Press.

Stone, D. & Colella, A. (1996). A Model of Factors Affecting the Treatment of Disabled Individuals in Organizations. *Academy of Management Review* 21(2), 352–401.

Stone, D.L. & Michaels, C. (1993). Factors Affecting the Acceptance of Disabled Individuals in Organizations. Paper presented at the Annual Meeting of the Academy of Management. 8–11 August 1993. Atlanta GA.

Stone, D.L. & Michaels, C. (1994). Effects of Nature of the Disability and Competitiveness of Reward System on Selection of Disabled Team Members. Paper presented at the Annual Meeting of the Academy of Management. 14–17 August 1994. Dallas TX.

Stone-Romero, E.F., Stone, D.L. & Lukaszewski, K. (2006). The Influence of Disability on Role-Taking in Organizations. In A.M. Konrad, P. Prasad & J.K. Pringle (eds), *Handbook of Workplace Diversity* (401–30). London: Sage.

Tajfel, H. & Turner, J.C. (1986). The Social Identity Theory of Intergroup Behavior. In S. Worchel & W. Austin (eds), *Psychology of Intergroup Relations* (7–24). Chicago: Nelson-Hall.

Thomas, R.R. Jr. (1992). *Beyond Race and Gender: Unleashing the Power of Your Total Work Force by Managing Diversity*. New York: AMACOM.

Turner, J.C. (1987). *Rediscovering the Social Group: A Self-Categorization Theory*. New York: Basil Blackwell.

Van Knippenberg, D. & Schippers, M.C. (2007). Work Group Diversity. *Annual Review of Psychology* 58, 515–41.

Young, J.L. & James, E.H. (2001). Token Majority: The Work Attitudes of Male Flight Attendants. *Sex Roles* 45, 299–319.

Disability Management in Various Countries

8 *The Development of Disability Management in China*

IGNATIUS TAK SUN YU, DAN TANG, K.K. CHAN, F.K. IP AND KAREN Y.L. LO-HUI

Introduction

Since the late 1970s, the People's Republic of China (PRC) has been gradually transformed from a socialist economy into a capitalist one. Like other industrialized countries, the PRC has not escaped the huge social and economic burden and losses arising from occupational accidents and hazards. In an effort to minimize the impact of work disability on victims, employers and society as a whole, the Chinese government has begun to reform the work injury insurance system and adopt a disability management approach to occupational rehabilitation practice. As the disability management approach is new to the PRC, the central government has turned to professionals from outside Mainland China as part of its effort to promote this approach in Mainland provinces and cities. The Hong Kong Special Administrative Region (SAR) is one of the major sources of knowledge and skills in disability management because of its proximity and well-established social welfare system.

The purpose of this chapter is to review the development of work-related disability management reform in Mainland China and the Hong Kong SAR. A brief historical overview is followed by an exploration of the social, political and economic issues involved in promoting the idea and concept of disability management. This chapter also examines pilot initiatives that illustrate areas of advocacy in the future development of disability management in Mainland China and the Hong Kong SAR.

Development of Disability Management

From 1949 to 1978, the political, economic and social welfare system in the PRC was modelled on that of the Soviet Union. Characterized by inefficient centralized planning and a collective and universal provision of welfare flowing from ideological imperatives, the system began to experience severe stress as China opened its economy to the world. Following fierce political struggles, the PRC underwent a paradigm shift from a focus on political and ideological concerns to the economic reforms that began in 1978.

In an era of globalization and rapid economic growth, and with the emergence of local capitalists and foreign investment during the last two decades, China has become the world's factory. Ironically, rapid economic growth has brought growing social and environmental problems and a drastic increase in work-related injuries. According to statistics released by China's Work Injury Department in 2009, the country had around one million work injury cases in 2008 (Chen 2009). The Chinese Ministry of Health reported in 2007 more than 670,000 cases of work-related illness, 90 per cent of which were related to lung disease. Over 100,000 new cases of lung disease are reported in China every year (*People's Daily* 2007). The total estimated direct economic loss from work injuries and occupational diseases is over a hundred billion Renminbi (around 14 billion US$) (Chen 2009). It has been estimated that the coming decade or two will see the peak outbreak of occupational injury and disease in China. Occupational health and safety protection for migrant workers has also been identified as a critical issue.

The original communist model of social security could no longer deal with the increasing occupational health and safety issues, work injuries and diseases that accompanied China's economic reforms. For nearly half a century, with the enactment of the Labour Insurance Regulations (these regulations were subsequently amended in 1973, 1958 and 1978), the Chinese social security system was deeply rooted a socialist model developed by the Soviet Union. The system was highly decommodified, redistributive, universalistic, non-contributory and comprehensive in its distribution of occupational benefits and provisions. The workers who benefited from the system were assigned a work-unit or *Danwei*, and were centred largely in cities and state-owned enterprises. This socialist welfare regime was considered a uniquely Chinese model of occupational welfare (Lee 2000) given the extent to which it reflected the political and economic structure and context of the PRC at the time.

The drastic socio-economic changes and related income inequalities, unemployment, environmental and occupational diseases and injuries, etc., which arose from market reform and globalization since 1978, brought into question the sustainability of the traditional socialist welfare security system. The dismantling of central planning and the rise of a market-oriented economy had a great impact on occupational welfare. First of all, in order to survive in a competitive market-oriented economy, most of the state-owned enterprises adopted a neo-liberal approach to occupational welfare. Secondly, those working in non-state enterprises were left unprotected. Such factors made social welfare reform inevitable if social needs were to be adequately met.

In the face of enormous personal, social and economic losses caused by high rates of occupational injury and disease, occupational rehabilitation of disabled work injury workers who have been injured at work became a key issue in terms of the country's development. There was a growing consciousness of the need to preserve valuable human capital, restore the working capacity of people with work injuries and minimize the social and economic burden on society.

In this new context, reforms in occupational health and safety legislation and of the social security and injury insurance systems became a priority. In the past, the Labour Insurance Scheme and Government Employee Insurance covered comprehensive welfare benefits (e.g., pensions, medical care, occupational disease and injury compensation) for the workers in state-owned enterprises and government officials, as well as retirees and their dependents. In 1998, the Chinese government reorganized the Ministry of Labour as the Ministry of Labour and Social Security (which was subsequently reorganized as the Ministry of Human Resources and Social Security in 2009) to coordinate all social insurance programmes. In addition, the Chinese government enacted several pieces of labour legislation to protect and safeguard the well-being, health and safety of workers. These included the Occupational Disease Prevention and Control Law (enacted in 2002), the Work Injury Insurance Regulation (enacted in 2004) and the Labour Contract Law (enacted in 2008). These new laws and regulations laid out a macro-framework that clearly defined the responsibility of enterprises and the state when it came to the prevention, compensation and rehabilitation of work injuries and occupational disease.

The current work injury insurance system now being used in China is modelled on the one used in Germany, which adopts the principle of emphasizing prevention and rehabilitation. This approach attempts to integrate work injury prevention, occupational rehabilitation and compensation, with the focus placed on prevention and rehabilitation. Under the legal framework of the work insurance system, the development of work injury prevention programs and the provision of occupational rehabilitation services to people with disabilities due to injuries at work are considered the key concerns for future development. This well-conceptualized concern for the development of occupational rehabilitation within the work injury insurance system also laid the foundation for the introduction of disability management in China.

The introduction of return-to-work services for people with work injuries in Hong Kong by the Hong Kong Worker's Health Centre (HKWHC) highlights the differences in approach taken in the former British colony. As a Special Administrative Region of China under the 'one country, two systems' policy, the work injury system in Hong Kong has significant differences from that of Mainland China. Joint efforts, such as the one between the Guangdong Provincial Work Injury Rehabilitation Center (GPWIRC) and the HKWHC, provide a blueprint for exchanges of knowledge and skills and the training of local professionals engaged in disability management in Mainland China.

Developments in the Hong Kong Special Administrative Region of China and Mainland China

It was against the background of the macro-changes described above that a pilot project in South China was jointly initiated by the GPWIRC and the HKWHC.

DEVELOPMENTS IN THE HONG KONG SPECIAL ADMINISTRATIVE REGION OF CHINA

In the mid 1990s, a large public utility company in Hong Kong agreed with the Hong Kong Workers Health Centre to set up an occupational rehabilitation program for their employees with work injuries and those who were on prolonged sick leave. This effort became a hallmark in the development of occupational rehabilitation in Hong Kong SAR (Yu 2008). The HKWHC subsequently received government funding to provide vocational retraining services in the community for people with work injuries, and began promoting an early return to work case management program. For the past 10 years, the HKWHC has supported over a thousand people with work-related injuries to return to work.

The return-to-work service developed by the HKWHC has focused on facilitating the psychosocial and work adjustment to those with disabilities as a result of injuries at work.

The interventions are divided into early, middle and late phases (Hong Kong Workers Health Centre 2009). Early-phase intervention focuses on facilitating communication between stakeholders who manage medical treatment and medical rehabilitation, and providing work-site-based return-to-work support to employers and people with work injuries. Mid-phase intervention focuses mainly on lifestyle redesign and pain management support for those who have been on work-injury-related sick leave for over six months and who are not yet ready to return to work. Late-phase intervention focuses mainly on providing vocational retraining services for those with work injuries who may not be able to return to their original job. A case management approach based on an integrated bio-psychosocial model has been found helpful in facilitating the psychosocial and work adjustment of people with work injuries. The active involvement of employers is also critical in supporting the return to work of people with work injuries.

Nevertheless, due to the fact that the current Employees' Compensation Ordinance (ECO) in Hong Kong SAR does not prescribe occupational rehabilitation services, there are loopholes in the work injury rehabilitation system. In 2002, a Proposal on Occupational Rehabilitation was published by an alliance of professionals in the field, which highlighted the need to revamp the existing system for employees' compensation and the occupational rehabilitation service for workers injured at work or suffering from occupational diseases (Alliance of Professionals for the Rehabilitation of Workers with Occupational Injuries 2002:19).

The development of disability management by health professionals in Hong Kong SAR has lagged behind that of most developed countries. Obsolete concepts of injury, treatment, physical rehabilitation and settlement via compensation still prevail and influence strategies for managing work-related injuries. The concept of integrated rehabilitation, the management of disability and support for return to work are still not well known or accepted by the medical profession. There remains much to be done in helping medical professionals take up the mission of providing comprehensive disability management services to relevant clients.

Despite the relative lack of progress in the field, there have been some initial moves towards a more progressive model of disability management. Recent years have seen an increased demand by people with work injuries for new models of care. Pilot programs initiated by non-governmental organizations (NGOs), such as the HKWHC, insurance companies and the Labour Department have had an impact on changing attitudes within medical circles.

With the collaboration of the Hong Kong Hospital Authority, the Hong Kong Society of Occupational and Environmental Medicine, the Hong Kong Association of Rehabilitation Medicine, the Association of Private Orthopaedic Surgeons and the Chinese University of Hong Kong, the first training course on the American Medical Association Guides to the Evaluation of Permanent Impairment with Review of Principles of Disability Assessment was organized in May 2002. Some doctors, though just a few, successfully obtained the title of Independent Medical Examiner. This course provided an opportunity to address the long-neglected area of disability assessment and management in the medical profession.

As most clients have musculoskeletal problems as an element of their disability, the orthopaedic profession was the first to show interest in the field of disability management. In addition to the activities mentioned above, the Hong Kong College of Orthopaedic Surgeons commissioned a training programme in occupational rehabilitation for the profession in 2007 (Hong Kong College of Orthopaedic Surgeons 2007). They also set up the Orthopaedic Rehabilitation Sub-Specialty Board to provide training related to occupational rehabilitation and disability management. Orthopaedic surgeons have also begun to liaise with the Labour Department concerning employee compensation and rehabilitation issues. Though there has yet to be a major breakthrough, there have been incremental changes, such as improvements in communication, that facilitate the Assessment Board's role in settling compensation. In the past few years, there have also been collaborative programmes between NGOs to identify clients who might benefit from case management services that complement their medical treatment.

Some separate occupational rehabilitation services have been emerging in the past five years, provided by different bodies including the insurance companies and NGOs (Chan, Woo & Tang 2008: 6). The Voluntary Rehabilitation Programme for Employees Injured at Work was introduced in March of 2003 by the Hong Kong Federation of Insurers and the Labour Department of the Hong Kong SAR to encourage workers to accept alternative medical treatment provided by insurers (Labour Department n.d.). Private case managers have been employed by insurers to help manage selected claims for work injuries and to offer private medical treatment and rehabilitation. Nevertheless, these insurer-sponsored voluntary rehabilitation programs have focused mainly on medical treatment and rehabilitation with little importance given to arrangements for a return to work. Similarly, employers have not been actively involved in facilitating efforts to help those with workplace injuries or disabilities return to work.

Certain large companies/employers, including the Hong Kong Hospital Authority, have formed occupational medicine teams for disability management programs. By 2003, some momentum had been achieved and the Hong Kong Hospital Authority began an occupational medicine service, which sponsored the training of selected employees who would then provide disability management service training to the rest of the staff. The initial response was not satisfactory with only a few medical doctors joining the program. Currently, only three of seven service clusters have formally trained employees to coordinate the service for their staff. In light of the experience of these initial training efforts, however, more clusters have been willing to send employees for training, and some centres have started to provide services to outside partners. The Hong Kong Hospital Authority has also established a very good model for large corporations that are setting up disability management programs. By 2009, disability management services for employees who have been injured on duty have been extended to all seven clusters of public hospitals in Hong Kong SAR, potentially benefiting around 60,000 employees.

In summary, though it is a limited step and is still far from the standard of disability management found in other developing countries, these initial moves represent a positive step and the prospects for future collaboration are bright.

DEVELOPMENTS IN MAINLAND CHINA

Collaboration between the Guangdong Provincial Work Injury Rehabilitation Centre (GPWIRC) and the HKWHC began in 2003 in China's southern province of Guangdong. Their joint project established a work injury prevention and occupational rehabilitation resource centre in Guangzhou (the capital city of Guangdong Province) to explore work injury prevention and work and social rehabilitation support for people with work related injuries. The project introduced a much more proactive approach by engaging employers earlier in the rehabilitation process and encouraging their support for a return-to-work process for their injured employees. From 2003 to 2005, experts from the GPWIRC and the HKWHC worked together to study, explore and apply the case management model as a new pattern of occupational rehabilitation. Finally, an action research report on the occupational rehabilitation and community reintegration of migrant people with work injuries was published (Lo-Hui et al. 2005).

This pilot stage of the collaboration explored the psychosocial adjustment, work adjustment and return-to-work options for workers with work injuries. Questions included how people with work injuries and their family members accept and adjust to physical disability and they take care of themselves after being discharged from a medical rehabilitation hospital. Since some of these workers with work injuries were migrant labourers from poor areas of rural China, the pilot study also explored whether these injured workers could find sustainable livelihoods once they returned to their home villages.

During this pilot phase, data was collected on 400 workers with work injuries who were served by the program, and 14 cases were studied in-depth. Among the conclusions drawn from this study were: the importance of intervening with counselling support as early as possible to help injured workers adjust to their disability; the importance of providing support and training for the caregivers of people with severe work-related injuries; the importance of preparing workers for a return to work and reintegration into their community before their discharge from the GPWIRC; and the importance of increased support to people with work injuries as they return to their original job or go on to vocational retraining for re-employment.

The project also helped identify different phases in the work injury rehabilitation process and the differing needs to be addressed within each phase. These distinct phases include: hospital medical treatment and rehabilitation services; discharge from the hospital; readaptation to the working environment and reintegration into work and the community.

This study highlighted key concerns in the development of a holistic model of case management for occupational and community reintegration in the context of Mainland China. It was found that treatment needs to stress early intervention, integrative follow-up at both the rehabilitation centre and within the community, mediation among family members, rehabilitation counselling and employment support upon return to work (Lo-Hui et al. 2008: 44). The information provided by this pilot effort represents a major contribution to the further development of work injury rehabilitation (Chen 2005). Its validation of the importance of facilitating occupational rehabilitation and community reintegration of workers with work injuries has had a significant impact on the work injury insurance system in Mainland China.

Following this pilot project, a work and social rehabilitation department was formally set up within the GPWIRC in 2006. The department included a team made up of a medical doctor, a rehabilitation therapist, a nurse and a social worker – all committed to utilizing the case management model (Luo 2008). With the support of rehabilitation professionals from Hong Kong and South China, the department gradually developed protocols for service. These protocols included rehabilitation counselling for psychosocial adjustment, home modification for community reintegration, 'work hardening' and work-capacity-building, job analysis and outreach (workplace visits), liaison with employers return-to-work support including trial work arrangements and vocational retraining (Lo-Hui & Luo 2008: 3). The effort resulted in a more systematic service protocol for occupational rehabilitation and social rehabilitation for people with work-related injuries at the GPWIRC.

A small charitable emergency fund was jointly set up by the HKWHC and the GPWIRC as a pilot effort to financially assist 32 workers with home modifications, starting small businesses or other activities designed to sustain their livelihoods (e.g., household-based chicken farming for migrant workers returning to poor rural areas and suffering from spinal cord injuries or severe burns). Monitoring the outcome of this effort led to the creation of a database for research on the needs of these injured workers in their efforts to reintegrate back into their community and work.

Future Disability Management Developments in People's Republic of China

MAINLAND CHINA

China is a country that has comparatively large numbers of people who have suffer from serious work-related injuries. Within the past decade, the number of workers who have been physically handicapped due to work injuries has increased every year with serious consequences for China and its citizens. The prevalence of work injuries has brought poverty to many, slowing the country's efforts to achieve a better life for all. Given the scale of the problem, the challenge of developing an effective system of work injury prevention and rehabilitation is both complex and formidable.

Due to the fact that China's approach to work injury rehabilitation is still at an early stage, work injury rehabilitation concepts, policies and actual operations are still fresh ideas. Currently, China is searching for suitable strategies for local financing and implementation, and has developed the following three methods for medical rehabilitation (Tang 2009): establishing work injury rehabilitation centres, e.g., the GPWIRC in Guangdong Province, with direct funding support from work injury insurance; investing private capital in developing work injury rehabilitation centres, such as those in Xinjiang and Henan provinces, which provide work injury rehabilitation services reimbursed by work injury insurance; and selecting certain hospitals which already have good rehabilitation services, such as in Beijing, and designating them as centres of work injury medical rehabilitation.

The concept of work rehabilitation and return to work was unheard of in China 10 years ago (Tang & Chan 2008: 3). Despite the pilot work and social rehabilitation department set up by the GPWIRC, many difficulties were encountered in promoting this concept. The slowness with which these new ideas have been taken up has been due to a number of factors. There has been a lack of knowledge and understanding about work injury rehabilitation (and even about medical rehabilitation) among the general Chinese public, including people with work injuries and their employers. Nationally, there has also been insufficient rehabilitation facilities and resources to satisfy the increasing needs of people with work injuries. Loopholes in regulations and variations in funding reimbursement for rehabilitation services across different provinces and regions have also aggravated the problem. Insurance policies and bureaucratic management that do not reflect the goal of helping workers return to work and reintegrate into their communities is also a factor. Conflicting financial interests and competition among hospitals and rehabilitation centres often make early intervention difficult. Finally, unemployment and the general economic downturn in China have made a return to work for people with work injuries even more challenging.

In keeping with the established pattern of social development in Mainland China, successful pilot efforts in one region of the country serve to advocate for wider change, with the new model being replicated in other regions. After five years of collaboration between the GPWIRC and the HKWHC, the occupational rehabilitation pilot project was evaluated and summarized in a policy paper presented at the provincial level. The paper received a positive reception and the consideration, by higher levels of government, of incentives for employers to accommodate their workers' return to work may well frame the future development of disability management programs in China. The acceptance of these concepts by certain large corporations and state-owned enterprises is already an indication of a growing number of employers and their representatives willing to establish return-to-work policies for their employees with work injuries.

There are many challenges in developing occupational services in Mainland China that may undermine the potential development of disability management programs in the future (Lo-Hui & Luo 2008: 77). These challenges include the lack of training and understanding of occupational and social rehabilitation concepts by local rehabilitation professionals, which limits their focus to medical treatment and medical rehabilitation. Many local professionals are also unaware of the importance of psychosocial and work adjustment in the return-to-work process; furthermore. the reimbursement system of labour insurance for rehabilitation is still underdeveloped. Due to the fact that current labour insurance rehabilitation policy contains no requirement for employers to accommodate the return to work of workers with work injuries, many companies are reluctant to support return-to-work programs. Finally, the lack of formal training in rehabilitation counselling and disability management also hinders the development of disability management programs in Mainland China.

In May 2009, the Ministry of Human Resources and Social Security endorsed the GPWIRC status as National Work Injury Rehabilitation Base of People's Republic of China. In doing so, the provincial government of Guangdong Province provided financial support for its relocation as a work injury rehabilitation training centre in 2010. The new centre will support the development of a work injury rehabilitation model by integrating medical and occupational rehabilitation. The centre will also practise evidence-based rehabilitation services to provide the basis for the development of future labour insurance policy. The centre will work with partners, including the HKWHC, to further develop work and social rehabilitation and work injury prevention with the support of the labour insurance system.

HONG KONG SPECIAL ADMINISTRATIVE REGION OF CHINA

Experience in other countries have shown that only through the collaboration of government, employers, professionals and NGOs can effective disability management be delivered. Given the present situation in Mainland China, the development of a culture of disability management and service provision is still at an early stage. Despite the challenges, the imperative of creating an increasingly humane society makes a revolution in disability management a pressing priority.

Further movement in this direction will necessitate commitment from the government. Elements of disability management and return to work for people with work injuries should be included in the Employees' Compensation Ordinance and social welfare policy for work injury disability.

Economic factors at both the local and global level, such as the changing nature of job requirements, rates of unemployment, and other factors, all make a return to work for people with work injury more difficult. Motivated by a maximization of profit and the competitiveness of the market, employers have few incentives or obligations to set up disability management programs or accommodate a return to work for people with work injuries. Nevertheless, the HKWHC has found that efforts to liaise with employers can facilitate the rehiring of employees after injury through graded return-to-work programmes. This is especially true when the disability has been temporary. Appraisal of such efforts on the part of the government should be encouraged. In addition, enforcement of provisions for a graded return to work for people with work injuries, following proper medical assessment, could facilitate the development of a culture of disability management and return to work.

Insurance companies, governments and employers are the chief stakeholders in employee compensation. Although they pay insurance for their employees, employers are currently not required to pay the actual compensation, provided they are not found guilty of negligence in relation to the provision a safe working environment. Asking employers to share part of the medical and social insurance costs for employees' compensation should be explored. Such a measure would also facilitate work injury prevention and the adoption of disability management concepts. Without the provision of incentives or obligations to have employers set up disability management programs and accommodate a return to work for workers with disabilities, the development of disability management in the Hong Kong SAR will be slow. The fact that the majority of work injury accidents in the Hong Kong SAR result in only moderate to mild disability may make it easier for such policies to be put in place.

If there are not qualified disability management practitioners available, services providing disability management are little more than words. The responsibility for such training falls on universities, the government and other education providers. In 2004, the University of Hong Kong, in collaboration with the University of Montreal, Canada, attempted to organize a distance-learning certificate course on disability management; however, the program was not successful. Given a growing familiarity with the concept of disability management and increased demand for related training, universities should consider taking the lead in providing such courses. Collaboration with overseas universities with established programs should also be pursued. The international Certified Disability Management Professional (CDMP) certification examination organized by National Institute of Disability Management and Research (NIMDAR) in Canada was introduced in Hong Kong in 2008 and has been well received (International Disability Management Standards Council 2009). Only through the provision of training and manpower, will disability management be workable.

As the main stakeholder in the early phases of the management of people with work injuries, the medical profession has a key role in the success of disability management. Greater provision of training in disability management, disability assessment, occupational medicine and occupational rehabilitation for medical professionals will be needed. It will only be through the creation of a common language and philosophy that disability management will be successfully implemented on a wider scale. Currently, there are large organizations, including the Hong Kong Hospital Authority, which have formed teams for occupational medicine and disability management programs in order to facilitate disability management training for their staff. The initial results in the Hong Kong Hospital Authority have shown some positive signs, such as a decrease in the number of accidents and a shortened duration of sick leave for people with work injuries. The Hong Kong Hospital Authority has also begun working on the provision of such services to external partners. This effort has provided a good model for other large organizations in relation to the creation and implementation of disability management programs and generally increasing the knowledge and acceptance of the concepts that such programs embody.

Limitations remain in terms of the availability and quality of disability management due to existing priorities in the medical profession, among insurance companies and within the Labour Department. The demand for services from people with work injuries fluctuates in terms of type, degree, timing and urgency. Organizational flexibility is required to find workable solutions to fit gaps in service and coordinate care among various stakeholders, including the employers. The experience of the HKWHC as an NGO has been particularly helpful in modelling such flexibility and providing valuable information concerning disability management and return-to-work services. The role of NGOs in providing disability management should be supported as part of social welfare policy.

As a special administrative region of the People's Republic of China, Hong Kong is governed under a 'one country, two systems' arrangement that allows for sociocultural differences. For this reason, the future development of disability management in the Hong Kong SAR may be different from that of the Mainland. Currently, the lack of incentives or obligations for employers to set up disability management programs and to accommodate a return to work for workers with disabilities is a critical issue. Without the participation of employers, the development of disability management in the Hong Kong SAR will be slow. Past experience has shown that growth is taking place with NGOs and professionals providing the momentum. The government's commitment to facilitating and nurturing the culture of disability management remains the most critical element. With government leadership, the present lag behind Mainland China and the rest of the world can be overcome.

Conclusion

The integration of work injury prevention, compensation and rehabilitation in Mainland China was established in the work injury insurance policy of 2004. At the same time, the government worked out a clear policy to regulate all private and public enterprises that protected workers' health by locating occupational and safety health measures in the workplace. Most importantly, the government's support of return to work by people with work injuries established the clear and long-term direction for the development of the work injury insurance system. Challenges exist at various levels of rehabilitation development in Mainland China that make duplication of the same service model in South China difficult. Nevertheless, the willingness of large organizations, including state-owned enterprises, to support the return to work of their people with work injuries represents an important advance in the development of disability management in Mainland China.

The main challenge in the Hong Kong SAR remains the engagement of employers in vocational rehabilitation programs for people with work injuries. It is important to communicate to different stakeholders the importance of return-to-work programs and the ways these will benefit not only workers, but also employers and society at large.

The development of return-to-work support services for people with work injuries by the HKWHC and the GPWIRC in the Hong Kong SAR and Mainland China represents a helpful contextualized model of disability management. A review of the workers' compensation scheme as part of the labour insurance system will be crucial in providing the necessary incentives to develop a disability management program that supports the return to work of people with work injuries.

Bibliography

Alliance of Professionals for the Rehabilitation of Workers with Occupational Injuries. (2005). *Proposal on Occupational Rehabilitation*. Hong Kong: Hong Kong Workers' Health Centre.

Chan, E.Y.L., Woo, K.W.S. & Tang, T.M.Y. (2008). Occupational Rehabilitation Services Provided by a Community Workers' Health Centre in Hong Kong: A Case Study. *WORK* 30, 6–9.

Chen, G. (2009). *The Establishment of a Work Injury Insurance System in China*. Paper presented at the International Seminar for Work Injury Rehabilitation. Guangdong, China.

Chen G. (2005). Preface. In Lo-Hui, K.Y.L., Luo, X.Y., Lu, X.W. & Mai, G.Z. (eds), *Action Research on Occupational Rehabilitation & Community Re-integration of Migrant People with Work Injuries*. China: Hong Kong Workers' Health Centre & Guangdong Provincial Work Injury Rehabilitation Centre.

Guan, X.P. (2000). China's Social Policy: Reform and Development in the Context of Marketization and Globalization. *Social Policy and Administration* 34(1), 115–30.

Hong Kong College of Orthoapedic Surgeons. (2007). *Occupational Rehabilitation in the Orthopaedic Perspective: Prevention of Chronicity*. 4th Orthopaedic Rehabilitation Symposium and Conjoint Commissioned Training by Rehabilitation Subspecialty Board, HKCOS and Institute of Health Care, Hospital Authority, Hong Kong.

Hong Kong Workers' Health Centre. (2009). *Annual Report 2008–2009*. Hong Kong: Hong Kong Workers' Health Centre.

International Disability Management Standards Council. (2009). Hong Kong offers CDMP Examinations – First in Asia. *Newsletter of IDMSC* 3, 1–2.

Labour Department. (n.d.). Voluntary Rehabilitation Programme for Employees Injured at Work. Available at: http://www.labour.gov.hk/eng/public/ecd/WorkInjuries2.htm, accessed 23 July 2009.

Lee, M.K. (2000). *Chinese Occupational Welfare in Market Transition*. Basingstoke: Macmillan Press.

Li, X. (1999). The Transformation of Ideology from Mao to Deng: Impact on China's Social Welfare Outcome. *International Social Welfare* 8, 86–96.

Li, Z. (2007). Realistic Options for the Work Injury Rehabilitation System in China. *Work* 30, 67–71.

Lo-Hui, K.Y.L., Luo, X.Y., Lu, X.W. & Mai, G.Z. (2005). *Action Research on Occupational Rehabilitation & Community Re-integration of Migrant People with Work Injuries*. China: Hong Kong Workers' Health Centre & Guangdong Provincial Work Injury Rehabilitation Centre.

Lo-Hui, K.Y.L., Luo, X.Y., Lu, X.W. & Mai, G.Z. (2008). Summary Report of Action Research on Occupational Rehabilitation and Community Re-integration of Migrant Workers with Work Injuries in Mainland China. *WORK* 30, 39–45.

Lo-Hui, K.Y.L. & Luo, L. (2008). *Working Report of the Occupational and Social Rehabilitation*. China: Hong Kong Workers' Health Centre & Guangdong Provincial Work Injury Rehabilitation Centre.

Luo, L. (2008). *Work and Social Rehabilitation – Practice of the Case Management Mode*. The 2nd Mainland and Hong Kong SAR, China Work Injury Prevention and Rehabilitation Seminar. China: Hong Kong Workers' Health Centre & Guangdong Provincial Work Injury Rehabilitation Centre.

People's Daily. (2007). NPC Standing Committee Members Call for Occupational Disease Prevention to be Included in Draft Law. 26 April 2007. Available at: http://english.people.com.cn/200704/26/eng20070426_369807.html, accessed 23 July 2009.

Tang, D. (2009). *The Development of Work Injury Rehabilitation*. Paper presented at the Seminar of Guangdong Provincial Rehabilitation Medicine Association. 15 May 2009. Guangdong, China.

Tang, D. & Chan, C. (2008). Work Rehabilitation in Mainland China: Striving for Better Services and Research. *WORK* 30, 3.

Yu, I.T.S. (2008). From Concepts to Practice. *WORK* 30, 1.

Zhu, Y.K. (2002). Recent Developments in China's Social Security Reforms. *International Social Security Review* 55, 39–53.

9 A Framework for Success: CRS Australia's Approach to Disability Management

ALISON ANGLETON

Introduction

Disability management practice integrates traditional approaches to vocational rehabilitation with employers' strategic approaches to workplace health and safety. It brings together injury prevention, early intervention, workers compensation and vocational rehabilitation to provide a comprehensive response designed to facilitate employment of people with disabilities. Originally resulting from employer efforts to minimize the costs associated with workplace injury and illness (Shrey 1995; Kendall, Muenchberger & Clapton 2007), disability management frameworks have become central in workers compensation and injury management in North America (Rosenthal. et al 2007; Harder 2005; Westmorland & Buys 2002). The term disability management is not widely used in Australia (Westmorland & Buys 2002) and although many of the structures and services required of a disability management framework are in place, they are not integrated as part of a comprehensive national strategy. In Australia, the practice of disability management is generally known as injury management, occupational rehabilitation or vocational rehabilitation.

Vocational rehabilitation in Australia has undergone a number of significant paradigm shifts since its inception in the 1940s, though its primary measure of success, assisting people into work, has largely remained constant. Initially, it was a medically based service focused on functional restoration; then it moved towards an approach characterized by community-based rehabilitation, multidisciplinary teams and case management (Tipping 1992; CRS Australia 2006). Social policy and legislative changes in the 1970s led to a division between workers compensation and vocational rehabilitation services and although employment remained a principle measure of success for both schemes, the aim of vocational rehabilitation was expanded to include a broader social focus that included strategies aimed at achieving greater independence within the community and working with those who had no prior labour market attachment. Rather than reflect a substantive difference in goals and methods, however, the division of insurance-funded workers compensation schemes and government-funded vocational rehabilitation is largely a difference in emphasis and approach. Workers compensation schemes in Australia have by definition necessitated employer engagement, given the direct link to insurance premiums, whereas vocational rehabilitation services, by their nature, have not had the same access to or commitment from employers.

In recent years, the role of employers has been highlighted for those with non-compensable illnesses and disabilities as well as for people injured in the workplace (Commonwealth of Australia 2010b; Organisation for Economic Cooperation and Development 2007). Once the domain of insurers and compensation schemes, the term disability management is broadening to include service delivery to people who have never entered the workforce and have no pre-existing relationship with the employer (Harder 2008; O'Halloran & Innes 2005). This has implications for employers, including the need to accommodate illness prevention strategies, job modifications, flexible working hours and an increasingly diverse range of injuries, health conditions and disabilities. It also has implications for governments who are already taking measures that demand collaboration between employers, people with disabilities, disability employment service providers, insurers and unions (Commonwealth of Australia 2010b; Matthews et al. 2010).

Disability management, with its focus on workplace-based strategies and employer engagement, encompasses vocational rehabilitation and both approaches have the potential to strengthen and complement each other. Disability management, at its best, integrates vocational rehabilitation with employers' strategic management of workplace health and safety. Addressing risk and disability within the workplace is increasingly becoming a necessity for business, particularly with an ageing population and the growing incidence of chronic disease (Council of Australian Governments 2006; Harris 2008; Buys 2005). Engaging workplaces, assessing risk and making job modifications are central to CRS Australia's approach. Commonwealth Rehabilitation Service (CRS) Australia achieves this strong focus on employer responsibility and occupational health by adopting case management (CRS Australia 2006) as a mechanism to bring together employers and healthcare professionals to assist people with disabilities to find and retain work.

The longer someone is out of work because of ill health, the less likely they are to return to work (Hanson, Edlund & Henningsson 2006; Cotton 2006; Dunstan & Covic 2006; The Australasian Faculty of Occupational Medicine and the Royal Australian College of Physicians 2001). Without early intervention and appropriate referral to health care and employment services, people experience extended periods out of the workplace (Department of Work and Pensions 2004). This often leads to a range of related issues, including decreased self-esteem, secondary psychological issues and the erosion of work skills and competencies (Waddell, Burton & Aylward 2007; Mclean et al. 2005; Barnes et al. 2008). The subsequent impact on families through financial hardship, social exclusion and intergenerational poverty and unemployment is well documented (Black 2008; McClure 2000; Reinhardt, Pedersen & Madsen 2002; Vinson 2007). Employers also feel the effects through increased rates of sickness absences, decreased motivation and decreased productivity. Early intervention and health promotion have clear benefits with regard to minimizing the economic and social impact of disability, illness and injury (OECD 2007).

Primarily in response to a decline in employment participation of people with disabilities and the need to maximize social and economic participation, the Australian government has demonstrated an increased focus on these issues and is addressing them at a social policy level. For example, many of the initiatives outlined in the new Disability Employment Services model that took effect in 2010 (Commonwealth of Australia 2008), such as Job Access (which includes an advisory service for employers), flexible ongoing support (comprising short intensive support to the person with a disability in the workplace) and job-in-jeopardy assistance (assistance provided to 'at risk' workers), incorporate disability management principles. These initiatives also partially address the issue of job retention by people with injuries and disabilities, although that issue is not currently given the same level of attention as efforts to engage employers in the recruitment of people with a disability.

At the same time, research and reforms related to the welfare-to-work strategies in Australia and the United Kingdom (McClure 2000; Human Rights and Equal Opportunity Commission 2005; Evans, 2001; Bambra, Whitehead & Hamilton 2005) have heightened attention on employer engagement and responsibility. Expert assemblies such as the International Forum for Disability Management and the *International Journal of Disability Management Research* (Harder 2008) have contributed to a shared understanding and a platform in which disability management practices can be discussed and compared, thus giving rise to greater emphasis on the term disability management. Although the adoption of the term disability management is relatively recent, disability management practices, together with associated skills and knowledge, have been in operation in CRS Australia for decades.

This chapter explores the notion of disability management within the context of Australia's largest provider of disability management services, CRS Australia. CRS Australia has a network of over 170 offices in metropolitan, regional and remote locations and assists over 60,000 people with a disability, injury or health condition each year. It delivers services across the boundaries of insurer-funded workers' compensation, employer-funded injury prevention and government-funded disability employment services and, as such, offers a unique perspective on disability management in Australia.

Disability Management and Vocational Rehabilitation

Vocational rehabilitation is widely considered one of the most effective interventions for a person with an injury or disability (European Commission 2000; Organisation for Economic Co-operation and Development 2003; International Labour Organisation 2002; Institute for Research into International Competitiveness 2003). There are many terms used to describe both the interventions and theory of vocational rehabilitation. In Australia, vocational rehabilitation, workplace rehabilitation and injury management are commonly used terms. There is also growing use of the term disability management, reflecting the emergence of the disability management movement internationally (Harder 2005; Matthews et al. 2010). Originally developed in North America to refer to the prevention and management of injury and illness in the workplace (Westmorland & Buys 2002) and emerging largely in response to the rising costs associated with illness and injury in the workplace, disability management involves employer-led activities aimed at preventing illness and injury as well as strategies to minimize their impact. Disability management is an overarching and distinct approach that while encompassing vocational rehabilitation can also be differentiated from it. It is in this context that disability management is increasingly recognized as reflecting the practices of workplace rehabilitation, injury management and disability employment in Australia.

Westmorland and Buys (2002) describe disability management as an employer-based strategy that can be differentiated from traditional vocational rehabilitation on the basis of five key characteristics:

1. focus on injury prevention
2. employer-driven approach supported by organizational policy
3. management and staff collaboration around disability in the workplace
4. delivery of interventions within the workplace, and
5. early intervention irrespective of any claims liability determination.

Implementing disability management involves engaging employers in the prevention and management of injury and disability in the workplace regardless of whether the injury or disability is compensable or non-compensable. Current initiatives, like those seen in the United Kingdom's Health, Work and Wellbeing strategy (Department of Work and Pensions 2004), encompass a holistic approach and now extend to include conditions that have the potential to impact employee performance (e.g., flexible hours, work/life balance). This fundamental change in approach is increasingly being demanded of employers to meet the changing face of work and health. Whether driven by the broader social responsibility of employing people with disabilities or simply a business necessity to raise productivity, there is an increasing realization that managing disability in the workplace is sound business practice (Lewis 2008). The growing numbers of workers with chronic health conditions, increasing rates of mental illness and a rapidly ageing population all demand organizational policy and processes to prevent and manage disability.

Disability management usually assumes a pre-existing relationship with the employer and therefore a connection to workers' compensation systems (O'Halloran & Innes 2005); however, a pre-existing relationship with an employer is not a necessary requirement when applying disability management principles. Indeed, the principles and key characteristics of disability management, namely the strong focus on employer responsibility and organizational policy as drivers for occupational health, provide important insights about the direction of vocational rehabilitation, injury prevention and disability employment services in Australia. They have the potential to complement and strengthen traditional vocational rehabilitation approaches.

The traditional rehabilitation approach has been to assess barriers to employment and social participation, provide counselling to modify behaviour and promote adjustment to disability, treat the health condition(s), teach job search skills and secure competitive employment (Shrey, 1996). While this has certainly improved the economic and social participation of people with disabilities, historical emphasis on assessing, treating and restoring physical and psychological function, for the most part, excluded active engagement with employers and missed opportunities for workplace assessment and modification. Perhaps more importantly, referral processes between hospital, general practitioners, employers, workers compensation insurers and vocational rehabilitation providers have, in the past, missed the opportunity for early intervention (CRS Australia 2008).

Although recognized as integral in achieving the goals of vocational rehabilitation, there does not appear to be the same level of engagement with employers or demand on employers from governments in Australia to become actively involved in the early intervention vocational rehabilitation processes as in countries such as the United States. A recent OECD report stated that Australia's 'current policy pays little attention to the issue of early identification of health problems and the role of employers in this initial period, thereby missing the opportunity to intervene early' (OECD 2007). As a consequence, people who are injured or sick at work are often not effectively assisted by their employers or the workers compensation schemes and by the time they reach the Australian government income support and employment services systems the opportunity for early intervention and retention of the person in the workplace is lost (CRS Australia 2008).

History of Disability Management in Australia

Emerging largely in response to the rising costs associated with illness and injury in the workplace, disability management involves employer-led activities aimed at preventing illness and injury, as well as strategies to minimize their impact. The disability management movement, however, has its history in traditional approaches to occupational health and rehabilitation (Shrey 1996; Rosenthal et al. 2007). In Australia, these approaches have historically been linked with employment services and have at their basis the philosophy that employment is a measurable and effective means of social inclusion and economic participation for people with disabilities (O'Halloran 2002; Kendall, Muenchberger & Clapton 2007; Humpage 2007; Marston & McDonald 2007; Barnes 1999).

Many of the initiatives aimed at increasing employment in Australia have, until recently, formed the basis of Australia's welfare system. Like governments in the United States and United Kingdom responding to the aftermath of WWI and WWII, Australia was committed to increasing its employment rates, including of people in receipt of 'invalid pensions' (Tipping 1992). However, unlike many countries with different tiers of government, the Australian federal (Commonwealth) government assumed responsibility for the administration and delivery of vocational rehabilitation services (O'Halloran 2002; CRS Australia 2004).

The concept of rehabilitation has its origins in the medical profession's ideology of physical and functional restoration (O'Halloran 2002; Dunstan & Covic 2006; Barnes 1999; Humpage 2007) and the assumption that disability can be remedied or overcome with appropriate intervention and by motivation on the part of the injured person. This changed in the 1970s and 1980s when policy was influenced by international social movements, including those of de-institutionalisation, anti-discrimination, social justice and service consumer rights.

Originally established to address the physical and medical needs of injured war veterans and provide work for the physically rehabilitated, the primary purpose, from the outset of the Commonwealth Rehabilitation Service rehabilitation centres in Australia, was to get people back to work. Its success was measured by the numbers of people who gained employment having been provided with rehabilitation.

Following the National Committee of Enquiry into Compensation and Rehabilitation in Australia (NCECRA) (in 1974), rehabilitation was defined to include the medical, social and psychological needs of the person, not just those related to employment. The Disability Services Act 1986 consolidated the social rehabilitation focus and enshrined values of empowerment, dignity and choice for people with disabilities. While maintaining a focus on employment, it also broadened the aim of vocational rehabilitation to the provision of independent-living services to enable independence within the community, where employment was not possible and existing community supports were not available.

This reform enabled a move away from institutional settings to models of service delivery based in the community. It also recognized the importance of working with employers across the spectrum of services. A new emphasis on services emerged which included injury prevention, early intervention, job retention, return to work and recruitment of people with disabilities with appropriate skills. As a result, vocational rehabilitation became a recognized service delivery model that focused on managing disability and addressing the barriers to both social and economic participation.

The NCECRA report also recommended improvements in the rehabilitation and compensation systems for people injured at work or in motor vehicle accidents. In response to steadily increasing costs of work injury, together with the associated social impacts, rehabilitation began to include early intervention and injury prevention. By the 1980s and 1990s, Australia's Commonwealth, states' and territories' governments amended legislation and vocational rehabilitation programs to emphasize return-to-work interventions that also addressed related psychosocial issues. These models were based on CRS programs and were adopted by the state and Commonwealth compensation bodies for their approach to disability management (Tipping 1992). The separation of legislation and responsibility for workers compensation from that for broader disability employment services in Australia has differentiated employer obligations and responsibilities according to whether the injury or condition took place within a workplace or the injury or condition predated the employee's employment.

In an effort to address unemployment of people with a disability and an ageing population and in response to observations such as that from the Organisation for Economic Co-operation and Development (OECD), there has been significant change to welfare in Australia over the last 20 years. The Australian government's Disability Reform Package of 1991 (Commonwealth of Australia 1991) once again emphasized employment as the desired outcome of vocational rehabilitation assistance, and was complemented by an agreement in which state governments took over primary responsibility for non-vocational rehabilitation. In 1998, policy reform introduced mutual obligation requirements whereby those in receipt of certain welfare benefits were required to engage in job-seeking activities in order to receive welfare payments. These reforms together with changes to administration and funding arrangements transformed the vocational rehabilitation market, opening it up to competition and separating the purchaser and provider of services (Kendall & Clapton 2006). In the course of these changes, the Commonwealth Rehabilitation Service was renamed CRS Australia.

The Australian government's recent social inclusion agenda has begun another paradigm shift in the provision of services. It promotes a joined-up solution to policy and program provision across levels of government to deliver targeted and tailored interventions to address systemic disadvantage (Gillard & Wong 2007). A key aspect of the agenda is the development of a national employment strategy for those with a disability or mental illness. The Future of Disability Employment Services (Commonwealth of Australia 2008) consultations and the Disability Employment Services model (Commonwealth of Australia 2010a) outline the future direction of disability employment services in Australia and promote early intervention, flexible ongoing support and greater emphasis on employer engagement in disability employment. The new Disability Employment

Service model implemented in March 2010 replaced the Disability Employment Network and Vocational Rehabilitation Services aims to increase access to individually tailored disability employment services. The model includes an employee assistance fund intended to better support employers with broader access to workplace modifications and an intermittent post-placement support option. The model also acknowledges the importance of early intervention by increasing opportunities for services to work directly with schools, hospitals and community organizations.

These recent changes have seen greater emphasis placed on employer and workplace engagement, thus reflecting the principles of disability management. The term disability management is now used to define one stream of disability employment services in Australia, and the core concepts and principles of disability management are embedded in Australian government policies. As a portfolio agency of the Australian government Department of Human Services, CRS Australia deliver services across the boundaries of insurer-funded workers compensation, employer-funded injury prevention and government-funded disability employment services. It is in this context that CRS Australia provides a unique perspective on disability management and has the potential to play a significant role in the direction of disability management in Australia.

Current Operational Context

Australia has a federal (Commonwealth) government as well as governments in each of its states and territories, all of which have jurisdiction for social policies and legislation. Workers compensation schemes and broader disability employment initiatives operate in different jurisdictions.

Workers compensation, motor vehicle accident, income protection and superannuation schemes are legislated by the state and territory governments. Compensation schemes provide benefits based on pre-injury earnings that are financed by premiums paid by employers to commercial insurers. Insurers purchase or provide their own occupational rehabilitation services with the aim of returning people to the same job with the same employer or a new job with a new employer. Managing injury and disability in the workplace to achieve early return to work is the primary objective of the workers compensation systems. Clear guidelines outlining workplace rehabilitation policy and procedures are put in place by each authority. There are also a number of self-insured employers who take on responsibility for their workers' compensation liabilities themselves.

The Australian government funds a broader Disability Employment Service program. Within this Australian government-funded Disability Employment Service (DES) there are two streams: the Disability Management Service and the Employment Support Service. Although both provide specialist help for people with disability, injury or health conditions who require support to find and maintain sustainable employment, the Disability Management Service provides assistance to those with an injury, disability or health condition and who are not expected to need long-term or regular support in the workplace, whereas the Employment Support Service provides assistance to those with a permanent disability who need regular long-term ongoing support in order to gain and maintain their job.

In order to access the government-funded Disability Employment Service, an assessment of an individual's ability to work is undertaken by job capacity assessors who identify all barriers to participation and recommend interventions to help overcome those barriers. Assessors consider the impact of medical conditions and/or disability on an individual's work capacity and wherever possible directly connect them to services to assist them to maximize their workforce participation. It is regarded as a more comprehensive approach than in other countries (OECD 2007) and minimizes the number of interviews and assessments the person is subjected to before services are provided.

There is a broad range of providers delivering disability management services either within the workers compensation schemes or the Disability Employment Service program; however, CRS Australia is unique in that it is the largest provider of specialized expertise in both areas. CRS Australia services are largely delivered at the workplace and include work-related assessment, job modification, coordination of rehabilitation interventions, identification and arrangement of retraining and/or placement in alternative employment.

Disability Management in CRS Australia

The engagement of employers as part of the return-to-work process is a fundamental aspect of the approach to vocational rehabilitation and for some parts of CRS Australia's business, as already noted, employer engagement is mandated in workers compensation legislation. Teaching people work skills that include safe work practices, appropriate management of health conditions, interaction with supervisors and co-workers and, when necessary, job modification is a key part of CRS Australia's service delivery and is central to any disability management framework. The strength of CRS Australia's service delivery model is that it combines activities aimed at injury prevention, return to work and workforce participation with specialized vocational rehabilitation and disability employment interventions.

Unlike many traditional rehabilitation approaches, CRS Australia incorporates injury prevention strategies in its suite of interventions and regards this aspect of its work as central to the quality of employment outcomes. Strategies to manage existing disability-related issues to minimize further exacerbation of conditions, as well as strategies aimed to prevent the occurrence of new conditions, are ideally developed with employers and employees. Early intervention in the workplace allows the opportunity for people whose employment is affected and/or in jeopardy due to their injury, disability or health condition to maintain their employment and avoid their condition progressing to a compensable claim or to losing their job (Arnetz et al. 2003; Wyatt & Sher 2003).

However, although employers engage CRS Australia to undertake a range of assessments and workplace interventions aimed at preventing or minimizing the incidence of workplace injuries, the majority of work with employers is still undertaken within the framework of managing a compensable claim. This is in large part due to the pervasive negative beliefs about disability, which are held by the community and reflected by employers (Hernandez, Keys & Balcazar 2000; Peck & Kirkbride 2001), and the mistaken belief that productivity will be lower and costs higher if people with disabilities are recruited and supported to remain in work (Graffam et al. 2002). For those with mental illness, the stigma, low expectations and reluctance by employers to recruit people with a disability are heightened (Butterworth, Crosier & Rodgers 2004). As a result of these beliefs, many people with disabilities remain cautious of disclosing their disability for fear of the employer's response. Reluctance on the part of the injured person to disclose and on the part of the employer to intervene means the opportunity for early intervention is often lost. An important change required in both the broader community as well as with employers is an understanding and recognition about the positive contribution people with disabilities can make to workplaces in particular and the community in general. The recently introduced government initiatives aimed at engaging employers in the recruitment and retention of people with a disability (Commonwealth of Australia 2010c) indicates a trend toward disability management practice in Australia.

Case Management in CRS Australia

In CRS Australia, case management is a process of working in partnership with people with disabilities to achieve their goals through timely and effective delivery of an individually designed rehabilitation program (CRS Australia 2006; Woodside & McClan 2007; Scully, Habeck & Leahy 1999; Grubbs, Cassell & Mulkey 2006). Within this case management model, allied health professionals, referred to in CRS Australia as rehabilitation consultants, have primary accountability for the delivery of vocational rehabilitation services.

This approach requires rehabilitation consultants (case managers, to confirm, through a comprehensive assessment undertaken by job capacity assessors, a person's strengths and barriers. It also requires the rehabilitation consultants to provide targeted, individualized assistance to enhance the person's strengths and manage the barriers so that they can obtain a suitable job or reach another identified goal (CRS Australia 2006). The focal point of a vocational rehabilitation program is to obtain suitable and sustainable employment. In this process, the key principles of disability management, disability awareness, adjustment to disability, disclosure and training are addressed (CRS Australia 2006; ILO 2002).

At the foundation of CRS Australia practice is a belief in the positive effects of work. Gainful employment provides a sense of identity, promotes good mental health and enables people to participate in social and economic life (Waddell & Burton 2006; Barnes et al. 2008; Mclean et al. 2005; Bartley 1994; Ross & Mirowsky 1995; Provencher et al. 2002; Nice 2008). Although some work can present a risk to health, in general, employed people enjoy better physical and mental health (Murphy & Athanasou 1999). In addition to the individual's responsibility for health and well-being, employers and health professionals can also play a key role in promoting and enabling good health (The Australasian Faculty of Occupational Medicine and the Royal Australasian College of Physicians 2010)

CRS Australia's model of case management, whereby program activities or services are delivered concurrently rather than following a linear progression from one discrete stage/phase of the program to the next, enables better coordination and efficiency in service delivery (CRS Australia 2006). When the provision of vocational interventions and support to manage personal and disability-related barriers is undertaken simultaneously, it allows for a better understanding of the impact of health and disability and is better able to respond to the individual and their changing circumstances. For example, the cyclic nature of mental health conditions can require reassessment of a person's needs and stage of rehabilitation (Farkas et al. 2000). Concurrent programming accommodates these changing needs and enables people to continue job-seeking or employment while simultaneously addressing barriers.

The use of such a framework maximizes client participation and strengthens the relationship between program activities and the employment goal from the outset. Immediate or graduated return to work, while at the same time addressing barriers to employment and social participation, also allows workers to experience therapeutic gains and appropriate adjustment at work. Moreover, this approach can enable the active engagement of employers, thus leading to better accommodation of disability-related issues and increased job retention.

The framework for the delivery of CRS Australia vocational rehabilitation services, as illustrated in Figure 9.1, is designed to comply with legislation while achieving sustainable outcomes for people with disabilities. CRS Australia's framework includes:

- early intervention and early return to work
- multidisciplinary interventions (psychological, physical, ergonomic, vocational)
- individualized case management
- utilization of employer and community resources
- workplace assessment and modification
- job matching and skill development
- injury prevention strategies
- post-placement support
- employment retention strategies.

The CRS Australia vocational rehabilitation process has very similar goals and methods to the key characteristics of disability management.

CRS Australia has developed an integrated model consistent with client-centred practice whilst also applying the principles of motivational interviewing (Miller & Rollnick 2002) and the trans-theoretical model of behavioural change (Prochaska & DiClemente 1984). In this way people are engaged and supported to take an active part in the planning, implementation and review of their vocational rehabilitation program within a model designed to promote empowerment and self-determination.

Of central focus to the CRS Australia model of vocational rehabilitation is the use of multidisciplinary teams of professionally qualified allied health staff, including occupational therapists, physiotherapists, psychologists, social workers and rehabilitation counsellors. These rehabilitation consultants collaborate with medical providers to carefully manage the transition from medical and therapeutic services to interventions that optimize work-related functional capacity, adjustment to disability and employability. A wide range of specialist services, including cognitive and physical assessment, functional upgrading, adjustment-to-disability counselling, vocational and worksite assessments, and workplace assessment and job redesign, are undertaken to ensure the person's existing condition is not aggravated as a result of the job placement or return-to-work strategies. Following work-related injury consultation with employers and insurers in the process of return to work is also central to the Rehabilitation Consultant role to ensure the safe and early return to work.

CRS Australia also employs employment service consultants with specialist labour market knowledge, in recognition of the importance of developing employer relationships

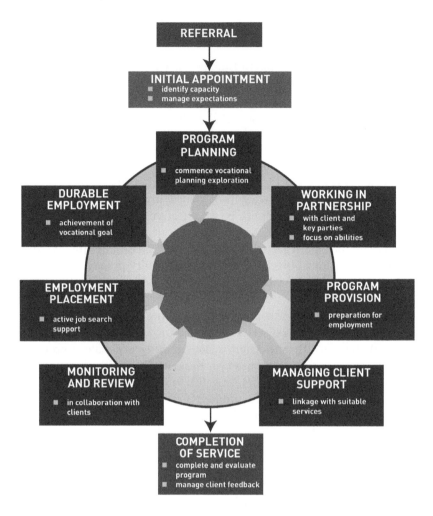

Figure 9.1 CRS Australia's vocational rehabilitation model

and understanding local employer needs. Appropriate job matching and knowledge of local skills shortages informs program planning, employment preparation and increases the likelihood of employment.

Disability Management Principles and Strategies in CRS Australia

In addition to case management practice, counselling and psychological interventions (such as pain management, stress management, anger management), physical conditioning and adjustment to disability, disability management in CRS Australia involves a range of employer-focused and workplace-based activities aimed at securing employment. CRS Australia practice demonstrates a commitment to the principles identified by the International Labour Organisation (ILO 2002) in terms of managing disability in the workplace by tailoring education, support, advice and services to people with disabilities as well as employers.

As part of its disability management framework, CRS Australia works with employers to negotiate safe and sustainable work placements and delivers a range of flexible services customized to meet organizational needs (ILO 2002; Shrey 1995). Services are designed to complement employers' strategic approaches to workplace health and safety. Injury prevention services include interventions designed to avoid exacerbation of existing conditions. Training in manual handling, office ergonomics and workstation ergonomics, while designed to prevent injuries occurring, are just as applicable to those with existing injuries and health conditions as those without. Whether instructing people about the most effective ways to lift and carry weights or identifying correct posture and workstation configuration, training and awareness is an effective way for employers to achieve reductions in workplace injuries. Workplace safety services, such as workplace inspections, auditing of safety management systems, specialist risk assessments and workplace design, are also provided to organizations as part of their disability management strategy. These safety services help to minimize workplace accidents and injuries by identifying hazards in the workplace – task, system or process – and recommending strategies to either eliminate or reduce the level of risk. Employee assistance programs (EAP), return-to-work programs and other psychological services are also provided as part of a comprehensive response to workplace health and safety risks. Training and safety programs adopt a risk management approach and are based on the relevant national standards and codes of practice. By delivering such services, benefits to organizations can be demonstrated by fewer injuries, reduced symptoms, reduced sick leave, absences and turnover, and increased job satisfaction and work engagement.

After an injury takes place or while a person is adjusting to disability, recovery and employment prospects can be enhanced by a range of workplace interventions. Work-related assessments aimed at facilitating the safe return to work or start of a new job analyze and match the individual to the critical job demands, work environment and work practices. It is during this process that an assessment of the suitability of pre-injury or alternative duties is undertaken and, where required, an assessment of workplace modifications or job redesign. While issues and interventions may differ, the same approach is taken for physical injuries as for psychological, cognitive, communication and psychosocial injury or illness.

Instruction in the workplace and opportunities to develop experience on the job are also important contributions employers can make to the process. Work training and work experience placements are extremely effective tools used by CRS Australia to engage employers, enhance a person's work prospects and vocational skills, build confidence and encourage more active and effective participation of people with disabilities in the workforce (CRS Australia 2006). Work training has been used by CRS Australia as a key strategy in managing disability employment for more than 60 years.

All these workplace interventions are negotiated amongst the employer, the person with a disability and CRS Australia and, as a consequence, demand substantial cooperation and goodwill by each party. Communication between stakeholders and coordination of organizational policy, legislative requirements and health services demands that rehabilitation consultants possess a diverse and complex skill set. Even after the person with an injury or disability returns to work, these skills are still needed by the rehabilitation consultant because when people return to work, the associated rewards and challenges may not be realized for a number of months. Therefore, engaging the individual and maintaining their motivation to continue working is crucial (Farkas et al. 2000; Shinitzky & Kub 2001) as too is engaging the employer to ensure sustainable employment and effective transition to work. Post-placement assistance and support fosters the individual's independence in employment, alleviates concerns and addresses workplace adjustment issues identified by either the person with the disability or the employer (Egnew 1993).

Although all these activities occur within a workplace, the extent to which the employer is actively promoting and supporting the placement through organizational policy, procedures and culture is highly variable. The variation to which employers engage in the process is a major point of differentiation between and within workers compensations schemes and broader disability employment initiatives. However, the most crucial determinant of success is the degree to which the objectives of all parties (people with disabilities, vocational rehabilitation providers, insurers, health professionals) are integrated and a common goal agreed upon. Much greater emphasis needs to be developed on partnerships between employers and employees to promote and enhance health and well-being in the workplace. It is through these partnerships and collaborations that mutual respect and understanding are strengthened and positive attitudes to disability achieved.

Conclusions

CRS Australia has a long history of bringing employers and healthcare professionals together to help people with disabilities, injuries and health conditions find and retain employment. This has been achieved within changing social policy contexts and across different Commonwealth, state and territory jurisdictions. The current social inclusion agenda, reforms to the Disability Employment Service and plans to introduce a national workers compensation and occupational, health and safety and workers compensation framework are unprecedented steps in better aligning Commonwealth, state and territory programs and overcoming systemic barriers to assisting people with disabilities.

The future role of disability management in Australia depends to a large degree on the success of initiatives to join up government services and the ability to change government and community expectations of employers with regard to their role in workplace health and well-being. Once disability management practices are established, many more opportunities will exist for the integration of injury prevention and rehabilitation in the workplace as well as increased collaboration between management and staff to drive broader and more comprehensive organizational rehabilitation policy and practice.

Comprehensive and strategic approaches to workplace health and safety will be particularly important to address emerging health issues, such as chronic disease, and increasing rates of mental health conditions. These drivers will be compounded by factors including an ageing workforce, rates of locational disadvantage and the need to expand and bolster positive attitudes towards people with disabilities. In order to engage and retain working-aged Australians in work, it may be necessary to consider, once again, broadening the meaning of success to include improved personal well-being, community participation and reduced social exclusion.

Ideally, disability management integrates workplace programs with social participation, maximizing opportunities for health and well-being within workplaces and assisting people with disabilities to restore function and participate in employment that recognizes their ability. In this regard, CRS Australia is well placed to continue its work in vocational rehabilitation and disability management. It is CRS Australia's great strength that with its focus on employment, it continues to treat the individual as a whole whose physical, social and psychological needs must all be addressed. Indeed, as the largest provider of disability employment services and covering areas of insurer-funded workers compensation, employer-funded injury prevention and government-funded disability employment services, CRS Australia is a central player in the future development of Australian disability management practice.

Bibliography

Arnetz, B.B., Sjogren, B., Rydehn, B. & Meissel, R. (2003). Early Workplace Intervention for Employees with Musculoskeletal-Related Absenteeism: A Prospective Controlled Intervention Study. *Journal of Occupational & Environmental Medicine* 45, 499–50.

Australasian Faculty of Occupational Medicine and the Royal Australasian College of Physicians. (2001). *Compensable Injuries and Health Outcomes*. Sydney: Royal Australian College of Physicians.

Australasian Faculty of Occupational Medicine and the Royal Australasian College of Physicians. (2010). *Realizing the Health Benefits of Work. A Position Statement*. Sydney: Royal Australian College of Physicians.

Bambra, C., Whitehead, M. & Hamilton, V. (2005). Does 'Welfare-to-Work' Work? A Systemic Review of the Effectiveness of the UK's Welfare-to-Work Programmes for People with a Disability or Chronic Illness. *Social Science Medicine* 60, 1905–918.

Barnes, C. (1999). Extended Review: Disability and Paid Employment. *Work, Employment and Society* 13, 147–49.

Barnes, M.C., Buck, R., Williams, G., Webb, K. & Aylward, M. (2008). Beliefs About Common Health Problems and Work: A Quantitative Study. *Social Sciences & Medicine* 67, 657–65.

Bartley, M. (1994) Unemployment and Ill Health: Understanding the Relationship. *Journal of Epidemiology and Community Health* 45, 333–37.

Black, C. (2008). Working for a Healthier Tomorrow: Dame Carol Black's Review of the Health of Britain's Working Age Population. Available at: http://www.workingforhealth.gov.uk/documents/working-for-a-healthier-tomorrow-tagged.pdf, accessed 15 February 2009.

Butterworth, P., Crosier, T. & Rodgers, B. (2004). Mental Health Problems, Disability and Income Support Receipt: A Replication and Extension Using the HILDA Survey. *Australian Journal of Labour Economics* 7, 151–74.

Buys, N. (2005). Future of Disability Management in Australia. In H. Harder & L. Scott (eds), *Comprehensive Disability Management* (199–201). Edinburgh: Elsevier Science Ltd.

Council of Australian Governments (2006). National Reform Agenda (NRA): Human Capital, Competition and Regulatory Reform. Council of Australian Governments Meeting. 14 July 2006. Available at: http://www.coag.gov.au.coag_meeting_outcomes/2006-07/index.cfm, accessed 15 June 2010.

Commonwealth of Australia. (1974). Report of the National Committee of Inquiry Chairmen A.O. Woodhouse and C.L.D Meares – Compensation and Rehabilitation in Australia. Vol. 2. Canberra: Australian Government Publishing Service.

Commonwealth of Australia, Disability Reform Package, 31 May, 1991, House of Representatives, 1991. Canberra.

Commonwealth of Australia. (2008). The Future of Disability Employment Services in Australia Discussion Paper. Barton ACT: Australian Government Department of Education, Employment and Workplace Relations.

Commonwealth of Australia. (2009). Job Services Australia. Available at: http://www.deewr.gov.au/Employment/JSA/Pages/about.aspx, accessed 15 August 2009.

Commonwealth of Australia. (2010a). Disability Employment Services. Available at: http://www.deewr.gov.au/Employment/Programs/DES/Pages/about.aspx, accessed 15 June 2010.

Commonwealth of Australia. (2010b). Disability Employment Services. Available at: http://www.deewr.gov.au/Employment/Programs/DES/Employer_Support/Pages/about.aspx, accessed 15 June 2010.

Commonwealth of Australia. (2010). Government Launches New Disability Employment Services. Available at: http://www.deewr.gov.au/ministers/arbib/media/release/Pages/article.aspx, accessed 15 June 2010.

Cotton, P. (2006). Occupational Well-being – Management of Injured Workers with Psychosocial Barriers. *Australian Family Physician* 35, 958–61.

CRS Australia (2004). Australia's Experience in Vocational Rehabilitation for Unemployed People with a Disability. Unpublished report.

CRS Australia. (2006). *Case Management: A Framework for Success*. Canberra: CRS Australia.

CRS Australia (2008). Options for Improving Employment Services and Meeting the Objectives of the Social Inclusion and Skills Policies. Unpublished report.

Department for Work and Pensions (UK). (2004). *Building Capacity for Work: A UK Framework for Vocational Rehabilitation*. London: Department for Work and Pensions. Available at: http://www.dwp.gov.uk/docs/health-and-wellbeing.pdf, accessed 15 June 2010.

Dunstan, D.A. & Covic, T. (2006). Compensable Work Disability Management: A Literature Review of Bio-psychosocial Perspectives. *Australian Occupational Therapy Journal* 53, 67–77.

Egnew, R.C. (1993) Supported Education and Employment: An Integrated Approach. *Psychosocial Rehabilitation Journal* 17, 121–27

European Commission. (2000). *Benchmarking Employment Policies for People with Disabilities*. Brussels: European Commission. Employment and Social Affairs.

Evans, M. (2001). *Welfare to Work and the Organisation of Opportunity. Lessons from Abroad*. London: London School of Economics.

Farkas, M., Sullivan Soydan, A. & Gagne, C. (2000). *Introduction to Rehabilitation Readiness*. Boston: Boston University, Center for Psychiatric Rehabilitation.

Gillard, J. & Wong, P. (2007). An Australian Social Inclusion Agenda. Available at: http://www.alp.org.au./download/now/071122_social_inclusion.pdf, accessed 15 June 2009.

Graffam, J., Shinkfield, A., Smith, K. & Polzin, U. (2002) Employer Benefits and Costs of Employing People with Disability. *Journal of Vocational Rehabilitation* 17, 251–63.

Grubbs, L.A., Cassell, J. & Mulkey, S. (2006). *Rehabilitation Caseload Management Concepts and Practice*. New York: Springer Publishing Company.

Hansen, A., Edlund, C. & Henningsson, M. (2006). Factors Relevant to a Return to Work: A Multivariate Approach. *Work* 26, 179–90.

Harder, H.G. (2005). History and Evaluation of Disability Management. In H. Harder & L. Scott (eds) *Comprehensive Disability Management* (1-11). Edinburgh: Elsevier Science Ltd.

Harder, H.G. (2008). History of the International Forum on Disability Management and the International Journal of Disability Management Research in Context. *International Journal of Disability Management Research* 3, iii–iv.

Harris, A. (2008). *Chronic Disease and Labour Force Participation in Australia: An Endogenous Multivariate Probit Analysis of Clinical Prevalence Data*. Montash: Centre for Health Economics, Monash University.

Heads of Workers' Compensation Authorities. (2009). Draft Position Paper, Nationally Consistent Approval Framework for Workplace Rehabilitation Providers. Melbourne: Heads of Workers' Compensation Authorities.

Hernandez, B., Keys, C. & Balcazar, F. (2000). Employer Attitudes toward Workers with Disabilities and Their ADA Employment Rights: A Literature Review. *The Journal of Rehabilitation* 66, 4–16.

Human Rights and Equal Opportunity Commission (HREOC). (2005). Submission to the Senate Employment and Workplace Relations and Education Legislation Committee Inquiry into the Workplace Amendment (Work Choices) Bill 2005. Sydney: Human Rights and Equal Opportunity Commission.

Humpage, L. (2007). Models of Disability, Work and Welfare in Australia. *Social Policy & Administration* 41, 215–31.

Institute for Research into International Competitiveness. (2003). *Cost Benefit Analysis of Rehabilitation Services provided by CRS Australia*. Curtain Business School: Curtain University of Technology.

International Labour Organisation. (2002) Code of Practice: Managing Disability in the Workplace. Geneva: International Labour Organisation.

Kendall, E. & Clapton, J. (2006). Time for a Shift in Australian Rehabilitation? *Disability & Rehabilitation* 28(17), 1097–101.

Kendall, E., Muenchberger, H. & Clapton, J. (2007). Trends in Australian Rehabilitation: Reviving its Humanitarian Core. *Disability & Rehabilitation* 29(10), 817–23.

Lewis, A. (2008). Vocational Rehabilitation in the 21st Century: Skills Professionals Need for Systems Success. *Work* 31, 345–56.

Marston, G. & McDonald, C. (2007). Assessing the Policy Trajectory of Welfare Reform in Australia. *Benefits* 15, 233–45.

Matthews, L., Buys, N. Randall, C., Biggs, H. & Hazelwood, Z. (2010). Evolution of Vocational Rehabilitation Competencies in Australia. *International Journal of Rehabilitation Research* 33, 124–33.

McClure, P. (2000). *Participation Report for a More Equitable Society, Final Report of the Reference Group on Welfare Reform* (The McClure Report). Available at: http://www.workplace.gov.au, accessed 15 June 2009.

Mclean, C., Carmona, C., Francis, S., Wohlgemuth, C. & Mulvihill, C. (2005). *Worklessness and Health – What do we Know about the Causal Relationship? Evidence Review*. London: Health Department Agency. Available at: http://www.hda.nhs.uk/evidence, accessed 15 June 2010.

Miller W.R. & Rollnick, S. (2002). *Motivational Interviewing. Preparing People for Change*. New York: The Guildford Press.

Murphy, G.C. & Athanasou, J.A. (1999). The Effects of Unemployment on Mental Health. *Journal of Occupational and Organisational Psychology* 72, 83–99.

Nice, K. (2008). Changing Perceptions about Sickness and Work: Judging Capacity for Work and Locating Responsibility for Rehabilitation. *Social and Public Policy Review* 2, 1.

O'Halloran, D. (2002). An Historical Overview of Australia's Largest and Oldest Provider of Vocational Rehabilitation – CRS Australia. *Work* 19, 211–18.

O'Halloran, D. & Innes, E. (2005). Understanding Work in Society. In G. Whiteford & V. Wright-St Clair (eds), *Occupation and Practice in Context* (299–316). Sydney: Elsevier.

Organisation for Economic Co-operation and Development (2003). *Transforming Disability into Ability: Policies to Promote Work and Income Security for Disabled People.* Paris: OECD.

Organisation for Economic Co-operation and Development (2007). *Sickness, Disability and Work: Breaking the Barriers.* Vol. 2. Australia, Luxembourg, Spain and the United Kingdom.

Peck, B. & Kirkbride, L.T. (2001). Why Businesses don't Employ People with Disabilities. *Journal of Vocational Rehabilitation,* 16, 71–75.

Prochanka, J.O. & DiClemente, C.C. (1984). *The Transtheorectical Approach: Crossing the Traditional Boundaries of Therapy.* Malabar FL: Kreiger.

Provencher, H., Gregg, R., Mead, S. and Mueser, K. (2002) The Role of Work in the Recovery of Persons with Psychiatric Disabilities. *Psychiatric Rehabilitation Journal 26,* 132–44.

Reinhardt Pedersen, C. & Madsen, M. (2002). Parents' Labour Market Participation as a Predictor of Children's Health and Well-Being: A Comparative Study in Five Nordic Countries. *Journal of Epidemiology and Community Health* 56, 861–67.

Rosenthal, D., Hursh, N., Lui, J., Isom, R. & Sasson, J. (2007). A Survey of Current Disability Management Practice: Emerging Trends and Implications for Certification. *Rehabilitation Counseling Bulletin* 50, 76–86.

Ross, C. & Mirowsky, J. (1995). Does Employment Affect Health? *Journal of Health and Social Behaviour* 36, 230–43.

Scully, S., Habeck, R. & Leahy, M. (1999). Knowledge and Skill Areas Associated with Disability Management Practice for Rehabilitation Counsellors. *Rehabilitation Counseling Bulletin* 43, 20–29.

Shinitzky, H. & Kub, J. (2001). The Art of Motivating Behaviour Change: The Use of Motivational Interviewing to Promote Health. *Public Health Nursing* 18(3), 178–85.

Shrey, D.E. (1995). Worksite Disability Management and Industrial Rehabilitation: An Overview. In D.E. Shrey and M. Lacerte (eds), *Principles and Practices of Disability Management in Industry* (3–53). Winter Park FL: PMD Publishers Group.

Shrey, DE. (1996). Disability Management in Industry: The New Paradigm in Injured Worker Rehabilitation. *Disability and Rehabilitation* 18(8), 408–14.

Tipping, J. (1992). *Back on Their Feet: A History of the Commonwealth Rehabilitation Service 1941–1991.* Canberra, ACT: Australian Government Printing Service.

Vinson, T. (2007). *Dropping off the Edge: The Distribution of Disadvantage in Australia.* Richmond VIC: Jesuit Social Services; Catholic Social Services.

Waddell, G. & Burton, A. (2006) *Is Work Good for Your Health and Well-Being?* London: The Stationery Office.

Waddell, G., Burton, K. & Aylward, M. (2007). Work and Common Health Problems. *Journal of Insurance Medicine* 39, 109–20

Westmorland, M., & Buys, N. (2002). Disability Management in a Sample of Australian Self-Insured Companies. *Disability and Rehabilitation* 24(14), 746–54.

Woodside, M. & McClam, T. (2007). *Generalist Case Management: A Workbook for Skill Development.* Belmont CA: Thomson Brooks/Cole.

Wyatt, M. & Sher, C. (2003). *An Integrated Early Intervention Model Produces Results. A Report for the Productivity Commission.* Melbourne: OccCorp.

10 Disability Management: New Methodology to Support Workplace Reintegration in Belgium

MARTHE VERJANS, AN ROMMEL, ELIZABETH TIJTGAT
AND KATRIEN BRUYNINX

Introduction

The occupational safety and health, and work-life balance of employees should be highly prioritized in an employment policy adapted to the labour market of the twenty-first century. In Belgium, the basis for such a policy can be found in the regulation concerning the protection of the well-being of employees' Well-being at work regulation (1996). The focus of this regulation is the prevention of exposure to workplace risks and thus the avoidance of injuries and diseases. The target is a continuous and permanent decrease of occupational accidents and sickness (Milquet 2008). However, it is one thing to be able to guarantee health and safety standards at work, yet quite another to deal with the long-term consequences of accidents and health problems that do happen – especially in terms of having a regulatory framework and specific company policies to promote the reintegration of the employees who are confronted with long-term health problems or disabilities. In Belgium, there is insufficient focus on this target group. The employees who acquire long-term health problems and/or functional limitations during the course of their career often receive benefits for extended periods and are, in effect, consequently excluded from the job market. This is all the more concerning in the view of the following data. The 2006 SILC survey shows that around 15 per cent of workers report long-term health problems, and around 13 per cent are hindered at work due to these problems (SILC 2006). These long-term health problems are pointed out as the main causes of unemployment and exclusion from the labour market. These are the autonomous factors that reduce the probability of employment (Wynne & McAnaney 2004). Data from the National Institute for Health and Disability Insurance (INAMI/RIZIV) – the federal institute for health insurance – demonstrate that mainly older workers are leaving the job market following long-standing health problems or disabilities. Besides this, the data show that most exclusions from the workforce are due to mental or musculoskeletal disorders (RIZIV 2007). Investing in keeping these people at work or in getting them back to work with their employer, and thus avoiding a permanent withdrawal from the job market, is both an ethical and an economic necessity.

Job retention and reintegration can be a partial response to the problems which confront the labour market, and which are caused by the ageing of the working population and the new work situations that cause new risks and challenges for workers and employers. This policy has to be elaborated on two levels. On the one hand, it requires the encouragement of employers to develop a policy that facilitates the return to work of workers with long-standing health problems or disabilities. On the other hand, job retention and reintegration processes need to become more tailor-made in order to help employees to stay active on the job market.

Disability management methodology is developed to increase the employability of employees, taking into account their possible work restrictions. On the international level, this methodology is increasingly recognized (Piek & Reijenga 2004). Disability management is a systematic and goal-oriented approach at the workplace which aims to simplify the reintegration process of persons with occupational disabilities through coordinated efforts, taking into account individual needs, workplace conditions and the legal framework (NIDMAR 2000). This methodology has a twofold approach: the coaching of employees who are faced with a prolonged absence from the job market due to health problems or disabilities and the structural implementation of a reintegration policy within the company.

Key concepts in the framework of an effective disability management programme are:

1. ensuring that there is an early contact between the employer/company and the employee who had to leave work due to an injury or illness,
2. providing accommodations within the workplace,
3. stimulating contact between the curative sector and the work floor,
4. mapping the characteristics of the job, and
5. coordinating the process of reintegration through a disability case manager (DCM).

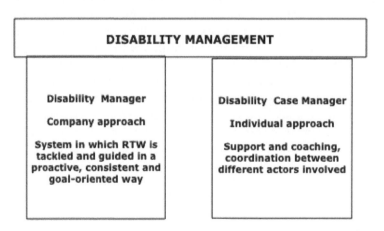

Figure 10.1 Disability management

Companies that implement these interventions at the structural level can reduce the length of period of inability to work and the related costs (Franche et al. 2005b). The benefits from assisting people to return to work outweigh the costs, consequently resulting in a financial profit for the company (Tompa et al. 2008).

Intro_DM: Introduction of Disability Management in Belgium

In order to introduce the disability management methodology in Belgium and to adapt it to the Belgian context, the Intro_DM project (Introduction to Disability Management) was launched in June 2005. The purpose of the project was to facilitate the processes of reintegration and job retention. To achieve this, actions were undertaken on three levels:

- Micro-level (employee): development of tools and a training course in order to implement the methodology of disability case management.
- Meso-level (employer): development of tools and a training course in order to implement the methodology of disability management. On the basis of these tools, the employer can develop a systematic approach concerning job retention and reintegration in the company.
- Macro-level (society): formulation of policy recommendations to optimize the employment policy regarding persons who are confronted with long-standing health problems or disabilities.

The strength of the Intro_DM project is in the specific experience of a wide range of organizations and the interesting synergies provided by these mutually enriching relationships. Prevent, the institute for occupational health and safety, was the manager of the project. A core group was set up, consisting of UCBO – University of Ghent, a vocational training and coaching centre for people with disabilities, and Arbeids Consulting Team Desiron who pioneered scientific approaches to the reintegration of employees after occupational accidents. Aside from these three lead organizations, the partnership included the social partners – two trade unions (Algemeen Belgisch Vakverbond (ABVV) (Belgian General Federation of Labour) and Christian Trade Union, Belgium (ACV-CSC)), and the Belgian Federation of Enterprises (VBO) – as well as organizations with specific knowledge within the field of integration, such as Jobcentrum West-Vlaanderen, that focus on the sustainable integration of job-seekers with a disability through training and personal job coaching, and Job & Co, a company established to assist minority groups (such as migrants, disabled people, long-time unemployed, low-skilled workers, etc.) with integration into the labour market. This unusual and innovative mix of organizations with specific areas of expertise has helped the partnership to spark innovative ideas and synergies. The main financial partners of the project were the European Social Fund[1] and Cera.[2]

---

1   The European Social Fund (ESF) funded the project as a part of the EQUAL program (http://www.equal.be/). The mission of the EQUAL initiative is to promote a more inclusive work life through fighting discrimination and exclusion based on sex, racial or ethnic origin, religion or belief, disability, age or sexual orientation (http://ec.europa.eu/employment_social/esf2000/index_en.html).

2   The projects supported by Cera reflect the cooperative values of the organization: collaboration, solidarity, participation and respect for the individual (http://www.cera.be/).

Methodology

This chapter is mainly based on empirical research to determine the added value of disability case management in reintegration processes. Within this scope, the following steps were considered:

- Training of disability case managers: 17 professionals from various professions (vocational training, human resources, occupational accident insurance, etc.) took part in a ten-day training course. The main themes of this course were the complex Belgian legal framework, communication channels with different actors and job-matching. A roadmap, developed by researchers of Prevent and UCBO-Ugent, provided guidance to the 17 professionals about the processes of reintegration/job retention. The steps steps in the roadmap are: (1) identification of the problem, (2) clarification of the problem/assessment, (3) planning, (4) interventions, implementation of the plan of action and monitoring, and (5) follow-up and final evaluation.
- Coordination of 43 case studies by the disability case managers: employees who are absent or are faced with a prolonged absence from the job market due to health problems or functional limitations were asked to take part in the research. From May 2006 to February 2008, the trained DCMs guided this heterogeneous group of employees on the taught methodology. Of the 43 employees, 25 (58 per cent) returned to work at their previous places of employment after a process of reintegration coordinated by a DCM. Five employees (12 per cent) were insufficiently recovered to return to the workplace. The outcome of two processes of reintegration/job retention were not known by the end of the project. Eleven employees (26 per cent) didn't return to their workplace, but were further supported by professional organizations.
- In order to optimize the disability case management methodology and to be able to investigate whether the disability case manager is considered to be an added value in the process of reintegration, several research sources were combined: in each case the DCM made a journal in which he/she registered all actions taken. In addition, telephone interviews and in-depth interviews were conducted by the researchers. The different actors involved were questioned about their perception of the value of a coordinating actor in the process of reintegration/job retention. Beside this, semi-structured interviews took place with four core groups of actors: occupational physicians, advising physicians from health insurance companies, rehabilitation centres and labour unions. Finally, the results were discussed with the partners and experts of the project Intro_DM.

International standard models were used for the development of tools for a structural implementation of a reintegration policy within a company. The practical implementation will be further elaborated during a new project DM@Work. The actions laid out in this new project will be described below.

Based on the practical experiences on the level of the individual employee and of the company, policy recommendations were formulated in order to optimize the process of reintegration and job retention.

Disability Case Management: Added Value in the Process of Reintegration

In this chapter we describe how the disability case management methodology can be added value in the process of reintegration. By elaborating and testing the methodology in 43 cases during the Intro_DM project, different fields of knowledge and skills which play a crucial role in a process of reintegration and job retention have been defined. Therefore it is crucial that the one in charge of coordinating this process, namely the DCM, masters this knowledge and skills.

In order to stimulate a safe and sustainable return to the workplace, the DCM facilitates the steps in the path back to work. The DCM should stimulate communication and collaboration between the different actors involved and coordinate the process of job matching (Shaw et al. 2008). This coordination is necessary because the process of reintegration is characterized by a complex interaction between different actors with their own visions and priorities (Pransky et al. 2004). During each process, a particular network is established between: (1) the employee: the person who is absent or threatened by a prolonged absence from the job market due to health problems or disabilities; (2) the employer: the person who employs the person with health problems or disabilities, as well as other individuals at the company related to the employee, such as the human resources management (HRM), supervisor, colleagues, occupational physician, etc.; (3) the health sector: those who take care of the employee in order to achieve recovery and rehabilitation; and (4) the institutions concerned with the benefits: those who compensate the employee during his/her absence from the workplace (Young et al. 2005). The employee has a central position in this network. By applying the disability case management methodology, the DCM works closely with/counsels the employee in order to stimulate the collaboration between the different players involved and coordinates the process (Verjans & Rommel 2008).

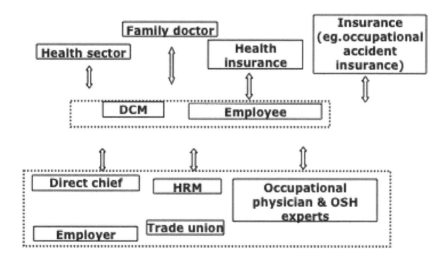

Figure 10.2 Network of involved actors

The goal of a process of reintegration/job retention needs to be that the employee returns to the highest level possible, that is, the same job with the same employer, an accommodated job with the same employer, a new job with the same employer, an accommodated job with a new employer, or a new job with a new employer (Russo & Innes 2002).

The Added Value of Disability Case Management in a Process of Job Retention/Reintegration: Three Roles

CONVERSION OF THE LEGAL FRAMEWORK INTO PRACTICAL GUIDELINES ABOUT JOB RETENTION/REINTEGRATION

The interviewed actors confirmed that the disability case manager has an important role to play as an interpreter of the legal framework into concrete guidelines concerning reintegration/job retention. The legal framework in Belgium is complex, being split on federal and regional levels, and it is difficult for employers and employees to know all the specific measures that facilitate reintegration.

For the employee, the clarification of the financial consequences of returning or not returning to the workplace – also from a long-term perspective – is essential. Even when the process does not lead to re-employment, this clarification can signify the end of an uncertain financial situation. After all, a guaranteed income is one of the main reasons for people to take up work again (Franche et al. 2005a). Furthermore, employees emphasize the importance of the administrative support by the DCM; being dependent on compensatory systems often implies finding your way through an administrative tangle.

Also for the employer, it is important to have a clear view of the financial implications of re-employment. Some measures can take away the possible negative consequences of re-employment. By elucidating this, the DCM can motivate the employer to cooperate fully in the process of reintegration. The economic factors cannot be neglected in the case of a possible return to work, nor can social and legal motives (Franche et al. 2005a).

In their own field each actor has a good knowledge of the measures facilitating a process of reintegration, but often lacks a general perspective. This can harm the process because a successful return to work is often the result of a creative combination of several measures. Different studies confirm that an extensive comprehension of all possible measures existing within the legal framework stimulates the process of job retention/ reintegration (Davis, Badi & Yassi 2004; Linz et al. 2001).

In the literature this aspect is not mentioned explicitly as an important competence that a DCM should have (Shaw et al. 2008). However, in Belgium, coordinating a process of reintegration/job retention means being confronted with a complex legal framework. There are laws, on both the federal and regional levels, influencing a process of reintegration and the implementation of different measures depends on the cause of the inability to work (disease, occupational disease, occupational accident) (Verjans & Rommel 2008). Knowledge about the legal framework, the different compensatory systems and the various institutions involved is necessary in order to be able to coordinate the process of job retention/reintegration. By translating this knowledge into practical guidelines the DCM can play an important part that adds value.

STIMULATION OF COOPERATION WITHIN THE NETWORK

Another significant role of the DCM, as indicated by the interviewed actors, is the stimulation of cooperation within the network. A lack of exchange of information between the different actors can lead to a prolongation of the absence and hence a lower rate of people returning to work. For example, a more efficient communication and information exchange between the different doctors can accelerate a return (Mortelmans, Donceel & Lahaye 2006).

Every case is characterized by a network, each with its own particularities. It is not easy for both the employer and employee to make the actors in the network collaborate since the actors involved are often unknown to each other. However, a process has a greater chance of being successful when everyone works together towards one defined goal. This requires a complex interaction between the different partners, all of whom have their own visions and priorities (Pransky et al. 2004). The DCM can get a view on the (im)possibilities of collaboration within the network and he/she can assess which options should be excluded or offer opportunities. The different actors involved in a return-to-work process – also the DCM – are interdependent. It is essential that the DCM clarifies these relations of dependence and speaks with the partners about their roles and responsibilities. The disability case manager needs to master techniques to negotiate with and convince the different actors.

Important to mention here is the fact that in a process of reintegration/job retention it is crucial that the DCM facilitates the collaboration and stimulates communication. However, he/she should not simply play the role of messenger taking messages from one person to the other.

JOB MATCHING

The third role of the DCM in a process of reintegration, considered to be important by the other actors involved, is the formulation of advice on the practical realization of the processes that guide the return to work. Essentially, keeping an optimal balance between the demands of the job and the capability of the worker is crucial in this. This exercise is difficult for the actors as they often lack sufficient information to find a durable solution.

Employees are often not aware of the different options existing within the company for job accommodation or of the willingness of the employer to take action. The DCM can clarify these uncertainties.

The employer and occupational physician have an overview of the different functions and tasks existing within the company. However, employers have indicated that it is not easy to find solutions at the workplace. Employers often find it hard to broaden their perspective to look beyond the restrictions of the employee, caused by long-standing health problems or disabilities and to focus on the capabilities of the employee involved. This negative outlook is often the cause of fewer opportunities in the labour market (Nijhuis & Van Lierop 2007).

The lack of understanding regarding the specific job demands in the curative sector, on the one hand, and the negative perception of the workers' capabilities, on the other hand, may impede the return to work (Isernhagen 2006). The majority of the occupational physicians involved in this research indicated that their knowledge of the workplace and job demands is often insufficient to propose appropriate solutions to facilitate a return to work. Also the focus on the capabilities of the worker seems to be lacking. The DCM can gather information for this purpose from the curative sector, or can stimulate the interaction between the curative sector and the workplace. Secondly, the disability case manager can inform the curative sector and the consultant physician (health insurance) about the job demands.

To find a solution for this bottleneck impeding the return to work, the model of job matching provides a useful framework (Pransky et al. 2004). This model searches for possibilities of reintegration by comparing the job demands and job capabilities of the employee. In doing this, and by exchanging information, possible bottlenecks become clear. The ideal match will be reached by interventions on different levels, such as the improvement of the capabilities and skills of the employer (e.g., training), the adaptation of the job demands (e.g., more variation in job content), accommodation of the workplace (e.g., ergonomic adaptations) and/or the implementation of organizational changes (e.g., teamwork).

During the process of reintegration/job retention, the disability case manager will bring together all the information necessary for job matching on the basis of meetings, observations and job analysis. With this information in mind the DCM can put forward practical and specific proposals about the ideal match. Knowledge about ergonomics is crucial here (Shaw et al. 2008). Moreover, it is advisable that the DCM visits the workplace. However, in some case studies certain employers showed resistance towards this. Hence, disability case managers need to have sufficient methods, techniques and skills related to job matching, as well as to learn how to deal with resistance to change.

When the disability case manager combines these different fields of knowledge and skills, he/she can be a significant stimulating factor in the process of returning the employee to the workforce. Besides aiding on an individual level, action is needed on the meso-level as well – in other words in the policy of the company. Individual processes of job retention and reintegration have more chance of being successful when there is a systematic approach concerning return to work at the company level.

Disability Management: A Systematic Approach in Companies

Employers initially have a positive attitude towards employees willing to return to work after an occupational accident (Prevent 2001). In order to expand this positive attitude to all workers with long-term health problems or disabilities, employers need to be encouraged to take responsibility. Awareness-raising actions focusing on the advantages that spring from investing in people need to be organized.

Workers and employers share the final responsibility for the outcome of the process of reintegration/job retention. However, due to a lack of concrete reference points and specific knowledge in this area, employers are not able to properly integrate job retention and reintegration of workers as a priority in their company policy. In addition, every reintegration process has its own particularities, so it is difficult for companies to acquire expertise in this field. A structured approach at company level is needed. Efforts in the areas of health and safety, job retention and reintegration are essential for the future.

Effective personnel and health and safety policies provide the framework for this. We recommend that this integrated approach should be increasingly encouraged in the future. The concept of disability management could constitute an essential tool in the implementation of this approach. Final responsibility for the implementation and monitoring of a disability management policy lies with the disability manager. This person must be able to unite the employer, the health and safety department, the human resources department, the trade unions, the management team and other actors around the common agenda of job retention and reintegration. The disability manager can be the employer, the human resources manager or the health and safety adviser.

One of the actions taken during the Intro_DM project was the development of a roadmap on how to develop and implement such a systematic approach (Verjans & Rommel 2008).[3]

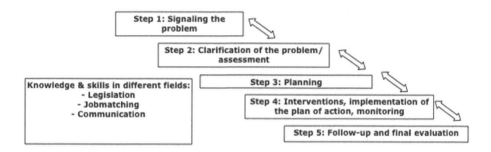

Figure 10.3 Roadmap for a DM policy

This roadmap forms a good base and starting point when a company wants to set up a systematic policy on job retention and reintegration in order to support its employees with long-term health problems or disabilities. However, companies still need more specific tools that take into account the characteristics of their sector and business. These tools will be developed during the project DM@Work (April 2009–November 2010)[4] for four sectors: construction, chemical, health, and public.

The new project has following focus points:

• The harmonization of the human resources management and health and safety policy.
• The development and establishment of a disability management policy in agreement with the actions taken in other policy fields such as ergonomics, diversity and

3   The roadmap is developed on the basis of internationally recognized models. National Institute of Disability Management and Research (NIDMAR), Disability Management in the Workplace, 2003, Piek & Reijenga (2004), Workplace Health, Safety and Compensation Commission of New Brunswick (WHSCC) & Commission de la santé, de la sécurité et de l'indemnisation des accidents au travail (CSSIAT) du Nouveau-Brunswick.

4   The European Social Fund is the main financial partner in the project DM@Work. The project is coordinated by Prevent. Prevent, together with ACT Désiron, forms the core group. Other partners are the occupational health and safety services Idewe, Adhesia and Mensura. The social partners that support the project are: the trade unions ABVV, ACV, ACLVB, and the employer organizations the Belgian Federation of Enterprises and UNIZO, the organization for small and medium enterprises. The project also relies on the expertise of the specialists who put into practice the Flemish policy about equal labour participation and diversity.

absenteeism policy. These actions can be part of a systematic approach of job retention and reintegration. They need to be listed and harmonized so that the human resources management and health and safety policy is streamlined and can serve as a framework for a disability management policy.

- The full collaboration between the actors in these two fields (i.e., human resources and health and safety) is vital in order to achieve this goal. A first step in this collaboration can be the establishment of a socio-medical team within the company, consisting of the HRM and the health and safety department.
- The health and safety department to have the principal role.

The occupational health and safety experts could play an important role in the introduction and implementation of a company policy on reintegration and job retention. Currently, these experts are not actively enough involved. To be able to fulfil this role in an optimal manner, it is essential that the health and safety departments realize that job retention and reintegration are inseparable from occupational welfare policy.

In the new project DM@Work, tools will be developed by and offered to health and safety departments in order for them to play a crucial role in the development of a systematic approach to reintegration and job retention of employees who are confronted with long-term health problems and/or functional limitations. These tools consist of: standard procedures for sickness and reintegration, roles and responsibilities of the different actors involved; a database with analysis of risks, jobs, tasks, possibilities of workplace accommodations; a communication strategy to develop support for the theme of reintegration in the whole company; a return-on-investment instrument; an argumentation-tool to achieve the involvement of the whole company; and disability case management.

With the optimization of the disability management and disability case management methodologies, the processes of job retention/reintegration of employees who are confronted with long-term health problems and/or functional limitations will be facilitated. However, these actions are not sufficient. The legal reality in which individual cases need to be resolved is a determining factor in the outcome of the return-to-work efforts. The way regulations and legislation are developed influences the possibilities of returning to work of employees with long-term health problems and/or functional limitations. That is why, within the scope of the Intro_DM project, policy recommendations were formulated in order to optimize the employment policy regarding persons who are confronted with long-term health problems and/or functional limitations.

Conclusion

This chapter focuses on the achievements made in the scope of disability management in Belgium. In Belgium, job retention and reintegration of employees with long-term health problems and/or functional limitations needs to become a priority, because it can be a partial response to the problems the labour market is confronted by today, which are caused by the ageing of the working population and the new work situations which cause new risks and challenges for workers and employers.

Certain changes in the law and recent initiatives indicate that the theme of job retention and reintegration is increasingly recognized. For example the National Strategy of Well-being at Work, 2008–2012, an initiative from the Belgian Deputy Prime Minister and Minister for Employment Joëlle Milquet, explicitly states that the facilitation of the professional reintegration of employees currently incapable of working is one of the priorities. The reintegration of employees will be stimulated by energizing all of the processes that are likely to keep workers in the labour market or find them a job. This is a welcome and necessary step in the right direction. However, further action needs to be taken to develop a global and integrated vision on socio-professional reintegration.

In order to increase the employability of employees with long-standing health problems or disabilities, a specific action plan was set up by the DM@Work project to introduce the disability management methodology in the Belgian context. These actions were situated on three levels.

The disability case management methodology was developed on the micro-level. Processes of job retention/reintegration have more chance of being successful when they are coordinated by a disability case manager. This actor needs to combine different fields of knowledge and skills in order to realize an added value in a return-to-work process, namely the interpretation of the legal framework into usable practical guidelines concerning job retention/reintegration, the stimulation of cooperation between the different actors involved and finding an optimal balance between the demands of the job and the capabilities of the worker. Individual cases have more chance of a durable and safe solution when there is a systematic approach at the company level. The concept of disability management constitutes an essential instrument in the implementation of this approach. However, employers need more specific tools to establish an efficient policy for job retention and reintegration, such as standard procedures for absenteeism and reintegration, a database with analysis of risks and workplace accommodations and the roles and responsibilities of the different actors involved. These tools will be developed during the project DM@Work, taking into account the specific characteristics of the sector and the company.

With the actions available on these two levels, the return to work of employees confronted with long-standing health problems or disabilities will be facilitated. However, research shows that the federal laws, as well as laws at the regional level, are a determining factor on each individual case. In Belgium, at least, there is a need for a global and integrated vision on socio-professional reintegration so that responsibilities can be defined and the links between the workplace, workers and service-providers can be strengthened. The development of this vision is slowed down by the existence of two parallel systems/policy fields: on the one hand, there are strategies particular to the Belgian Well-being at work regulation – that focus on prevention while, on the other hand, there are strategies existing in the social security system. Amongst the strategies that emanate from the social security system are a number that focus mainly on the curative aspect. Others aim to encourage social and professional integration. Between the two systems – the employment and social security systems – there is a gap. Political decision-makers should therefore be encouraged to opt for a more dynamic and integrated approach, as well as for a rationalization of the existing systems and access to benefits and services. Policies should explicitly be directed at the principle that workers with long-term health problems and/or functional limitations will return to work.

Bibliography

Davis, P.M., Badi, M. & Yassi, A. (2004). Preventing Disability from Occupational Musculoskeletal Injuries in an Urban, Acute and Tertiary Care Hospital: Results from a Prevention and Early Active Return-to-Work Safety Program. *Journal of Occupational & Environmental Medicine* 46, 1253–262.

Federal Government of Belgium. Wet betreffende het welzijn van de werknemers bij de uitvoering van hun werk. Available at: http://www.werk.belgie.be/WorkArea/showcontent.aspx?id=8346, accessed 4 August 1996.

Franche, R.L., Baril, R., Shaw, W., Nicholas, M. & Loisel, P. (2005a). Workplace-Based Return-to-Work Interventions: Optimizing the Role of Stakeholders in Implementation Research. *Journal of Occupational Rehabilitation* 15, 525–42.

Franche, R.L., Cullen, K., Clarke, J., Irvin, E., Sinclair, S. & Frank, J. (2005b). Workplace-Based Return-to-Work Interventions: A Systematic Review of the Quantitative Literature. *Journal of Occupational Rehabilitation* 15, 607–31.

Isernhagen, S.J. (2006). Job Matching and Return to Work: Occupational Rehabilitation as the Link. *Work* 26, 237–42.

Linz, D.H., Ford, L.F., Nightingale, M.J., Shannon, P.L., Davin, J.S., Bradford, C.O. & Shepherd, C.D. (2001). *Journal of Occupational & Environmental Medicine* 43(11), 959–68.

Milquet, J. (2008). Nationale strategie inzake welzijn op het werk 2008–2012. Available at: www.werk.belgie.be/home, accessed 25 November 2008.

Mortelmans, K., Donceel, P. & Lahaye, D. (2006). Disability Management through Positive Intervention in Stakeholders' Information Asymmetry. A Pilot Study. *Occupational Medicine* 56, 129–36

National Institute of Disability Management and Research (NIDMAR). (2000). *Code of Practice for Disability Management.* Geneve: ILO.

National Institute of Disability Management and Research NIDMAR (2003): Disability Management in the Workplace: A Guide to Establishing a Joint Workplace Program. Port Alberni, BC: NIDMAR.

Nijhuis, F. & Van Lierop, B. (2007). Arbeidsreïntegratie en arbeidsrehabilitatie. In: W. Schaufeli & A. Bakker (eds). *De psychologie van arbeid en gezondheid* (169–91). Houten: Bohn Stafleu Van Loghum.

Piek, P. & Reijenga, F. (2004). *Disability management als nieuwe insteek voor HRM.* Den Haag: Sdu Uitgevers.

Pransky, G.S., Shaw, W.S., Franche, R.L. & Clarke, A. (2004). Disability Prevention and Communication among Workers, Physicians, Employers, and Insurers – Current Models and Opportunities for Improvement. *Disability and Rehabilitation* 26, 625–34.

Prevent, (2001). *Study on Accidents at Work and Employability – Factors Influencing Successful Reintegration of Injured Workers.* Available at: http://osha.europa.eu/en/publications/forum/4, accessed 15 July 2011.

RIZIV. (2007). Jaarverslag 2007. Available at: www.riziv.fgov.be/presentation/nl/publications/annual-report/index.htm, accessed 8 May 2009.

Russo, D. & Innes, E. (2002). An Organisational Case Study of the Case Manager's Role in a Client's Return-to-Work Programme in Australia. *Occupational Therapy International* 9, 57–75.

Shaw, W., Hong, Q., Pransky, G. & Loisel, P. (2008). A Literature Review Describing the Role of Return-to-Work Coordinators in Trial Programs and Interventions Designed to Prevent Workplace Disability. *Journal of Occupational Rehabilitation* 18, 2–15.

SILC. (2006). *European Union Statistics on Income and Living Conditions.* Available at: http://ec.europa.eu/eurostat, accessed 8 May 2009.

Tompa, E., de Oliveira, C., Dolinschi, R. & Irvin, E. (2008). A Systematic Review of Disability Management Interventions with Economic Evaluations. *Journal of Occupational Rehabilitation* 18, 16–26.

Verjans, M. & Rommel, A. (2008). *Disability Management als meerwaarde bij jobbehoud & re-integratie.* Brussels: Prevent.

Wynne, R. & McAnaney, D. (2004). *Employment and Disability: Back to Work Strategies.* Luxembourg: European Foundation for the Improvement of Living and Working Conditions.

Young, A., Wasiak, R., Roessler, R., McPherson, K., Anema, J. & van Poppel, N. (2005). Return-to-Work Outcomes Following Work Disability: Stakeholder Motivations, Interests and Concerns. *Journal of Occupational Rehabilitation* 15, 543–56.

11 *Workplace Disability Management: Findings of an Empirical Investigation of Swiss Companies*

THOMAS GEISEN, ANNETTE LICHTENAUER,
CHRISTOPHE ROULIN AND GEORG SCHIELKE

Introduction

Since the 1990s, increasing efforts have been undertaken in Western industrialized nations to reduce the number of redundancies due to sickness or accidents. While the reasons for these growing efforts are manifold, they differ from country to country (see OECD 2003). They range from economic reasons through social policy to demographic factors (among other things, ageing workforces). A new approach that has arisen in this context is disability management. It has gained international acceptance and support, not only in social policy but also among companies and social security providers. Disability management is an 'intervention and consultancy' approach. It aims to promote and support integration and reintegration processes among the gainfully employed (Geisen 2010: 76 (author translation)).

Important steps towards international use of disability management included the founding of the National Institute of Disability Management and Research (NIDMAR) in Canada in 1994 (see NIDMAR 2008), and the ratification of a code of practice by the International Labor Organization (ILO) (see ILO 2002).[1] At the end of the 1990s, disability management became more widespread in European countries, particularly in Switzerland. However, to date, disability management is not sufficiently established in European companies.

To begin with, disability management developed in countries where individuals or companies are largely responsible for making basic social security arrangements, and where these arrangements are tied to gainful employment, such as in Canada, the United States and Australia (see Harder & Scott 2005). In the United States and Canada,

---

1   Disability management is also closely linked to workplace health promotion; see WHO (1986); ENWHP (2007); Badura, Ritter & Scherf (1999); Gröben & Bös (1999); Münch, Walter & Badura (2004).

for instance, this is true not only for health and accident insurance, but also for other social benefits. Discussing the close relationship between social security and full-time employment in the United States, Ilona Ostner observes:

> Statutory social insurance exists only for the risk of old age. In case of redundancy, social security as a rule presupposes full-time employment, that is, where such support is provided at all. If granted at all, other workplace welfare measures are tied to full-time employment – in the United States, such measures include social security benefits for the gainfully employed and their families in case of sickness, as well as other benefits. Such, 'fringe benefits' make up an ever greater proportion of (full-time) salaries. (Ostner 1998: 236 (author translation)).

This also means that a higher sickness and accident rate is a direct cost factor for companies, and includes the higher private insurance contributions they are obliged to pay. Social costs arising from absences due to sickness and accidents, for instance, thus become increasingly evident to companies, which perceive them as a relevant business cost.

The situation is different in Western European social welfare states and their strongly developed social security systems (see Kraus & Geisen 2001). In these countries, companies have only a limited influence on the business costs resulting from sickness or accident. Health insurance contributions are thus not calculated on the basis of concrete company performance, such as the number of sick-leave days, but rather on an amount determined under applicable law. Espring-Andersen (1998: 43f) places the Swiss welfare state in the group of liberal welfare states. Unlike the United States, Great Britain, Canada or Australia, however, Switzerland is not an archetypal example of this regime, but comes close to it (Esping-Andersen 1998: 44). In Switzerland, a well-developed system of basic state provision is combined with elements of private insurance (for instance, the three-pillar model regulating old age provision) and fringe benefits paid by companies (such as contributions to daily sickness-allowance insurance schemes) (see Wicki 2001). In the event of accident or sickness, individuals living in Switzerland can thus rely on support from mandatory health insurance, accident insurance and disability insurance (Wicki 2001). While companies are unable to influence the costs of mandatory social security, some private insurance costs come under direct corporate influence. One example is the contributions paid by companies towards daily sickness-allowance insurance.[2] Companies themselves identify starting points for reducing costs, more by enhancing HR management than by increasing insurance contributions, and this is particularly the case in relation to absentee rates. In recent years, companies have therefore stepped up their absentee management (see Staub 2007; Zeltner 2003). Moreover, since 2000, Swiss companies have introduced workplace disability management.

The study on Disability Management in der Schweiz (Geisen et al. 2008) marked the first extensive investigation of workplace disability management in Switzerland. The study focused particularly on the reasons for introducing disability management in companies, the actual processes this involved and the effects of such schemes. This

---

2   Esping-Andersen argues that welfare states differ 'considerably with regard to their principles of entitlement and stratification. These differences entail qualitatively different arrangements between state, market, and family. Identifiable variations between individual welfare states are therefore not subject to linear distribution, but can be grouped into types of regimes' (Esping-Andersen,1998: 43 (author translation)). He distinguishes liberal, corporatist,and social democratic welfare state regimes (Esping-Andersen 1998: 43ff).

chapter presents the key findings of the 2008 study, with a discussion of the relevant theoretical foundations, the findings of various empirical analyses of workplace disability management in Switzerland and relevant aspects of its social framework.

Theoretical Foundations and Empirical Findings

The term 'disability management' is used in various ways in theory (see Geisen 2010; Harder & Scott 2005; Wermuth & Woodtly 2008). Concretizations of the term and the conception of disability management itself refer both to the concept and to process design. In Switzerland, terms such as integration management and case management are frequently used synonymously. Wermuth and Woodtly criticize this practice insofar as it addresses only one facet of disability management, namely, case management (Wermuth & Woodtly 2008: 16). They call for a conception of disability management as 'workplace health management', which encompasses the various measures and activities designed to promote employee health in both conceptual and structural terms (Wermuth & Woodtly 2008: 15f). Wermuth and Woodtly argue that conceiving disability management along these lines would enable a better engagement in the international debate.

The notion of disability management as workplace health management has been criticized by, among others, Geisen who considers disability management synonymous with workplace integration management (see Geisen 2010). He understands the latter as an area-specific form of case management. This perspective systematically interrelates the case and system levels. Adopting a case management approach to disability management would have the advantage of basing approaches to workplace health promotion, and the implementation of corresponding measures, on a systematic analysis of cases. Such approaches would not exclude the provision of general health promotion measures, such as in areas as nutrition and physical activity. Within disability management, however, in-company measures are based on the analysis of concrete problems, and their use is aligned with such measures (Geisen 2010).

However, the only study on disability management in Switzerland (from 2008) has shown (Geisen et al. 2008) that the term disability management is neither used in practice nor widely known among practitioners. Instead, companies implementing workplace disability management programs have recourse to already established terms such as health management, integration management or case management. Besides workplace disability management programs, in Switzerland various forms of external disability management have been established which means that companies do not introduce disability management themselves but instead use external service providers. Such providers also include health and life insurers in particular. Occasionally, occupational pension funds are also active in this area, not only by funding the casework undertaken by companies and external service providers, but also by (partly) rendering disability management services themselves. Rather than referring to disability management, these actors speak of case management. Thus, the term disability management has not become established in Switzerland, nor has there been sharp distinction between the competing terms. Accordingly, the model hitherto lacks clear boundaries. In Switzerland, disability management is conceived as a pragmatic approach to providing care and support for staff in the event of sickness or accident rather than as a substantiated theoretical concept.

Workplace Disability Management in Switzerland

There is a lack of reliable data regarding the success and the concrete design of disability management, in practice, in Switzerland. The study reported in this chapter (Geisen et al. 2008) attempts to contribute to the closing of this gap by analyzing how disability management was implemented in eight Swiss companies. On behalf of the Federal Social Insurance Office (BSV), the authors of this chapter conducted a pilot study on disability management in Switzerland during the period from May 2007 to July 2008. The study aimed to reconstruct the processes involved in introducing disability management in companies, to identify the reasons for introducing such programs and to describe and compare the structures and procedures involved. It also studied the outcome of disability management in the companies surveyed.

The research team first identified 62 companies, public offices and government departments that had adopted internal measures to support staff members suffering illness or injury. Since no statistical data on workplace disability management are available in Switzerland, companies providing disability management were identified by contacting individuals working for return-to-work schemes, and subsequently by adopting the snowball principle as a sampling strategy (see Patton 2002). The companies thus identified were first asked to answer various questions about their in-house support for employees with an illness or injury. Based on the data obtained, the research team subsequently determined whether the measures adopted satisfied the criteria of workplace disability management. From the overall set of companies providing workplace disability management, eight companies were selected on the basis of theoretical sampling (Glaser & Strauss 2005; see Strauss 1998; see Strübing, 2004). The criteria included sector affiliation and the number of staff. The investigated sample comprised eight companies: Klinik Barmelweid (rehabilitation, 250 employees), Migros Basel (retail, 3,800 employees), PostFinance (financial services, 3,000 employees), PostMail (postal services, 16,000 employees), ISS (facility management, 9,000 employees), Basler Verkehrsbetriebe BVB (logistics, 1,000 employees), Siemens (industry, 6,000 employees) and Implenia (construction, 4,800 employees).

Qualitative interviews were conducted in the selected companies with, among others, members of their human resources (HR) or executive management, a workplace disability management supervisor and two employees receiving disability management support. In order to contrast cases, we investigated one successful and one less successful case of disability management, as defined by the disability manager. A total number of 31 interviews were held.

In addition to qualitative interviews, in seven out of the eight companies a written survey was carried out among employees supported by a disability management program.[3] A written questionnaire was used to enable those employees to provide details on their working and living conditions, the condition of their health and the workplace assistance provided by their employer. In the companies surveyed – totalling 37,850 employees – 740 persons were receiving workplace disability management support. The written questionnaire was sent to these individuals. There was a response rate of 26 per

---

3   'Under the Swiss Code of Obligations (OR), employers are obliged, in the case of sickness or accident, to continue the remuneration of gainfully employed staff for a limited period of time. ... Employers may absolve themselves under certain conditions from their duty to recompense such employees through entering into a collective daily sickness-allowance insurance' (Bundesamt für Sozialversicherungen BSV 2010:1 (author translation)).

cent, with 198 of the questionnaires being completed and returned.[4] The number of questionnaires returned enables the extrapolation of representative comments on the total number of employees involved in workplace disability management programs. The average age of employees supported by such programs in the companies surveyed is 48. Older persons are slightly overrepresented. Slightly more men (58 per cent) responded to the survey than women. Of the respondents, 68 per cent indicated that they were born in Switzerland. The majority had completed an occupational apprenticeship. Compared to the normal population, a high percentage of respondents have a low education level (having completed compulsory schooling or primary education as their highest qualification). Most survey respondents live in suburban districts or in urban centres.

The qualitative interviews and the standardized written survey were conducted between 31 May and 28 November 2007. Grounded theory (Glaser & Strauss 2005; Strauss 1998; Strauss & Corbin 1996) was used to evaluate the qualitative interviews; the results of the quantitative survey were assessed by means of description and inferential statistics.

Although the term disability management is not well known in Switzerland and finds no application in corporate practice, it was nevertheless used in the study to ensure cross-linkage with the relevant international debate. This is important particularly for undertaking further, comparative research in this area. The 2008 study also found that as a term and concept disability management introduces an important *tertium comparationis*[5] into the research process, through which the various terms, concepts and practices encountered in the area of return-to-work schemes could be verified and their differences presented in detail.

Drawing on the work of Wendt (2001) and Guransky et al. (2003) on case management, and on that of Harder & Scott (2005) and of the ILO (2002) on disability management, a working definition of disability management was developed for the study. This definition includes four key aspects:

1. recording and assessing staff absences with the help of systematic absentee management, thus enabling the early identification of health risks;
2. advising and supporting employees suffering illness or injury;
3. coordinating return-to-work activities and services;
4. prevention within the framework of workplace health promotion (see Geisen et al. 2008: 1).

The working definition includes those workplace measures and activities that must be in place to let one speak of comprehensive disability management. Case management is thereby understood as a fundamental basis for running disability management programs (Harder & Scott 2005; see Wendt 2001). Following the case management approach, disability management refers to the concrete case and its management, as well as to the organizational and institutional conditions (on the systems and organizational levels) of gainful employment prevailing in a given company. On the basis of case management, disability management thus constitutes an institutional framework within the company for providing staff suffering sickness or accident with information, advice and support

---

4   One company declined involvement in the written survey.

5   In relation to the total number of persons suffering illness or accident during the last five years in the companies surveyed, the 740 individuals contacted constitute a complete survey.

aimed at continued employment in the company. However, disability management should not be reduced to an approach adopted to optimize case management in the event of sickness or accident – even if this is at the forefront of practice. Other important aspects in this respect include prevention, health maintenance and early detection. Disability management exists only with reference to all four aspects, and thereby distinguishes the concept from one-dimensional models, as applied, in part, within absentee management (see Zeltner 2003) or workplace health management (see Ulich & Wülser 2009). Such fourfold underpinning also clearly distinguishes disability management from approaches aimed only at (re)integrating staff into gainful employment. Harder and Scott therefore refer to such encompassing disability management, which includes both case management and workplace organization, as comprehensive disability management (Harder & Scott 2005).

REASONS FOR INTRODUCING DISABILITY MANAGEMENT

Staff absences pose a serious challenge to companies. Long or only temporary absences due to sickness or accident may entail a loss of productivity. Increasingly, companies are seeking to counter the threat of losing manpower and skills by adopting reintegrative measures that begin with the employees who suffer an illness or injury. The management of the eight companies surveyed often cited the costs associated with sickness or accident as the principal reason for introducing workplace disability management. Costs resulting from staff absences are the key issue. In one case, Barmelweid Clinic, disability management was also introduced when the provider terminated of the daily contract. Cancellation prompted the clinic to review its staff absentee rate and subsequently to introduce a disability management scheme.

In addition to the objective cost savings achieved by reducing the absentee rate, other in-house motives for introducing internal disability management were found. Disability management can contribute to strengthening employee ties with the employer. If employees are convinced that their employer treats staff fairly, and if they trust their employer to support them in overcoming the difficulties arising from sickness or accident, then they will also be more motivated to contribute as much as possible to coping with the situation. While the costs resulting from lost working hours can be calculated, the benefits of strengthening corporate culture, enhanced employee identification with the company and greater employee job satisfaction are only partly quantifiable, particularly as preventive measures.

Another reason for introducing disability management is the competition between companies for customers, contracts and qualified employees. Companies believe that introducing workplace disability management affords them a strategic advantage, which they also consider to strengthen their public image as a socially minded employer. For instance, this was an important reason for ISS, a cleaning contractor, to introduce workplace disability management. Against the background of foreseeable bottlenecks on the labour market for qualified staff, greater importance will be attached to providing employees with increasing support, particularly in the event of sickness or accident. Such support is aimed at retaining employees over the long term. Some of the companies surveyed, such as Migros Basel, explicitly cited employee retention as a principal reason for introducing disability management.

In summary, workplace disability management is implemented for three principal reasons: costs, corporate culture and competition. In principle, it took between one and two years to introduce and implement such programs in the companies surveyed. Thus, adjusting workplace routines for performance-impaired staff can be neither envisaged nor achieved on a short-term basis. Instead, such adjustments must be made over a longer time period. One decisive reason necessitating the longer view concerns the complexity of workplace disability management itself. On the one hand, its success depends on full commitment from executive management and the various levels of company hierarchy, particularly immediate superiors; on the other, success also depends on employee trust in such internal support.

INTRODUCING DISABILITY MANAGEMENT

The 2008 study identified three approaches to incorporating disability management into company structure: first, as an HR subunit; second, as an integral part of HR; and third, as part of the social counselling unit. Disability management was generally positioned close to HR. Some of the companies also had an independent social counselling unit. In principle, the danger of linking disability management with HR is that supportive measures blend with disciplinary ones. Disability management thereby turns from being a client-related, advocatory and mediating process for supporting employees in the event of sickness or accident into an internal lobbying and control device. Indeed, the qualitative interviews conducted with staff receiving disability management support variously indicate an unfavourable linkage in this respect. Interestingly, these indications occur irrespectively of where disability management is situated within a company. Overall, no advantages or disadvantages of any particular positioning of disability management within company structure were identified. Moreover, no sector-specific differences in relation to a preferred internal disability management structure were found.

IMPLEMENTING DISABILITY MANAGEMENT

In principle, the eight companies surveyed in the 2008 study adopt a case management approach to disability management. However, significant differences exist between companies regarding aspects relevant to implementation. Thus, the point at which disability management goes into action varies considerably among the various companies, in a bandwidth ranging from seven to ninety days of absence. In most companies, however, disability management commences after one month of absence. Neither the qualitative nor standardized survey revealed any influence of program initiation on the satisfaction of staff members receiving such support. Staff expressed satisfaction with disability management being initiated regardless of when this occurred.

Not all employees suffering from illness are offered workplace disability management. What is defined as a 'case' varies from company to company. Varying or even missing systematic triage processes in the companies surveyed resulted in differing case numbers, and thus make it more difficult to compare established disability management concepts. As a rule, disability management is initiated by general or line managers. In all the companies surveyed, general or line managers play a key role in the disability management process. The study also found, however, that employees affected by sickness or accident quite frequently initiate disability management themselves.

Companies as a rule provide for discussions to be conducted on a graded scale of approximately three to six levels. Not all companies initiate disability management on the first level, instead opting for line managers and affected staff to discuss matters first. Significant differences exist among the companies surveyed with regard to the actual structure of the disability management implementation process. Strongly prestructured and standardized procedures contrast with more loosely structured and mostly open organizational forms of disability management. The former can be attributed to *systems-centred* forms of organization. Their advantage is that they enable the disability management process to be controlled. In contrast, less stringently structured and more open formats exhibit a *client-centred* approach. Their advantage is that they start from the concrete situation of the affected employees, adjusting a support and promotion strategy to individual needs. Of the companies surveyed, one half adopts a more client-centred approach while the other half prefers a systems-centred one.

In the companies surveyed, exactly when and how disability management is initiated proceeds along reasonably well-structured and standardized lines. Concrete case management, however, reveals substantial differences. Some companies have procedures that exhibit limited standardization. Generally, affected staff are obliged to participate in disability management. In contrast, one company, which adopts strongly client-centred disability management, characterized by a highly individual procedure, explicitly considers voluntary participation a prerequisite for successful disability management.

In the companies surveyed, disability management is confined largely to counselling interviews and information sessions. Survey respondents found these measures useful. However, other supportive measures seem to have been offered far less frequently, and were also found to be far less useful by employees involved in disability management programs. Generally, disability management merely provides guidance on medical, financial or legal assistance, or on counselling and retraining; such advisory services are rendered by third parties. In addition to case management, early detection and preventive measures are also implemented as part of workplace disability management.

The resources allocated to disability management vary significantly across the companies surveyed. Disability management staff have limited additional funds at their disposal. In the companies surveyed, the ratio of one full-time disability management staff member to other company staff members ranges between 1143 and 4310. On average, one disability manager is responsible for 1,717 staff members. While the relevant literature provides no precise details on optimal resource allocation, experience from disability management pilot projects undertaken in Switzerland suggests an ideal ratio of at least one full-time disability management position for every 1,000 staff members (see Schmidt & Kessler 2006; Stadt_Zürich 2006). Correspondingly, staff responsible for disability management in the companies surveyed criticized the level of resources provided. Additional resources are mobilized through both internal and external networks.

DISABILITY MANAGEMENT ACTORS AND THEIR ROLES

Disability management provides employees with important assistance in their endeavours to overcome performance restrictions and their inability to work. Within the company environment, those responsible for workplace disability management perform a key function in supporting employees in the event of sickness or accident. Employees rate this support more positively than the support provided by line managers and executive management. Surprisingly, no less than 16 per cent of the employees involved in a disability management program in the companies surveyed failed to perceive such management positively, and explicitly denied receiving disability management support. Evidently, this means that such support is not always perceived as such by those concerned. This might be related to a weak anchoring of disability management in the workplace. The findings of the qualitative interviews suggest that, in some cases, only the line manager was perceived as the initiator of disability management, whereas disability management was seen to constitute an independent organizational unit, or indeed that those involved had hoped to receive more far-reaching support. Additional comments made by respondents in the standardized survey show, moreover, that disability management does not entirely replace the commitment of immediate superiors.

Line managers are among the key actors in workplace disability management. The fact that line managers were the second most frequent category mentioned in the qualitative survey, in response to the question of who exactly had initiated disability management in the individual case, points to the important role played by immediate superiors. Line managers will as a rule seek initial clarification and conduct discussions with affected employees before a decision to initiate disability management is taken. For the most part, immediate superiors remain involved in the process for the duration of the individual case. They have close contact with the staff concerned from the outset, and serve as an important employee liaison throughout the process. To ensure that disability management is initiated independently of the arbitrariness of the immediate superior, most companies operate a systematic absence recording and reporting system.

The study found that social security providers also play an important role in successful disability management. Possible solutions for the individual case can be discussed and return-to-work programs initiated with the assistance of social security providers. In the best case, social security benefits and support can be actively integrated into the reintegration (return-to-work) process. Overall, while companies positively assess existing cooperation with social security providers, daily sickness-allowance insurance, the Swiss Accident Insurance Fund (SUVA) and occupational pension funds, they also identify a need for improvement. Most companies criticize cooperation with disability insurance on account of extended case processing times and lengthy medical assessments. The fact that such cases come under federal jurisdiction also requires additional effort, since companies must maintain contacts with a large number of disability insurance offices.

The important role played by family doctors in the integration process should not be underestimated either. Employees on disability management schemes highlighted the assistance provided by their family doctors as being particularly helpful. In the final analysis, this support was considered more important than their employer's. Company representatives, however, assessed cooperation with family doctors very differently and described it as rather difficult.

Disability Management and its Effects

The companies surveyed use various methods to establish and rate the success of their disability management activities. As a rule, the absentee rate and the direct and indirect costs arising from absences serve as indicators for measuring systematic performance. However, the costs and benefits of disability management are neither recorded in a standard fashion nor systematically documented. Nor are the impacts on company culture or competitiveness subject to any systematic review.

No direct causal link can be established between the introduction of disability management, its specific design and the lowering of the absentee rate or the reduction of costs. Limited in-house performance measurement figures are available, and none of the companies surveyed kept a disability management profit and loss account. No attempts to improve performance measurement can be found in the companies surveyed, and such schemes are in part not considered feasible by HR management. The effort required to record factors relevant to success is considered either too great or unreasonable.[6] Determining the success of disability management therefore relies particularly on the appraisal and assessment of those involved, that is, by the representatives of the companies surveyed on the one hand, and by employees receiving disability management support on the other.

Since only two companies determined the return-to-work rate, it was established after the fact within the standardized survey of the employees receiving disability management support. Employees were asked to report their original and current activity rates in order to determine both the extent of stoppage and the degree of reintegration (return to work) attained. Comparing both sets of data shows that on the one hand survey respondents were absent at a rate of 77 per cent of their original workload. On the other, stoppage caused by sickness or accident could be offset again at a rate of 60 per cent in the average number of cases at the time of the survey; staff suffering sickness or accident thus returned to work almost to a corresponding extent, and without requiring significant workplace restructuring.

Based on the success attained by helping employees with illness or injury return to work, the companies surveyed are convinced of the importance of disability management and consider it worthwhile. Companies reported that disability management had largely enabled them to reach the envisaged goals, namely, to provide staff with assistance and support, to intervene at an early stage, to strengthen corporate culture, to enhance their public image, to reduce or at least maintain absences at a stable level, to increase productivity and to lower costs.

However, a range of factors capable of hindering successful disability management was reported: insufficiently qualified disability management staff, scant resources for running disability management programs, the low autonomy of disability management with company structure and a demanding attitude of either company management or the staff concerned.

Besides lowering the absentee rate and the costs associated with this, introducing disability management also affects company culture. Disability management can contribute to strengthening employee-employer ties, as well as positively influence employee motivation. The employee survey conducted in the 2008 study revealed that staff members affected by sickness or accident were glad to receive support in their predicament. They indicated a range of positive company culture factors, including security, esteem and respect, confidence and future prospects. This clearly shows the great significance of interaction and communication for disability management. Criticism

---

6   *Tertium comparationis* (the third part of the comparison) is a key concept of comparative research. It involves the illustrative or evaluative comparison of objects or actions with the help of a third entity or quality. Following Burdorf (1995: 150), such comparison presupposes that two non-identical matters have at least one feature in common.

was levelled less often at the concrete forms of support than at a lack of support. The qualitative interviews revealed that strongly systematized disability management can also be perceived as constituting coercion and pressure. However, the standardized survey failed to confirm this finding. Most of the employees surveyed considered the support provided by workplace disability management not as a means of control, but rather as highly welcome assistance on the part of the company, including in those cases where no successful return to work could be achieved. While the majority of respondents still do not feel fit and well after receiving disability management support, they are motivated to resume work. Thus, return to work (that is, workplace reintegration) is relatively frequent. Workplace disability management thus contributes to improving the situation of employees on such programs, even if those concerned attach greater significance to other actors. On the whole, while employees consider workplace disability management helpful, such assistance is not deemed decisive. Personal surroundings are regarded as more important for coping with difficulties in the event of sickness or accident than the company environment. Family members and the family doctor are the principal contacts for employees under such circumstances. Importance is also attached to the support provided by health insurance, daily sickness-allowance insurance, occupational pension funds, and disability insurance. Cooperation between these agencies is therefore crucial for the success of disability management.

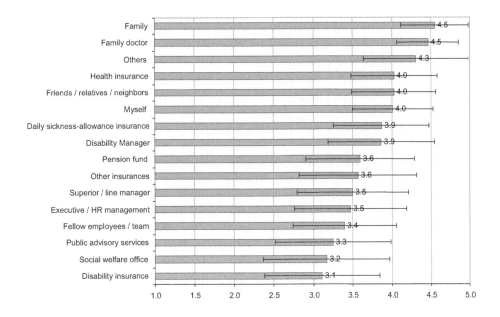

Figure 11.1 Importance of the support received

Survey Conclusions and Recommendations

One of the main findings of the 2008 study on disability management schemes in eight Swiss companies is that company size is a decisive factor for either setting up an in-house program or using an external provider. However, cases must be considered separately. For instance, one company (with 250 employees) established a successful disability management program because it could draw on staff already holding professional qualifications in this area.

Overall, the companies surveyed indicated that disability management had been introduced primarily for economic reasons. One striking feature, however, is that most companies fail to measure the economic success of their disability management programs. For instance, the companies surveyed gathered no data on the return-to-work (or reintegration) rate. The reasons for this shortcoming could be explained only to a limited extent: in one case, HR management referred to the complexity and effort required to collect data on the various factors relevant to furnishing a cost-benefit account of disability management; another company indicated that disability management was integral to its endeavour to create the image of modern and social enterprise. Besides the actual long-term economic benefit, disability management also served a more immediate public relations strategy.

The study was unable to establish to what extent the increasing social policy debates waged in Switzerland since the late 1990s and the various welfare state reforms undertaken, for instance in the context of various overhauls of disability insurance, played a role in the introduction of disability management. Whether stricter legal requirements should be imposed on companies to promote return-to-work schemes or whether they should commit themselves to such a strategy of their own accord, coupled with providing employees with incentives and support, remained a controversial issue throughout these debates. To date, those advocating corporate self-commitment have maintained the upper hand in shaping welfare state reforms, particularly with regard to the overhaul of disability insurance.

Where in the company structure disability management is incorporated has no influence on its success. The 2008 study found various approaches in this respect, with a strong preference for situating disability management close to HR. Nevertheless, the study found that the location of disability management within a corporate structure did not influence disability management practice. The limited scope of the reported study, however, only allows for limited findings in this respect. When introducing disability management, however, companies should ensure that such programs receive comprehensive in-house commitment, particularly from management.

The study found that while companies without exception adopt a case management approach, actual implementation and organization are very different. Employees receiving disability management support also quite often experience more stringently standardized procedures as coercive and controlling. Lower standardization better meets the needs of affected employees and enables solutions tailored to individual requirements. At the same time, less structuring also involves the risk of arbitrariness. On the one hand, disability management procedures should therefore be clearly structured, so as to ensure as much transparency as possible for superiors and staff alike. This is particularly important for channelling access to disability management and determining requirements and aims. On the other hand, an open-minded approach to individual case management should be maintained, so that unconventional solutions also remain possible. Moreover, successful program implementation and execution presuppose sufficient resources.

Generally speaking, the study found that employees consider the support received from their personal surroundings and their family doctor as decisive. In contrast, less significance is attached to company support. Given a good network of workplace actors and external agents, workplace disability management can contribute to successful integration. Immediate superiors play a key role in this regard. However, some consider themselves overburdened by attending to and supporting employees in the event of sickness or accident. Disability management provides superiors with important support under such circumstances. On the one hand, disability management staff can provide direct professional support and advice on how to approach employees in the event of sickness or accident. On the other, disability management can come as a relief to line managers in complex cases.

Cooperation with social security providers makes a decisive contribution to the success of disability management. Improving cooperation between companies and social security providers is therefore advantageous. Moreover, closer cooperation with family doctors should also be envisaged to do justice to the crucial role they play for employees in the event of sickness or accident.

Introducing workplace disability management enables companies to reduce their absentee rate and to lower costs. Two factors are decisive in this respect: first, disability management provides employees, suffering from illness or injury, with better supervision and support; and secondly, it helps better coordinate possibilities existing within the company to arrive at appropriate and sustainable solutions within the disability management process. Overall, the study reveals that interpersonal factors are crucial, particularly the showing of esteem and respect for the employees concerned.

Conclusion

Harder and Scott emphasize that disability management has undergone continuous further development in the past decades, 'and there is no disputing its positive intentions' (Harder & Scott, 2005: 29). In Switzerland, there is only limited empirical evidence to substantiate their finding. The study reported in this chapter has shown that no comprehensive efficiency review and monitoring of the success of workplace disability management can be guaranteed. Although disability management has increasingly been implemented in public and private enterprises in Switzerland since the turn of the millennium, there is a lack of research, particularly focusing on disabled workers and their needs to enable them to keep their jobs. To date, only a few isolated reports on pilot projects that include details on the impact achieved have been published (see Stadt_Zürich 2006). Further research is therefore urgently needed to ensure the systematic further development of disability management. International comparative research can make an important contribution in this respect. No such research on disability management exists yet.

The study reported here serves as a pilot study for Switzerland. Its comprehensive analysis of the processes involved in successfully establishing workplace disability management serves as a model and initiative for the further development of practice in Switzerland.

Bibliography

Badura, B., Ritter, W. & Scherf, M. (1999). *Betriebliches Gesundheitsmanagement. Ein Leitfaden für die Praxis*. Berlin: edition sigma.

BSV. (2010). Krankentaggeldversicherung. Available at: http://www.bsv.admin.ch/kmu/ ratgeber/00773/00783/index.html?lang=de, accessed 11 July 2010.

Bundesamt für Sozialversicherungen BSV. (2010). KMU Ratgeber. Kündigungsschutz. Available at: http://www.bsv.admin.ch/kmu/ratgeber/00903/00905/index.html?lang=de, accessed 15 October 2010.

Burdorf, D. (1995). *Einführung in die Gedichtanalyse*. Stuttgart: Metzler.

ENWHP. (2007). European Network for Workplace Health Promotion. Available at: http://www. enwhp.org/index.php?id=5:, accessed 5 December 2001.

Esping-Andersen, G. (1998). Die drei Welten des Wohlfahrtskapitalismus. Zur Politischen Ökonomie des Wohlfahrtsstaates. In S. Lessenich & I. Ostner (eds), *Welten des Wohlfahrtskapitalismus. Der Sozialstaat in vergleichender Perspektive* (19–58). Frankfurt am Main: Campus.

Geisen, T. (2010). Disability Management und Personalentwicklung. Neue Perspektiven im Umgang mit leistungsveränderten Mitarbeitenden im Unternehmen. In G. Ochsenbein, U. Prekruhl & R. Spaar (eds), *Human Ressource Management. Jahrbuch 2010* (73–91). Zürich: WEKA Business Media AG.

Geisen, T., Lichtenauer, A., Roulin, C. & Schielke, G. (2008). *Disability Management in Unternehmen in der Schweiz*. Bern: Bundesamt für Sozialversicherungen.

Glaser, B.G. & Strauss, A.L. (2005). *Grounded Theory. Strategien qualitativer Forschung*. Bern: Hans Huber.

Gröben, F. & Bös, K. (1999). *Praxis betrieblicher Gesundheitsförderung*. Berlin: edition sigma.

Gursansky, D., Harvey, J. & Kennedy, R. (2003). *Case Management. Policy, Practice and Professional Business*. New York: Columbia University Press.

Harder, H.G. & Scott, L.R. (2005). *Comprehensive Disability Management*. Toronto: Elsevier.

ILO. (2002). *Managing Disability in the Workplace. ILO Code of Practice*. Geneva: International Labour Office.

Kraus, K. & Geisen, T. (eds). (2001). *Sozialstaat in Europa. Geschichte – Entwicklung – Perspektiven*. Wiesbaden: Westdeutscher Verlag.

Münch, E., Walter, U. & Badura, B. (2004). *Führungsaufgabe Gesundheitsmanagement*. Berlin: edition sigma.

NIDMAR. (2008). About the Institute. Available at: http://www.nidmar.ca/about/about_institute/ institute_info.asp, accessed 10 February 2008.

Niehaus, M., Magin, J., Marfels, B., Vater, G.E. & Werkstetter, E. (2008). *Betriebliches Eingliederungsmanagement. Studie zur Umsetzung des Betrieblichen Eingliederungsmanagements nach § 84 Abs. 2 SGB IX*. Köln: Universität Köln.

OECD. (2003). *Behindertenpolitik zwischen Beschäftigung und Versorgung*. Frankfurt am Main: Campus.

Ostner, I. (1998). Quadraturen im Wohlfahrtsdreieck. Die USA, Schweden und die Bundesrepublik im Vergleich. In S. Lessenich & I. Ostner (eds), *Weltern des Wohlfahrtskapitalismus. Der Sozialstaat in vergleichender Perspektive* (225–54). Frankfurt am Main: Campus.

Patton, M.Q. (2002). *Qualitative Research and Evaluation Methods*. Thousand Oaks CA: SAGE.

Schmidt, H. & Kessler, S. (2006). 'Ability Management' – Erfahrungen in der Schweiz. In P. Löcherbach & W.R. Wendt (eds), *Case Management in der Entwicklung. Stand und Perspektiven in der Praxis* (192–208). Heidelberg: Economica.

Stadt_Zürich. (2006). *Schlussbericht Case Management am Arbeitsplatz*. Zürich: Stadt Zürich.

Staub, B. (2007). *Business Dossier Absenzenmanagement*. Zürich: WEKA Business Media AG.

Strauss, A. (1998). *Grundlagen qualitativer Sozialforschung*. München: Wilhelm Fink Verlag.

Strauss, A. & Corbin, J. (1996). *Grounded Theory. Grundlagen Qualitativer Sozialforschung*. Weinheim: Juventa.

Strübing, J. (2004). *Grounded Theory*. Wiesbaden: VS Verlag.

Ulich, E. & Wülser, M. (eds). (2009). *Gesundheitsmanagement in Unternehmen. Arbetspsychologische Perspektiven*. Wiesbaden: Gabler.

Wendt, W.R. (2001). *Case Management im Sozial- und Gesundheitswesen*. Freiburg im Breisgau: Lambertus.

Wermuth, E. & Woodtly, R. (2008). An der Schnittstelle zwischen Ökonomie, Gesundheit und Sozialem. Disability Management: Klärung des Begriffs und der Rolle der Sozialen Arbeit. *Sozial Aktuell*, Nr. 2 Februar 2008, 14–18.

WHO (1986). Ottawa Charter for Health Promotion. Charter Adopted at an International Conference on Health Promotion. The Move towards a New Public Health. 17–21 November 1986. Ottawa, Ontario, Canada. Available at: http://whqlibdoc.who.int/hq/1995/WHO_HPR_HEP_95.1.pdf, accessed 2 August 2010..

Wicki, M. (2001). Soziale Sicherheit in der Schweiz: Ein europäischer Sonderfall? In K. Kraus & T. Geisen (eds), *Sozialstaat in Europa. Geschichte – Entwicklung – Perspektiven* (249–72). Wiesbaden: Westdeutscher Verlag.

Zeltner, H. (2003). *Absenzenmanagement*. Aarau: Baldegger.

12 European Perspectives on Disability Management (1999–2009): Insights and Developments

DONAL F. MCANANEY

Introduction

This chapter is based on a series of studies incorporating eight EU Member States carried out over a ten-year period, all of which explored the barriers and facilitators of job retention and reintegration. The chapter addresses the development of disability management (DM) within a selection of EU Member States at a number of levels. The RETURN project (in 1999–2001) and the 2004 Employment and Disability Report for the European Foundation (Wynne & McAnaney 2004) both provide a useful insight into the policy and regulatory factors which have inhibited or enhanced the development of DM in certain jurisdictions rather than others. Key findings of the Stress Impact study that took place from 2001 to 2003 (Stress Impact Consortium 2006) provide an insight into the experiences of Land Transport Authority (LTA) workers, their families and professionals in five Member States. Finally, the Re-Integrate project (from 2007–2009) has provided an opportunity to explore the views of employers in six countries, some of which are located in the new Member States of the EU. This chapter explores, on the basis of policy, quantitative and qualitative research, the role that EU and state regulation plays in the retention and reintegration of disabled workers and the broader factors that influence a person to go back to work.

Disability Management from an EU Perspective

Since the term disability management was coined in the early 1990s (Bruyere & Shrey 1991) in Canada and the USA it has evolved and developed at very different rates in different jurisdictions internationally and its acknowledgement by stakeholders, policymakers, and particularly employers, as a viable strategy for reducing disability in the workplace and in wider society has been inconsistent. In some jurisdictions, e.g., UK and Australia, even the term itself is unpopular and has been replaced by other terms such as absence management and injury management, which are not exact synonyms for DM (e.g., Australian National Audit Office 2003; UNUM UK 2007; CIPD 2009,). In parallel, different interpretations of the exact nature of DM have emerged, e.g., the ILO Code on Managing Disability in the Workplace (International Labor Organization 2001) and the International Disability Management Standards Council Occupational Standards (National Institute of Disability Management and Research 1999).

An employee, who is at risk of exiting employment as a result of an illness or injury which occurred outside of work, but who does not have a pre-existing disability designation, is rarely covered by disability policy, much less disability legislation, in most jurisdictions. As a result, workers that experience a reduction in capacity due to illness or injury do not register as disabled in national statistics, social security records or agendas of representative organizations of people with disability or disability policies. Nevertheless, they constitute the highest percentage of people leaving the labour market, particularly in the older age groups. Even the UN Convention on the Rights of Persons with Disabilities (UNCRPD) is ambiguous on the rights of people who are 'not disabled yet'. Article 27 of the Convention clearly specifies job retention and return to work as important elements of the right of persons with disabilities to work, on an equal basis with others in the employment domain. This could well be interpreted, by a Member State or employer, to specify that only persons with a pre-existing disability designation are covered under the Convention (United Nations 2006). If this interpretation were to be adopted then vocational and professional rehabilitation, job retention and return-to-work programmes would not be a right for ill or injured workers who have not been officially designated as persons with disabilities. This is the current status of such workers in the majority of countries surveyed.

A case in point is the EU Disability Strategy (2008–2009) and its consequent Disability Action Plans, which are clearly focused on 'person with disabilities' (European Commission, 2007a). There is an underpinning assumption that this term has a constant meaning across cultures and legislative domains. A similar assumption underpins disability non-discrimination legislation, although the majority of cases taken under the Americans with Disabilities Act (ADA) in the early stages were job retention cases, many of which were brought by people who had no official disability designation (European Disability Forum 2001). It is often too late to protect a person's job when he or she has taken a non-discrimination case against the employer. This legal and administrative disregard on the part of many Member States must be viewed in a context in which there is mounting evidence that prevention and early intervention have an important role to play responding to disability in society (e.g., Bloch & Prins 2001; Stress Impact Consortium 2006).

While disability policy has remained neutral on the reintegration of long-term absent workers into employment, other drivers have increased the focus on this issue. Macroeconomic concerns, including the changing age profile of the labour market (Gramenos 2003), the need to maintain people in employment for longer (European Commission 2008a), unsustainable increases in social protection costs (EUROSTAT 2008) and a realization that the costs of absence have a major impact on the productivity of industry (Confederation of British Industry, 2008), are particularly important drivers. Many of these are well documented in EU policy documents but have yet to be reflected unambiguously in regulations and mechanisms targeted at the labour market (European Commission 2007b; Council of the European Union 2007). For example, the term 'return to work' is usually taken to mean the placement in employment of people who were previously employed but are currently long-term unemployed rather than long-term absent employees. In response to this the term 'reintegration' has been adopted to refer to long-term absent workers (Wynne & McAnaney 2004).

While measures targeted at people at risk of unemployment due to structural factors have been in place for many years and have been promoted by the EU Employment Guidelines which provide Member States with guidance on employment priorities on an annual basis, there has been no individual guideline that targets workers at risk of unemployment as a result of illness or injury (Council of the European Union 2005). Given the nature of the governance relationship between the EU and its Member States, even this would not provide a strong guarantee that action would be taken, but its absence reflects upon the status of DM within an EU policy context.

This is not to imply that the EU has been ignoring the issue of long-term absence and disability. In fact the European Commission has through a number of initiatives provided support to a number of projects, research studies and initiatives over a period of 15 years. These explored the distinction between measures targeted at people with disabilities who were economically inactive and employees who were out of work for an extended period of time but who still had an attachment to their employer (Wynne & McAnaney 2004; Wynne et al. 2005; Stress Impact Consortium 2006).

This chapter builds on the accumulated experience from these studies and initiatives to provide a description of the challenges encountered, the lessons learnt and some potentially useful and viable DM initiatives and approaches currently being adopted in some Member States.

For the purposes of this chapter the scope of DM is considered to cover two primary pillars of action at both system and company level. The first of these relates to the services, supports and interventions, at system and company levels, aimed at maintaining the workability of employees who are at work and have yet to cross the threshold into absence, i.e., job retention. This pillar includes such domains of action as occupational safety and health (OSH), workplace health promotion (WHP) and employee and family assistance programmes (EFAP). The second pillar incorporates those interventions, at both levels, targeted at people who have experienced injury or illness and who have been long-term absent (i.e., over six weeks) and which aim to reintegrate the person back into the workplace in their previous position (adapted or unadapted) or by redeployment (Wynne & McAnaney 2004).

EU policy and regulatory processes in relation to disability are strongly influenced by the way in which the EU and its Member States operate. The relationship between the institutions of the EU and its Member States is constrained by the concepts of 'competence' and 'subsidiarity'. The demarcation between those aspects of policy that are within the competence of the Union and those that are within the competence of its Member States is clearly delineated.

Where the EU has competence to act, e.g., the single market or non-discrimination in work, the European Commission (EC) (the administrative arm of the EU), the European Council of Ministers (the decision-making body) and the European Parliament (a body with oversight), can implement binding legislation by issuing directives with which Member States must comply.

In areas where there is a shared competence the EU can influence the actions of Members States using what is termed the open method of coordination (OMC) (European Commission 2008b). This involves the EC issuing guidelines (e.g., the Employment

Guidelines and Guidelines for Social Inclusion) that form a framework within which the Member States produce national action plans (NAPs). The OMC operates on an annual cycle of review and revision. Support for the NAPs is provided by structural funds administered by the EC, which provide co-financing for actions at the Member State level. Of particular importance in the current context is the European Social Fund (ESF), which supports actions in relation to both employment and social inclusion.

Finally, in those areas where the Member States have sole competence (e.g., social protection, education and health), the EC can assist by implementing measures to promote a better understanding and shared experience and knowledge amongst Member States.

From an overall policy perspective the EU has set itself a number of targets in relation to employment that could be supported by more proactive job retention and reintegration efforts by Member States and employers. Known as the Lisbon, Stockholm and Barcelona targets, they commit the Union to increasing the employment rate of older workers to 50 per cent (Stockholm target in 2001) and delay by five years the age at which older workers stop working (Barcelona target in 2002) by 2010 (Kanesci 2007). After the Lisbon Economic Council, a new target was set to raise the employment rate for people with disabilities to that of those without disabilities by 2010 (Van Lin, Prins & De Kok 2002). The EU Employment Summit, held in Prague on 7 May 2009, agreed on ways to tackle rising unemployment. Ten concrete actions, addressing both short-term and long-term challenges, were suggested that should be implemented at national and European levels in concert with the social partners. Three of these could be interpreted as having relevance to DM (European Commission 2009):

- Maintaining as many people as possible in jobs, with temporary adjustment of working hours combined with retraining and supported by public funding (including from the European Social Fund).
- Improving the efficiency of national employment services by providing intensive counselling, training and job search in the first weeks of unemployment, especially for the young unemployed.
- Promoting more inclusive labour markets by ensuring work incentives, effective active labour market policies and modernization of social protection systems that also lead to a better integration of disadvantaged groups including the disabled, the low skilled and migrants.

However, the first of these does not specifically cover people at risk of unemployment as a result of illness or injury, the second is primarily focused on the unemployed and the third in the main refers to people who are economically inactive.

This reflects a general pattern in EU policy development that tends to miss the target when it comes to DM. For example, from a DM perspective, OSH falls within the competence of the EU and as such is well regulated and monitored. However, the content and approach of current instruments to regulate health and safety in the EU do not extend beyond the prevention of occupational injuries or diseases to the domains of job retention or the maintenance of workability. While there is recognition by most agencies with responsibility for OSH at Member State level that there is a need to extend the meaning of occupational health to include at least the promotion of workplace health, the idea that this extends to absent workers is rare. Thus action in this area is still based on voluntary codes of practice and depends on the efforts of committed individuals and organizations. It is also very much focused on workplace injuries and thus has little to contribute to job retention for people at risk of exclusion arising from non-occupational injuries or illness.

It is fair to conclude that European policy, which addresses disability in a broad range of areas from anti-discrimination to transport or telecommunications, doesn't address the specific target group who need effective DM to retain or return to their jobs. For example, the Employment Equality Directive, which prohibits discrimination and mandates that employers must provide 'reasonable accommodation' for people with disabilities, is mainly applied to people with pre-determined or apparent disabilities as determined by national social protection or Equality Authorities (Whittle 2002). From a DM perspective, these approaches are less than relevant as they mostly apply when people with existing impairments achieve an official disability designation.

For example, many EU Member States have created financial incentives for employers and provide services to recruit and retain disabled people. However, this is more about placing inactive people in the competitive labour market through employment subsidies rather than protecting the employment of long-term absent workers (Hyde 1998; FAS 2010). Ultimately, there is, as of 2010, no EU legislative or policy instrument which addresses DM in any direct way. Further, it is highly unlikely, in the short term, that DM can be addressed at an EU level by a directive requiring Member State compliance.

The most promising area for policy action to promote DM at EU level is the OMC process, which is currently in operation in three domains relevant to DM, i.e., employment, social exclusion and public health. The approach of the EU to employment is set in the Integrated EU Guidelines for Growth and Jobs (Council of the European Union 2008). There are some promising references to retaining more people in employment, increasing labour supply and modernizing social protection systems in the Guidelines, but from the detail it is evident that retaining people in employment is about responding to structural change rather than individual differences arising from injury or illness. The reference to disabled people is more about reducing the unemployment gap rather than protecting employability. The most potentially relevant Guideline is Guideline 17, which aims at achieving full employment and addresses the needs of older workers. This guideline promotes measures for improved occupational health in order to reduce the sickness burden, increase labour productivity and prolong working life. This provides a basis for enhancing WHP programmes, but is far short of an endorsement of a full DM approach for older workers.

The EU social inclusion program aimed to impact on the eradication of poverty, raise the employment rate to 67 per cent by January 2005 and to 70 per cent by 2010, but made no reference to preventing people losing their jobs as a result of illness or injury. Public health policy bears no relationship to employment, but aims to respond to concerns about the safety and quality of food, use of chemicals and issues related to outbreak of infectious diseases and resistance to antibiotics (European Commission 2004).

The 2008–2009 EU Disability Action Plan (DAP) focuses on accessibility. The aim is to stimulate inclusive participation of people with disabilities and to work towards full enjoyment of fundamental rights. It includes fostering accessibility to the labour market through flexibility and social security (flexicurity), supported employment and working with public employment services, boosting accessibility of goods, services and infrastructures, consolidating the Commission's analytical capacity to support accessibility, complementing the Community legislative framework of protection against discrimination and facilitating the implementation of the UNCRPD (European Commission 2007c).

Given that Article 27 of the UNCRPD makes specific reference to promoting vocational and professional rehabilitation, job retention and return-to-work programs for persons with disabilities, one could assume that this would provide opportunities for implementing DM actions. However, it appears that the primary focus of the DAP is upon Article 19 – living independently and being included in the community – which is only peripherally related to the domain of DM.

Return to Work in the EU Member States

Given the relatively slow pace of policy and system change in the EU and its Member States, the results of a random sample of long-term absent workers carried out between 2003 and 2006 in Europe can still be considered relevant (Stress Impact Consortium 2006). The Stress Impact study surveyed over 2,000 long-term absent employees in five Members States, each of which had a different approach to responding to reintegration. The participating countries were: Austria, which operates a workers' compensation system; Ireland and the UK, which operate systems based on the welfare state model; Finland, where maintenance of workability and rehabilitation were the main pillars of action; and the Netherlands, in which employer responsibility for absence was key. The study was a Time 1-Time 2 study in which the long-term absent workers were randomly sampled and surveyed after 12 weeks in Ireland and the Netherlands or 26 weeks in the UK, Finland and Austria. Respondents were resurveyed 26 weeks after Time 1 to review reintegration outcomes. At Time 1, the respondents were surveyed in relation to their reasons for absence, employer responses, access to services and challenges to returning to work. At Time 2, they were asked to indicate whether or not they had returned to work and what they perceived as the facilitators and barriers in the process. The study was supported by a qualitative survey of 350 families of the respondents and 229 professional interviews, including health professionals, work-based professionals and mediating professionals in the return-to-work process.

The relative performance of the participating Member States is presented in Table 12.1. It was clear that the Netherlands outperformed other Member States in terms of return-to-work outcomes. It is not easy to propose any clear conclusions from this given that the sampling process and the demographics differed in each Member state. Nevertheless, some of the findings have relevance to the factors that influence return to work.

In the Netherlands, 63 per cent of respondents returned to full-time work in comparison to an average of 30 per cent across all participating countries. The highest proportion of respondents returning to part-time employment was also recorded in the Netherlands (16 per cent compared to an average of 10 per cent). Overall, 79 per cent of the Dutch sample had returned to part-time or full-time employment 26 weeks after the first survey. To place this in context, equivalent figures for Finland and the UK were 24 per cent and 17 per cent respectively. The average for all participating countries was 33 per cent.

Table 12.1   The relative performance of five EU Member States on return-to-work terms

	Return to work full-time	Return to work part-time	Return to work total
Austria	25%	8%	33%
Finland	17%	7%	24%
Ireland	34%	8%	42%
Netherlands	63%	16%	79%
United Kingdom	9%	8%	17%
Total	30%	17%	47%

Dutch respondents reported more frequently being in good health (56 per cent in comparison to an average of 32 per cent). Finnish respondents reported poor health most often (17 per cent reported good health). Older workers predominated in the sample: 38 per cent of respondents were less than 45 years of age compared to 62 per cent over that age.

Health conditions reported were classified in terms of physical, mental and co-morbid conditions. Across all participating countries the average number of respondents reporting mental health as the primary reason for absence was 9 per cent. Of the respondents, 9 per cent reported mental distress as a co-morbid condition. In comparison, 43 per cent of Dutch respondents reported mental health as either the primary or the co-morbid condition implicated in their absence (22 per cent and 21 per cent respectively).

The majority of workers who did return to work did so through redeployment. Of the respondents who returned to work, 68 per cent did so to a different job. In the Netherlands this figure was 73 per cent. In the UK, 2 per cent of respondents redeployed to a different job.

From a service perspective it is interesting to note the types of professionals with which the respondents reported having contact. The vast majority of respondents had contact with their general practitioner (GP) (87 per cent). Contact with other professionals was reported less frequently. Occupational physicians were referred to in 43 per cent of responses and rehabilitation professionals were cited in 32 per cent of cases. In contrast, return-to-work coordinators were specified by 3 per cent of respondents.

From an employer perspective, the majority of respondents were working for companies with fewer than 50 employees (58 per cent). This was highest in Finland (78 per cent). Employer commitment to long-term absent employees was evident in the fact that 42 per cent of respondents reported that their jobs were being held open for them. This commitment was not evident in the number of employers that had, according to the respondents, a formal approach to return to work.

From an employee perspective, 50 per cent of respondents had been contemplating going absent for a period of time prior to taking sick leave and 32 per cent reported elevated levels of stress as a factor in their absence.

The data from the Stress Impact study were analyzed using multiple regression in which return to work was the independent factor. A content analysis of the responses from the family interviews served to add detail to these findings.

The findings of the multiple regression analysis are less than surprising. Gender and age emerged as contributing factors to return to work. Female respondents reported a higher rate of return to work whereas those over 55 years of age returned to work less often. People with a higher level of education were more likely to return to work. Depression and longer duration of absence were also predictors of non-return to work. The existence of a formal integrated system for supporting return to work was a factor in positive outcomes.

The family study revealed some insights into the workers' perspectives. The factors that improved the likelihood of return to work included some of those identified by the multiple regression analysis, such as the presence of a formal return-to-work system, improved health and low income. In addition, it revealed that absent workers were more likely to consider going back to work if they were bored, feared the loss of their job, felt that they were needed by the employer, had good communication with their workplaces and practical work-based support for return to work. On the basis of the family interviews, absent workers were less likely to return to work if they had low income, had delayed in going absent in the first place, faced an increased or changed workload or new conditions, had failed to get work accommodations or negative conditions had not been rectified. Poor mental health was frequently cited as a reason for not returning to work.

Disability Management Developments in the EU Member States

Since the Stress Impact study, initiatives in promoting DM and reintegration at both policy and program levels have been implemented in a number of EU Member States. These have met with different degrees of success and in different forms depending on the characteristics of the social security and social protection systems in which they have developed and the organizations that have promoted change.

The most sustained and explicit DM developments have occurred in the workers compensation system in Germany (International Social Security Association 2008). Article 84 of Social Code Book 9 mandates the German Social Insurance to implement early intervention and reintegration interventions for employees at risk of exiting the workplace as a result of illness or injury. While this is equally applicable to the funds dealing with non-occupational injuries and ill health, the most substantial initiative has been taken by the German Accident Insurance agencies. The International Disability Management Standards Council Code of Practice for Employers and the Occupational Standards for DM Professionals and Return-to-Work Coordinators have been adopted. The workers compensation agencies are in a particularly strong position to promote the full spectrum of DM mechanisms as their remit incorporates occupational health & safety, workplace health promotion and rehabilitation.

The certification of front-line professionals with responsibility for the reintegration of injured workers and the accreditation of employing organizations using the consensus-based disability management audit (CBDMA) tool has been promoted by a number of like-minded organizations.

Between 2003 and 2008, 700 professionals undertook the exam for Certified Disability Manager Professional certification. Less progress has been made in convincing employers to engage with the DM Code of Practice for employers and the company audit. Twelve occupational rehabilitation centres and three commercial companies have chosen to undergo the audit to date.

In parallel with the deployment of the IDMSC standards, the German government made significant progress in creating the conditions for more effective DM structures. Specifically, Section 83 of the Social Code Book 9 created the opportunity for employers to put in place integration agreements that specify the processes and procedures that govern the experience of disability within the work place. The agreements have no statutory force, but commit all workplace interests to operate in the best interests of the worker with impairment. The primary purpose of the integration agreement is to provide a way to manage the recruitment of people with disabilities and the return to work of employees with health problems. Integration agreements or work retention policies can be considered to be a useful strategy in terms of implementing a disability management program. However, the take up of quality and impact of integration agreements has yet to be established and the extent to which they embrace the principles of DM needs to be documented (Niehaus & Bernhard 2006).

While the existence of a workers compensation system is strongly associated with the growth of DM approaches in a number of jurisdictions internationally, e.g., US, Canada, Germany and Australia, it does not appear to be a sufficient condition for the emergence of an effective DM policy. The relatively slow progress made in Austria, which operates a very similar social insurance system to that in Germany, is evidence of this (Lang & Reischl 2005). Further, the concept of DM has emerged in a number of jurisdictions with very different approaches to workers compensation.

In other Member States, the IDMSC standards were adopted by non-governmental and private organizations in the absence of a strong statutory response. In the UK and Ireland, two jurisdictions that operate a welfare system in which income continuance for absent workers is funded partially through general taxation rather than employer payments or social insurance, the standards were promoted by private organizations. In the UK, a private permanent health insurer, which is a subsidiary of a US insurer, adopted the standards. It has actively promoted them to its customers (employers) and offered, in partnership with a university, certification as a DM professional to those with responsibility for managing retention and return to work. While the company audit was also promoted to employers, the take up has been slow in the UK.

Developments in the UK have been sporadic. Early initiatives included the EU co-funded project Get Back (in 1998–1999), which targeted return to work for those with occupational injuries, and the Get Back Plus project (in 2000–2001), which specifically targeted return to work for employees with brain injury (McAnaney et al. 2005). Both of these projects demonstrated the potential in a proactive approach to managing the reintegration of long-term absent employees. Very soon after these projects finished, the UK Department of Work and Pensions (DWP) commissioned the Job Retention and Rehabilitation Pilot (JRRP) which adopted a randomized control trial methodology (RCT) for evaluating the costs and benefits of early intervention for long-term absent employees in 12 pilot sites throughout the UK (Department of Work and Pensions 2004). The results of the JRRP were ambivalent at best and may well have impeded the introduction of more proactive DM policies and mechanisms in the UK.

More recently the issue of long-term absence has gradually gained greater recognition as an issue at policy level in the UK and was specifically addressed in a review of the health of Britain's working age population (Black 2008). One element of the government response to the review has been the establishment of the Fit for Work initiative, which offers employees who are absent from work the opportunity for an assessment of their return-to-work potential by the National Health Service (Department of Work and Pensions 2008). While this is a step forward from a DM perspective, it falls well short of a full DM approach.

If DM is to develop in the UK, it is likely that it will require individual employers and the trade unions to begin to take the concept on board. A significant deciding factor in this is the way that sick leave is administered. Individual employers are responsible for paying sick pay to absent employees for the first six months of their absence. However, employers have the potential to claim these costs as tax deductions at the end of the financial year. As a result, employers are not out of pocket and the DWP is unaware of those that are long-term absent until they make a claim for incapacity benefit as they approach the six-month threshold.

Both the Confederation of British Industry and the UK Chartered Institute of Personnel and Development (CIPD) are well aware of the costs of absence to productivity and industry as is evidenced by their annual reports (Chartered Institute of Personnel and Development 2009). According to research conducted by the Confederation of British Industry (CBI), long-term absence of 20 days or more accounted for 43 per cent of all working time lost in 2006 (public sector – 52 per cent; private sector – 38 per cent) and cost £5.8bn. In the same year, absence cost £537 per employee and accounted for 3.3 per cent of working time (Confederation of British Industry 2008).

A striking finding was that companies that offer rehabilitation programs and flexible working can help employees back to work and thus lose less time to absence. The best-performing organizations lost only 2.7 days per employee, while the worst lost 12 days. However, this recognition has yet to lead to a coherent approach to job retention and reintegration in the UK.

The organization that has taken up the challenge of promoting DM and the IDMSC standards in Ireland is a not-for-profit service provider of disability services. The pattern of take up of the audit and occupational standards is very similar to the UK in that while frontline professionals have begun to engage in the training and certification process, the number of employers opting to undergo the audit is negligible.

This is in a context where the policy framework in Ireland, as specified by the National Disability Strategy, provides a number of potential facilitators to DM. Not least of these is the attempt to develop a joined-up disability policy which engages the departments with responsibility for health, social protection and employment (FAS, 2005). Under the Disability Act (2004) each of these government departments has made an explicit commitment to early intervention and active measures to prevent people from entering the long-term disability net (Department of Justice, Equality and Law Reform 2004). There is little evidence that these commitments have had any impact on job retention and reintegration rates in Ireland.

The Finnish approach to health and job retention has a long history that is based on the concepts of the maintenance of workability and rehabilitation. Maintenance of workability is primarily focused on keeping people at work and places responsibility on both the employer and the worker to engage in activities to protect and promote the health, well-being and productivity of employees. Alongside this, the state provides easy access to rehabilitation services to those who are long-term absent from work. However, traditionally, the rehabilitation providers rarely intervene in the workplace (Joensuu,

Kivistö & Lindström 2005). In recent times the Finnish Institute for Occupational Health has begun to actively promote the concept of DM and a Code of Practice derived from the IDMSC standards. It is too early to assess the impact of this on job retention and reintegration rates.

Sweden operates a system that tends to emphasize early rehabilitation, but once again the values of the system are not fully supportive of work-based rehabilitation and reintegration. In particular, while OSH and WHP are well supported, there is a disconnect between health and safety and reintegration services. Sweden has moved to place greater responsibility for absence on employers by placing the onus on them to support absent workers financially in the first weeks of absence. This has had some impact in terms of reducing short-term absence, but does little to bridge the gap between long-term absence and return to work (Wynne & McAnaney 2004).

The Netherlands has adopted the strategy of enhancing employer responsibility for job retention and reintegration in a radical way (Brenninkmeijer, Raes & Houtman 2005). Dutch employers have accepted responsibility for financially supporting their employees who are long-term absent for a period of two year regardless of the cause (i.e., both occupational and non-occupational causes). This has resulted in a major change in the way employers in the Netherlands approach absenteeism and has resulted in a growth of job retention and reintegration service providers. In parallel with this, the state provides a personal budget to the absent worker or the employer to finance a reintegration plan on the basis of approval by an occupational physician. There is evidence that employees who opt for the personal budget have more sustainable outcomes. The Dutch authorities have created the conditions within which greater employer commitment to the reintegration of those absent is ensured. However, they have not adopted any particular DM model and the application of the principle of DM has not been adopted as a coherent approach at a policy level. Nevertheless, the Stress Impact findings provide evidence to support the view that employer responsibility for DM is an important factor in encouraging more effective return-to-work behaviours.

DM has been adopted enthusiastically in other Member States by individual organizations. One organization operating in Belgium in the field of occupational health and safety has taken on the IDMSC occupational standards and is currently promoting them in Belgium, the Netherlands, Luxembourg and France. Individual providers of disability services have set up business units to market DM services in Portugal, Italy and Slovenia. All these initiatives are struggling to promote DM as a valuable service to employers, workers and the state. All these organizations are operating in policy, legislative and regulatory environments in which there are fundamental disconnects amongst OSH, HRM, social security and rehabilitation.

The Reintegrate project (in 2008–2009), which was designed to make the concepts of DM more accessible to HR managers in the EU, carried out focus groups with employers and stakeholders in Hungary, Slovenia, Ireland, Portugal, Italy and the Netherlands. The feedback from employers in all cases was that the issues of job retention and long-term absence were of critical concern. The primary roadblocks to taking action were the policy and funding infrastructures and the lack of skilled and trained DM professionals.[1]

---

1   Re-integrate – An integrated e-learning environment. Available at: http://www.re-integrate.eu/

Conclusions and Recommendations

Intervening factors in the Stress Impact study, such as time of interventions, sampling procedures and demographics, make any robust conclusion impossible. Apart from variables associated with national context, those in the Dutch cohort rated themselves as being the healthiest; the age range varied systematically between countries with the Finnish sample being the oldest and the Irish sample having the youngest average age. Nevertheless, in combination with the other studies carried out prior and subsequently, a number of inferences can be drawn from the findings.

- Employer responsibility: Where employers were assigned responsibility for long-term absence, regardless of whether the causes were occupational or non-occupational, return to work outcomes were best.
- Older workers: Where the absent workforce profile was older, the return-to-work outcomes were the lowest and where the profile was the youngest return-to-work outcomes were better.
- Early intervention: In systems where early monitoring and intervention were in place, return-to-work outcomes were better than where interventions occurred at a later stage.
- Liability: Jurisdictions where no-fault systems were in place outperformed those where workers compensation required negligence on the part of the employer.
- System support for DM: In the two jurisdictions in which there are clear policies to support job retention and reintegration, i.e., Germany and the Netherlands, despite their different approaches, DM has developed and prospered.
- Lack of relevant data: A major challenge in documenting and evaluating job retention and reintegration outcomes in the EU is the lack of systematic monitoring and data collection in relation to long-term absence and return to work. Data systems are either targeted at occupational injuries or at the placement of economically inactive people with disabilities into employment. Generally, Member States do not systematically monitor the return to work of long-term absent employees.
- Policy fragmentation: At EU level and in most Member States, there is a disconnect between employment, health and social protection which results in long-term absent workers being deprived of much-needed DM services and supports.
- Return-to-work threshold: The complex factors and processes that lead a person to seek and succeed in reintegrating back to the workplace are best characterized as a threshold comprised of system, service, work-based, non-work, health and personal factors.

A number of other issues have emerged over the past 10 years that have implications for the development of effective DM programs in the EU, including the discontinuity between OSH and rehabilitation systems, the emerging burden of mental health conditions, the lack of quality DM services, the role of medical and allied health professionals in the return-to-work process and a lack of awareness of employers about what constitutes good DM practice.

On the basis of a review of policies and practices at EU and Member State levels in seven European countries, a survey of the views of long-term absent workers, their families and the professionals with whom they interact in five Member States, and a consultation with employers in six Member States it is possible to propose a number of factors that are central to the development of DM in any jurisdiction.

At the policy level:

- Disability must be explicitly acknowledged as a dynamic process, the pathway of which can be influenced through early intervention.
- The workability, job retention and reintegration of workers with health problems or impairments, regardless of their origin, needs to be reflected in both the guidelines for jobs and growth and Member States' national action plans.
- Eurostat, the official data source for the EU, needs to develop indicators on the reintegration of ill and injured workers.
- The link between work, ill health and pensions needs to be targeted explicitly in employment, health and social inclusion policies.

At the systems level:

- Systems to respond to work, ill health and absence need to include non-occupational illness and injuries, otherwise less than 25 per cent of long-term absent employees will have access to DM services.
- Employer responsibility needs to be enhanced in most EU jurisdictions in order to promote early intervention and work-based rehabilitation.
- Eligibility criteria for services need to be made more flexible so that they become available to at-risk workers.

At the service level:

- The quality of service providers and competence of professionals need to be standardized and accredited based on international standards.
- A market in DM services needs to be supported.

At the employer level:

- Human resources and occupational health professionals need to be educated about the benefits of DM.
- Education in DM for employers needs to include training in organizational change strategies.
- Financial supports and incentives are needed, including negative incentives where an employee does not return to work and positive incentives to encourage early intervention.
- Social partners need to accept that it is in the best interests of both workers and the company to aspire to safe and timely return to work.

Bibliography

Australian National Audit Office. (2003). *Absence Management in the Australian Public Service*. Available at: http://www.anao.gov.au/uploads/documents/2002-03_Audit_Report_52.pdf, accessed 15 July 2011.

Black. C. (2008). Working for a Healthier Tomorrow: Dame Carol Black's Review of the Health of Britain's Working Age Population. London: Parliamentary Press TSO. Available at: http://www.workingforhealth.gov.uk/documents/working-for-a-healthier-tomorrow-tagged.pdf, accessed 15 July 2011.

Bloch, F.S. & Prins, R. (2001). *Who Returns to Work and Why? A Six-Country Study on Work Incapacity and Reintegration*. London: Transaction Publishers.

Brenninkmeijer, V., Raes, A. & Houtman, I. (2005). Review and Inventory of National Systems and Policy: The Netherlands. Guildford: Stress Impact, Surrey University. Available at: http://www.surrey.ac.uk/Psychology/stress-impact/publications/wp2/wp2_reportNetherland.pdf, accessed 15 July 2011.

Bruyere, S. & Shrey, D. (1991). Disability Management in Industry: A Joint Labor-Management Process. *Rehabilitation Counselling Bulletin* 34(3): 27–41.

Chartered Institute for Personnel and Development. (2009). *Annual Survey Report 2009*. Available at: http://www.cipd.co.uk/subjects/hrpract/absence/_absence_management_summary.htm, accessed 15 July 2011.

Confederation of British Industry. (2008). *Sickies and Long-Term Absence give Employers a Headache – CBI/AXA SURVEY*. Available at: http://www.cbi.org.uk/ndbs/press.nsf/0363c1f07c6ca12a8025 671c00381cc7/90ab71d2f4d981da8025744200523b87?OpenDocument, accessed 15 July 2011.

Council of the European Union. (2005). Guidelines for the Employment Policies of the Member States, Council Decision 2005/600/EC, *Official Journal of the European Union* 205(21). Available at: http://europa.eu/legislation_summaries/employment_and_social_policy/growth_and_jobs/c11323_en.htm, accessed 15 July 2011.

Council of the European Union. (2007). *Joint Report on Social Protection and Social Inclusion 2007: Social Inclusion, Pensions, Healthcare and Long-Term Care*. European Council Employment, Social Policy, Health and Consumer Affairs. Available at: http://register.consilium.europa.eu/pdf/en/07/st06/st06694.en07.pdf, accessed 15 July 2011.

Council of the European Union. (2008.) Guidelines for the Employment Policies of the Member States, Council Decision 10614/2/08 REV 2. Available at: http://register.consilium.europa.eu/pdf/en/08/st10/st10614-re02.en08.pdf, accessed 15 July 2011.

Department of Justice Equality and Law Reform. (2004). National Disability Strategy. Available at: http://www.justice.ie/en/JELR/NDS.pdf/files/NDS.pdf, accessed 15 July 2011.

Department for Work and Pensions (2004). *Building Capacity for Work: A UK Framework for Vocational Rehabilitation*. London: UK Department of Work and Pensions. Available at: http://www.scmh.org.uk/pdfs/dwp_vocational_annex.pdf, accessed 15 July 2011.

Department for Work and Pensions. (2008). *Improving Health and Work: Changing Lives. The Government's Response to Dame Carol Black's Review of the Health of Britain's Working-Age Population*. Available at: http://www.workingforhealth.gov.uk/documents/improving-health-and-work-changing-lives.pdf, accessed 15 July 2011.

European Commission. (2004). *Public Consultation Review of the EU Sustainable Development Strategy*, SEC(2004)1042. Available at: http://ec.europa.eu/sustainable/docs/pc_docs/ngo/issi_eu_ec_consult_2004_part_2.pdf, accessed 15 July 2011.

European Commission. (2007a). *Situation of Disabled People in the European Union: The European Action Plan 2008–2009*, COM(2007) 738 final. Available at: http://ec.europa.eu/social/main. jsp?catId=429&langId=en, accessed 15 July 2011.

European Commission. (2007b). *Integrated Guidelines for Growth and Jobs 2008–2010*, COM(2007) 803. Available at: http://eur-lex.europa.eu/LexUriserv/LexUriserv.do?uri=OJ:C:2009:184E:0038:0 048:EN:PDF, accessed 15 July 2011.

European Commission. (2007c). *Improving Quality and Productivity at Work: Community Strategy 2007–2012 on Health and Safety at Work*, COM(2007) 62. Available at: http://eur-lex.europa.eu/ LexUriserv/LexUriserv.do?uri=COM:2007:0062:FIN:EN:PDF, accessed 15 July 2011.

European Commission. (2008a). *Growth and Jobs: Re-launch of the Lisbon Strategy*. Available at: http:// www.euractiv.com/en/innovation/growth-jobs-relaunch-lisbon-strategy/article-131891, accessed 15 July 2011.

European Commission. (2008b). *A Renewed Commitment to Social Europe: Reinforcing the Open Method of Coordination for Social Protection and Social Inclusion*, COM(2008) 418 final. Available at: http:// eur-lex.europa.eu/LexUriserv/LexUriserv.do?uri=COM:2008:0418:FIN:EN:PDF, accessed 15 July 2011.

European Commission. (2009). EU Employment Summit agrees on ways to tackle rising unemployment. Press Release. Available at: http://ec.europa.eu/social/main.jsp?catId=101&lan gId=en&newsId=507&furtherNews=yes, accessed 15 July 2011.

European Disability Forum. (2001). *Analysis of the EU Directive On Equal Treatment in Employment and Occupation*. Available at: http://cms.horus.be/files/99909/MediaArchive/pdf/EDF01-8-Empl%20 Dir%20analysis.doc, accessed 15 July 2011.

EUROSTAT. (2008). Social Protection Expenditure and Receipts Data 1997–2005, European Social Statistics. Available at: http://epp.eurostat.ec.europa.eu/cache/ITY_OFFPUB/KS-SF-08-046/EN/ KS-SF-08-046-EN.PDF, accessed 15 July 2011.

FAS. (2005). Disability Management – 'The New Kid on the Block'. In *Disability FÁS Disability Policy and Development Unit, Newsletter* January 2005 Issue 4. Available at: http://www.fas.ie/ NR/rdonlyres/6DED40F0-A5C1-4A68-A3FB-62D7558A561D/0/Newsletter4.pdf, accessed 15 July 2011.

FAS. (2010). *The Irish Wage Subsidy Scheme*. Dublin: Foras Aiseanna Saohthair. Available at: http:// www.fas.ie/en/Allowances+and+Grants/Wage+Subsidy+Scheme.htm, accessed 15 July 2011.

Grammenos, S. (2003). *Illness, Disability and Social Inclusion*. Luxembourg: Office for Official Publications of the European Communities.

Hyde, M. (1998). Sheltered and Supported Employment in the 1990s: The Experiences of Disabled Workers in the UK. *Disability & Society* 13(2): 199–215. DOI: 10.1080/09687599826786.

International Labor Organization. (2001). *Code of Practice on Managing Disability in the Workplace*. Tripartite Meeting of Experts on the Management of Disability in the Workplace. Geneva. October 2001. Available at: http://www.ilo.org/public/english/standards/relm/gb/docs/gb282/ pdf/tmemdw-2.pdf, accessed 15 July 2011.

International Social Security Association. (2008). *Implementing Disability Management and Return-to-Work Strategies: A Case of the German Social Accident Insurance, DGUV*. Available at: http://www. issa.int/aiss/Observatory/Good-Practices/Implementing-disability-management-and-return-to-work-strategies, accessed 15 July 2011.

Joensuu, M., Kivistö, S. & Lindström, K. (2005). Review and Inventory of National Systems and Policy: Finland. Guildford: Stress Impact, Surrey University. Available at: http://www.surrey.ac.uk/ Psychology/stress- impact/publications/wp2/wp2_reportFinland.pdf, accessed 15 July 2011.

Kasneci, D. (2007). *Active Ageing: the EU Policy Response to the Challenge of Population Ageing*. Paper No. 8. European Papers on the New Welfare. Geneva: The Risk Institute. Available at: http://eng.newwelfare.org/author/dede-kasneci/, accessed 15 July 2011.

Lang, G. & Reischl, B. (2005) *Review and Inventory of National Systems and Policy: Austria*. Guildford, UK: Surrey University. Available at: http://www.surrey.ac.uk/Psychology/stress-impact/publications/wp2/wp2_reportAustria.pdf, accessed 15 July 2011.

National Institute of Disability Management and Research (1999). *Ethical Standards and Professional Conduct. Occupational Standards in Disability Management*. Port Alberni, BC: NIDMAR.

Niehaus, M. & Bernhard, D. (2006). Corporate Integration Agreements and their Function in Disability Management. *The International Journal of Disability Management Research* 1(1):42–51. Available at: http://www.atypon-link.com/AAP/doi/abs/10.1375/jdmr.1.1.42, accessed 15 July 2011.

McAnaney, D., Webster, B., Lohan, M. & Wynne, R. (2001). Disability Management: A System of Response or a Response to a System? *The Australian Journal of Rehabilitation Counselling* 7(1): 1–22.

Stress Impact Consortium. (2006). *Integrated Report of Stress Impact: On the Impact of Changing Social Structures on Stress and Quality of Life: Individual and Social Perspectives*. Guildford: Surrey University. Available at: http://www.surrey.ac.uk/Psychology/stress-impact/publications/wp8/Stress%20Impact%20Integrated%20Report.pdf, accessed 15 July 2011.

United Nations. (2006). *United Nations Convention on the Rights of Persons with Disabilities*. Available at: http://www.un.org/disabilities/default.asp?navid=14&pid=150, accessed 15 July 2011.

UNUM UK. (2007). *Unique Absence Management Assessment Service Launched*. Available at: http://www.unum.co.uk/Home/Corporate_Information/Press_Releases/, accessed 15 July 2011.

Van Lin, M., Prins, R. & De Kok, J. (2002). *Active Labor Market Programmes for People with Disabilities*. Netherlands: EIM Business and Policy Research.

Whittle, R. (2002). The Framework Directive for Equal Treatment in Employment and Occupation: An Analysis from a Disability Rights Perspective. *European Law Review* 27(3): 303–26.

Wynne, R. & McAnaney, D. (2004). *Employment and Disability: Back to Work Strategies*. Dublin: The European Foundation for the Improvement of Living and Working Conditions. Available at: http://www.eurofound.europa.eu/publications/htmlfiles/ef04115.htm, accessed 15 July 2011.

Wynne, R., McAnaney, D., Thorne, J., Hinkka, K. & Jarvisalo, J. (2005). The RETURN Project – Between Work and Welfare: Improving Return-to-Work Strategies for Long-Term Absent Employees. In: S. Mannila & A. Jarvikoski (eds), *Disability and Working Life* (74–100). Helsinki: Helsinki University Press, Rehabilitation Foundation.

PART III

Illness, Rehabilitation and Disability Management

13 Occupational Integration Management at the Enzensberg Clinic

JOACHIM MAIER AND GISELA RIEDL

Introduction

Disability management (DM) was primarily developed by businesses with the objective of retaining and utilizing workers despite illness or disability. Occupational integration management (OIM) is a tool used by businesses in Germany to initiate solution-oriented action in the event of health-based deployment problems of their employees. Questions that crop up when using OIM include: What health problems need to be addressed and what is the best way to do so? What can the employee actually do within the business? Are technical aids and/or financial assistance available? (Hetzel, Flach & Mozdzanowski 2007). Some of the overriding questions for businesses include: Can the problems be solved by the occupational teams and with the resources available? Is external support required? Can a clinic contribute to disability management? When recording the answers to these questions, and questions like these, the employer must always remember the requirements of data protection legislation.

While disability management predominantly applies to companies (Mehrhoff & Schian 2009), rehab/case management support (RCMS) can play an important role in the disability management process when there are complex medical issues – particularly after the accident or illness of an employee – and can assist in the decision-making. RCMS takes place independently in a clinic, and utilizes all the clinic's resources, both internal and external. RCMS is not supposed to take over the disability management but, in a supportive function, provide the business with important assistance so that the business can optimize its disability management/OIM.

In order to take on the responsibility of RCMS, there are certain requirements, which include: operationally trained staff that cooperate closely on an interdisciplinary basis and are managed by certified disability management professionals (CDMP), close cooperation amongst network partners, experience cooperating with businesses (Haase et al. 2002), thorough experience with the 'interface problem' between medical rehabilitation and occupational reintegration. These focuses have been under development at Enzensberg Clinic (a 420-bed acute care and rehabilitation clinic located in Germany) since 2000 and have been successfully employed. Details on approaches and prerequisites of the clinic are provided in the following sections.

The objective of disability management and RCMS is to maintain an existing workforce in conjunction with all parties involved or, if this is not feasible, to create occupational alternatives in line with the particular employee's impairment.

German Law

OCCUPATIONAL INTEGRATION MANAGEMENT

On 1 May 2004, Germany's Social Security Code (SGB) IX was amended by the Act on the Promotion of Severely Disabled People's Vocational Training and Employment. In this Act, the legislators introduced OIM in section 84, which focused on the rights of persons with severe disabilities and the responsibilites of their employers. The OIM is a preventive provision. It is intended to secure the long-term employability of employees.

The areas of application of occupational integration management

The provision of OIM applies to all employees. The legislation uses the word 'employees', which means all employees, not only the severely disabled. This OIM applies equally if an employee is unable to work for a period in excess of six weeks or repeatedly unable to work within a one-year period. As the provision of OIM provides no details on the size of the businesses that are obliged to use OIM, it therefore applies to all employers. The provision focuses on the length of time that the employee is unable to work, and for the reasons for the inability to work (ITW).

The occupational integration management procedure

This legislation mentions employers, employees, representation (where applicable the representative body for the severely disabled), company medical officers, joint local service points and integration offices as parties involved in the procedure. The wording of the law ('shall be clarified by the employer') stipulates that the employer is obliged to act. As a result, the employer must initiate the OIM if the above-mentioned conditions are met. The employer must clarify what opportunities are available to overcome the ITW. Furthermore, the employer is responsible for involving the employee representative and, in the event of severely disabled employees, the representative body for severely disabled workers. When involving others in the OIM process, it must be taken into consideration that integration management may only be used with the agreement and the involvement of the employee affected. In accordance with the legislation, the person affected is to be advised of the objectives of OIM, as well as the type and scope of data collected and used for this purpose. The employer must explain the goal and process of integration management and offer integration to the employee. If the person affected does not agree with the use of OIM, the integration attempt ends at this point. In the context of OIM, and in accordance with the legislation, company medical officers can also be consulted, as required. Like other physicians, the company medical officer is subject to doctor-patient confidentiality. The involvement of the company medical officer can represent a confidence-building measure for the employee affected. 'Measures are to be developed or implemented that maintain, support and/or restore the person's employability. These include general vocational qualification measures, workplace health and safety measures, as well as measures for humane work design, health support and workplace-related rehabilitation' (Stegmann et al. 2005: 16).

> *Apart from the development of measures for the early recognition and for the prevention of disability and illness, as well as the development of an occupational catalog of preventive measures, elements of Occupational Integration Management should also always include the consideration of medical and professional rehabilitation services outside the company ... (Fuchs & Welti 2005: 5)*

In providing such services to the employee, companies can choose to use the company medical officer as a coordinator.

> *The company medical officer can, for example, initiate contact with the joint service point, the treating physician or, as already described, with Rehab/Case Management Support – with the affected person's consent. Furthermore, the company medical officer can ensure a concrete, individually oriented coordination of medical rehabilitation in ... day-to-day company operations. (Britschgi 2006: 39)*

Company medical officers thus hold a key position in OIM. Their competence and commitment can influence OIM significantly.

The need for occupational structures

In order to implement OIM so that it meets the goals set by the legislators, occupational structures need to be created and laid down in corresponding regulations. There are no binding terms of reference for this; however, in accordance with section 84(3) SGB IX, the rehabilitation funding organizations and the integration offices can provide incentives to employers who cooperate OIM by granting premiums and bonuses. For this purpose, requirements have been linked to the introduction of OIM, namely 'a system for the recognition of problems, tools for recording and specification, a switchpoint within the company for processing, decision-making, implementation, the implementation of concrete measures and a documentation and evaluation' (Adloch et al. 2005: 40).

The basic requirement for the introduction of OIM is that each employee's postion/ health is evaluated and recorded for each absence longer than a certain period of time. Without this, it cannot be determined which employees would benefit from OIM. It has been accepted that the conclusion of an integration agreement in accordance with section 83(2a) no. 5 SGB IX or a company agreement is the method of choice for regulating OIM (Britschgi, 2006). Such agreements must define who is responsible for OIM within the company, which approach is to be taken with regard to the integration process, who is to participate in the procedure and how data protection is to be handled (Gagel, 2004). The parties within the company to be taken into consideration are the employee affected, members of the representative body for severely disabled staff, human resources, the company medical officer, the workplace health and safety representative, as well as the direct superiors of the person affected. In addition, a network with external partners can be formed. Apart from the external parties specifically mentioned in the law, 'joint service points of funding organizations' (usually, one comprehensive service point per city or district is operated by a pension or health insurance fund) and the integration office, medical and professional rehabilitation organizations, in this case RCMS, and the directly responsible rehabilitation funding organizations and thus cost units should be taken into consideration. The initiation of contact with the family doctor of the employee affected may also prove worthwhile (Schinkel 2006; Zink 2006; Fuchs 2005). Ideally a disability manager coordinates the person affected and the approach taken.

STATUTORY PENSION INSURANCE FUND

The statutory pension insurance fund, known in Germany as the Deutsche Rentenversicherung (DRV) Schwaben, is currently establishing cooperative networks with businesses and statutory health insurance funds. These networks will incorporate suitable medical rehabilitation facilities. In the event of potential health problems, such as obesity or back problems, employees are to receive preventive medical treatment in accordance with a defined procedure, or, if illness or an accident has occurred, they are to receive targeted, workplace-oriented rehab. The process is to be triggered by the company medical officer of the business where the employee works; the medical officer will be closely involved in the entire procedure.

Survey of Regional Mechanical Engineering Companies Regarding OIM

The object of the survey was to ascertain the existing structures in a company's healthcare management, the readiness of a company to introduce new structures for OIM and to cooperate with an external partner, and the services that are of interest to a company and in relation to which conditions. Information on the reasons why an employee is unable to work, the employee's age and the level of physical impairment were also relevant as 'older employees are not ill more often than younger employees, but record significantly more days off work due to an inability to work and the share of persons with altered performance or employees with health restrictions grows with increasing age' (Dworschak & Buck 2006: 28).

In September and October 2007, in an anoymized study, mechanical engineering companies with more than 200 employees located in the Allgäu and southern Germany regions were surveyed (Schlechter, Riedl & Maier 2008).[1] Data was collected on an anonymous basis so that internal processes and structures were not made public. In general, the companies employ external medical officers. The company medical officers provide information on workplace design and companies' support reintegration measures, suggest therapeutic measures and plan rehabilitation measures. There is still a great demand for information on OIM on the part of the companies. Currently, the companies are generally in the process of developing structures, such as integration teams, and procedures. The companies are interested in an exchange of opinions with other

---

1   The survey and evaluation of data was conducted by Ms Kathrin Schlechter in the context of her thesis in social economy at the University of Applied Sciences Kempten. We wish to thank her for the excellent work on this topic.

businesses that have experience with OIM; they are interested in process descriptions and checklists and in support from external partners.

Most companies indicate a high level of readiness to cooperate with rehab clinics in the context of OIM. The companies could provide information on job demands for specific occupations, and/or even take on the role of providing physical screening opportunities prior to an employee being admitted to a rehab clinic.

In this context the following points are of particular significance and interest to companies:

1. A clear indication on the prospect of the future employability of the employee in question, including remaining physical ability, rehab potential and conditions necessary for the reemployment of the employee.
2. The identification of environment factors that could impact on the future employability of the employee.
3. Suggestions of measures for workplace organization and ergonomics, as well as for personal training and what qualifications are necessary for staff to be effective.

Therefore it is clear that the companies queried are extremely interested in reintegrating the employee with a disability. They display a high level of readiness to initiate and execute the necessary measures for reintegration.

As network partners of the rehab clinics, companies would primarily like to see cost units (particularly employers' liability insurance associations, health insurance funds, integration offices) as well as occupational physicians and psychologists alongside the services usually provided by rehab clinics. The companies are extremely interested in brief, vocation-specific trials and exposure to actual work duties by trials, tours of the workplace by occupational physicians, and in-house briefings (on processes, legal requirements, technical aids, etc.). The companies stressed the following as crucial:

- An integrated recovery plan that includes both rehabilitation and return-to-work performance outcomes, to be fostered by the rehab clinic.
- Educational events for all employees in order to increase the awareness and acceptance of healthcare management.
- A specific contact at the rehab clinic who acts in close agreement with the company.

Companies found areas of employment with more demanding physical work, demanding production quotas, dealing with musculoskeletal injuries and the increasingly incidence of mental health issues to be particularly challenging.

In the companies surveyed there is low staff turnover and, as a result, an aging workforce and an expected increase of staff with altered performance abilities. The need for OIM is therefore increasing for mechanical engineering companies in the Allgäu.

Rehab/Case Management Support by Enzensberg Clinic

In the context of German legal requirements, there has been a goal – for some decades – to maintain the employability of ill and persons with disabilities. The difficulty, however, is the reconciliation of legal requirements with company structures and the personal qualifications of employees with altered performance abilities. While company medical officers had a good knowledge of the situation within their own company, they had insufficient access to relevant information that would have allowed them to determine the fit between the requirements of the job and the residual abilities of the employee.

In the context of SGB IX legislation, businesses, social security and private insurance companies have received an enhanced legal mandate to counter such difficulties in sharing information in order to provide a seamless, rapid flow of information between all participating parties in the network (Froese 2009). As a result of this opportunity the clinic developed the RCMS program, which provides participants with disability management as well as with decision-making aids that can be useful especially with medically difficult cases.

DEVELOPMENT OF RCMS

In 1995, at Enzensberg Clinic initial consideration was given to seamless and rapid procedures for the return to work following medical rehabilitation of patients that were hard to assess. On this basis, initial contact was made with larger businesses and social insurance agencies. At that time the specialist area of rehab consultation in clinical social work was a relatively new area within the sector of holistic rehabilitation in specialist clinics. These efforts were considered as a hub to link the actual rehabilitation services of the clinic with the patient's professional life, thus rendering it sustainable on a permanent basis. Procedures and cooperation between different institutions were extrapolated and coordinated, e.g., between medical and professional rehabilitation facilities, the workplace and the social insurance agency.

Enzensberg Clinic used that model for a pilot scheme from 1998 to 2000 in cooperation with AUDI AG Ingolstadt. The following sections will include information on the project and a summary of the results. In addition, statistical surveys on patient satisfaction and sustainability of results, as well as the need for cooperation with businesses in the Allgäu region, were conducted. Between 2002 and 2009, further modules were introduced in the RCMS field, such as the Fahreignungszentrum Allgäu (driver aptitude centre) for mobility issues as a result of injuries suffered in road traffic accidents, assessment procedures such as the evaluation of functional performance (EFL), OIM and the medical, job-oriented rehabilitation.

RCMS CONCEPT AND APPROACH

The complicated and drawn-out procedures generally involved while professional and social integration is completed – following severe accidents and during chronic illness – negatively impact the insured person and generate high levels of costs for providers of social services, private insurance companies and public insurance companies, as well as for employers (wage replacement benefits, loss of production, medical and professional programs, compensation payments, etc.). The German Federal Institute for Occupational Safety and Health estimates that the national economic cost of lost production caused by the inability to work amounted to a total of €38 billion in Germany in 2005, and the loss of gross value-added totaled €66 billion in 2005. The expenditure by the statutory health insurance funds alone amounted to €12.47 billion in 2005. The statutory pension insurance funds paid €4.8 billion in 2005 in respect of benefits pertaining to medical and professional rehabilitation (Fed. Institute for Occupational Safety and Health 2007).

In the context of disability management, 'managers should not only pay attention to figures but need to care for the people who largely impact the company's productivity' (Mehrhoff & Schian 2009: 9). Against this background, in 2002 a concept was developed at the Enzensberg Clinic that focuses on particularly complex rehabilitation cases, which is usually referred to as rehab or case management, and is conducted on behalf of a specific funding organization. RCMS primarily targets special, complicated cases – persons who are unable to work long term and people with limited employment options, who are characterized by an unclear performance profile and in respect of whom disease progression and the resulting impairment are difficult to assess (e.g. neurological diseases, craniocerebral injuries, amputations, pain syndromes). Key components of the concept are the timely and comprehensive analysis of the situation, the analysis of employee's ability to perform specific job duties, the determination of their rehab potential, and solution-oriented interdisciplinary expert opinions and recommendations. In order to address these factors, job- and workplace-based therapy and training measures are offered. In addition, the opportunity exists to undertake a driver aptitude test, as well as the opportunity for driver training in different vehicle classes for both professional and personal mobility. All of this is performed with the assistance of the specifically developed network of internal and external partners. The objectives of this approach are:

• the determination of residual performance in the event of a reduced ability to work,
• the targeted identification of suitable forms of therapy,
• the adequate provision of necessary medical, therapeutic, nursing and other measures – while avoiding duplication of services,
• the maintenance of the employment relationship, the opening of new professional opportunities and/or the initiating of professional retraining programs,
• the maintenance or the regaining of personal mobility,
• the continuous improvement in the provision of seamless rehabilitation and social and employment reintegration.

A RCMS process commences with the initial contact and questions about the worker's condtions by the RCMS management group, which comprises an occupational physician and a qualified social worker/rehab consultant, who have both undergone further training as disability managers. It is clarified whether the person affected can be admitted by the clinic and whether the in-patient stay at the clinic is purely for diagnostic reasons or if it is to be combined with a rehabilitation or a stay in the interdisciplinary pain centre. The client sends a preliminary registration form with precise questions they would like answered. This is viewed and evaluated by the occupational physician, who decides which network partners need to be involved in the individual case.

Following admission, a cross-departmental examination by the physician, clinical social worker/rehab consultant and (neuro-)psychologist is conducted. Based on the results of this examination, an initial cross-departmental situation analysis is drawn up in accordance with medical, social and professional guidelines. An initial overview with respect to the person's participation in work life and society is developed in cooperation with the person affected and with the agreement with the client. Depending on the initial analysis, further investigations and asssessments may be performed by medical specialtists, or in relation to the level of care required, or into the person's psychosocial circumstances and, if necessary, neuropsychological testing. During this process the person's behavior and motivation are also assessed and all of these assessments are performed within the network. The clinic team clarifies the individual's unique conditions (social setting, family and job situation/outlook) and draws up a positive and negative social-medical performance profile of the insured person. The work-related functional performance is evaluated by means of job-oriented assessment tools such as IWS/EFL testing (Isernhagen work system/evaluation of functional performance) and IMBA (Integration von Menschen mit Behinderung in die Arbeitswelt (Integration of people with disabilities into the working environment)). If necessary, a driver aptitude assessment can be performed and the need for disability-related additional fittings for vehicles can be assessed.

After evaluating the overall situation, the members of the team define strategies for action in cooperation with the insured person and in agreement with the client, which are set out in a solution-oriented interdisciplinary final report and forwarded to the client in a timely manner.

FUNDING ORGANIZATIONS

The RCMS program can be utilized by the rehabilitation funding organizations as a special service in accordance with section 19(4) of the Social Security Code (SGB) IX. The RCMS program then becomes the 'third party' pursuant to section 97 SGB X, which is why a contract for the provision of services needs to be concluded with the rehabilitation funding organization on an individual basis for each employee. The statutory pension insurance funds (in this case, DRV Schwaben) negotiate cooperation agreements pursuant to section 31 SGB VI with companies and health insurance funds so that workers can be treated in workplace-oriented clinics. The Enzensberg Clinic is a contractual partner of the pension and health insurance fund and has been approved for the rehabilitation process by the employers' liability insurance associations. The resulting report is submitted via the rehabilitation funding organization and then to the client.

BUSINESSES AND COMPANIES

Problematic combination of issues, such as extended or repeated absences, a decline in performance, extreme fluctuations in efficiency or depressed moods in hitherto reliable workers, will initially result in a personal discussion between the employee and their direct supervisor and, if unresolved, with the human resources officer, employee representative and company medical officer. In this discussion the prospect of an assessment of the employee's abilities and rehabilitation potential can be suggested as a means whereby the employee may be able to retain their employment. The employer is thus given the opportunity to counteract unfavourable developments immediately and to focus specifically on the relevant issues. Following an illness or accident, the company medical officer or the relevant health insurance fund initiates OIM measures, such as workplace-oriented medical rehabilitation. In the context of the procedure, all measures required for medical rehabilitation and for participation in work life can then immediately be introduced, in cooperation with the relevant rehabilitation funding organization. The business can absorb some the costs for rehab/case management support, by providing the employee with time off while at the clinic or giving them permission to use vacation leave in order to attend rehabilitation. It may also be possible to attract funding through a health insurance fund, depending on the type of insurance coverage the employee has. Such co-financing is in accordance with the legislation.

COMPANY MEDICAL OFFICER

The company medical officer is well aware of the work requirements, activity options and operating procedures of the job. After a person has given consent for the medial officer to share their information, the company medical officer may propose a job analysis, determination of rehab potential or another workplace-oriented medical rehab measure to the funding organization and initiate it. The procedure then progresses in the way set out in the previous section.

PRIVATE CLIENTS

Private insurance funding organizations, such as liability, accident and occupational disability insurers, can also submit requests directly to the RCMS program. Self-paying patients can, of course, also submit requests directly to the RCMS program.

ENZENSBERG CLINIC'S DISABILITY MANAGEMENT SERVICES

RCMS services are provided by the Enzensberg Clinic itself and by its network partners. Where necessary, the network partners are commissioned by the Enzensberg Clinic or by the RCMS program for the provision of specific services. The network partners act as external service providers for the RCMS program. This system ensures that all client questions are answered as comprehensively as possible. The clinic involved in disability management must create its team with a view to answering questions and solving problems. Under the umbrella of occupational medicine and rehab consultation, staff trained in business needs must cooperate closely on an interdisciplinary basis. The following specialty clinic areas have proven particularly helpful to disability management:

- prosthetics consultation for fitting and use training for amputees
- conservative and acute orthopedic medical care for conditions that generally do not require surgery, for example, intervertebral disc problems or osteoporosis
- interdisciplinary pain centre and psychosomatic medicine, in close cooperation with orthopaedics, anesthetics, psychology, physiotherapy, rehab consultation and recreational therapy provided in a multimodal therapy context, for somatoform disorders, burnout syndrome and workplace bullying problems (Riedl et al. 2009)
- neurology, with a particular focus on neuropsychological disorders after brain injuries or diseases as well as aphasia
- internal medicine in cooperation with other disciplines to clarify multiple disorders in different areas (e.g., pelvic injury, hypertension, and sleep apnea in drivers)
- physiotherapy, sports therapy and fitness, massage, ergotherapy (i.e., a medical rehabilitative intervention such as physiotherapy), speech therapy, psychology and clinical social work/rehab consultation; also, available are EFL testing (two-

day, standardized testing system for the evaluation of work-related functional performance) and personalized work-related rehabilitation.

All of these services can be utilized in the RCMS program for diagnostic and/or therapeutic reasons.

ALLGÄU DRIVER APTITUDE CENTRE SERVICES

Professional and personal mobility is of ever-greater importance. This is why the Allgäu driver aptitude centre was created by the RCMS program in 2004. This centre focuses specifically on people with illness or accident-related physical impairments, on people with previous neurological problems and on people who have not driven for a long period of time. The services offered by the driver aptitude centre cover driver training for the physically impaired, driver's license training for different types of licenses for those seeking employment that requires driving, aptitude assessments for those with physical impairments, driving tests and driver safety training. Medical specialists in all relevant specialty areas, including doctors with a qualification in driver aptitude, neuropsychologists, driving schools, TÜV (German Association for Technical Inspection), and ADAC (a German automobile club), provide these services. The driver aptitude centre assesses the patients' ability to drive, provides them with information on the legal situation regarding vehicle modifications and conversions. The driver aptitude centre can also assess whether professional drivers can still do their job and, if not, under what conditions it may be possible for them to do so. If the services are provided to people who are professionally dependent on motor vehicles and their driver's license or to people who are undergoing retraining as a bus driver, the employers' liability insurance associations, pension insurance funds, Agentur für Arbeit, social security and liability insurance companies also provide funding.

EXISTING NETWORK PARTNERS

The RCMS network consists of: physicians, psychologists and therapists at the Enzensberg Clinic; specialist medical facilities and medical practitioners in private practice; educational institutions, such as occupational rehabilitation centers, vocational training centres, Bavarian Business Association technical and further education centres, Dekra Arbeit GmbH, KOLPING; workshops for persons with disabilities in order to provide job-related short- and long-term trials with TÜV, driving schools, the ADAC and AGCO/ Fendt (fleet of agricultural machinery) which facilitate driver aptitude assessments, driver training and vehicle conversions. Specialist rehab consultants and case managers from the Agentur für Arbeit, the pension insurance funds, the employers' liability insurance association and rehab services of private insurance companies are regularly present at the Enzensberg Clinic, as it is the agency that brings everyone together.

In the context of pilot schemes, a close and structured partnership with employers and company medical officers focused on workplace analysis and design as well as on medical rehabilitation, and occupational reintegration after illness/accidents was put into place with the car manufacturers Opel and Audi. The network partners were consulted individually for each RCMS case. If, during the preliminary registration, the client asks questions that cannot be clarified with the assistance of the existing network partners, the RCMS program will provide an external service provider who can provide an answer.

Case Study

A 40-year-old male, works as a milk-tank driver is the subject of this case study. His job involves frequent entry and exiting of the milk tank and the regular pulling and coupling of milk lines. The worker sustanined a crush injury to his left foot – several fractures of the metatarsal bones. Initially, conservative treatment was provided. However, there were complications: delayed osseous healing and surgical ankylosis of the lower ankle joint. Subsequently, the worker developed chronic pain syndrome, physical restrictions that included reduced weightbearing by the leg, and skin and soft-tissue changes in the context of a regional pain syndrome. He made repeated attempts to perform his job; however, he increasingly frequently took sick leave because of the severity of his injuries. As a result, he was at risk of losing his job and was suffering from increased tension within his family.

Interdisciplinary diagnostics in rehab/case management support concluded that a special in-patient type of pain therapy was needed. There was a reduction in the complaints as a result of this inpatient multimodal pain treatment. During this treatment, driver aptitude diagnostics specific to his job led to the conclusion that, in the long term, it was no longer possible for him to do his job as a milk-tank driver, but a job as a driver for a scheduled bus service would be possible. While receiving in-patient therapy the worker was retrained as a bus driver and is now employed with the same employer on a part-time basis as a bus driver on a scheduled service.

Results of the RCMS Program

PATIENT SATISFACTION AND RETURN TO WORK AFTER REHAB

The RCMS program was evaluated in the context of an explorative cross-sectional study with regard to patient satisfaction and return to work after rehab. For this purpose, 112 persons who underwent the RCMS program between 2002 and 2005 were questioned in written survey in November 2005. Of the people surveyed, 62 responded, which is a return rate of 55 per cent. The participants were predominantly male (46 out of 62, or 74 per cent) and on average 38 years of age. Prior to their respective accidents, all were employed or in training. Before commencing the program, only 13 (21 per cent) were employed or in training; the greatest share was, however, permanently unable to work (n=35 or 56 per cent) and had an unclear work outlook. Of this latter group, eight (23 per cent) were able to work again at the time the survey was conducted, a further three (9 per cent) were undergoing training or retraining and six (17 per cent) had been granted benefits because of a reduction in earning capacity. The RCMS program therefore improved or at least clarified the earnings status of half of this severely affected group.

The satisfaction of the persons surveyed was correspondingly high. On the common scale for the global assessment of patient satisfaction, 'ZUF-8', the average of the total scores for satisfaction with the RCMS process of the respondents was a very good 28 points, with a theoretically possible maximum score of 32. Only 4 per cent (n=2) of the respondents rated the program at under 20 points. This high level of satisfaction is also shown in relation to the network processes, which 24 persons assessed as 'excellent' (39 per cent), 27 assessed as 'good' (44 per cent) and five assessed as 'so-so' (8 per cent). No one rated the processes as 'bad'; only six persons (10 per cent) given an assessment. Of those surveyed, 60 per cent (n=37) considered the measures recommended to be 'clearly correct', 27 per cent (n=17) considered them to be 'generally correct'. Only 5 per cent (n=3) considered the measures recommended to be 'not actually relevant'. The remainder refrained from giving an opinion (n=5 or 8 per cent). The response to the RCMS program's work is, therefore, very positive.

With regard to the number of cases, an increase from five RCMS-program patients in 2001 to 148 in 2007 was recorded. Until December 2007, a total of 551 patients participated in the RCMS program. The employers' liability insurance associations (BG/GUV) commissioned the RCMS program for 204 cases, liability insurance companies for 190 and other organizations for 147 cases. Within the seven-year period, not only were new funding organizations acquired, but the utilization by existing funding organizations was increased, which can be taken as proof that the funders are satisfied with their return on investment.

EXPERIENCE GAINED FROM THE AUDI PILOT SCHEME

The establishment of a RCMS program is based on the pilot scheme 'interlocking of medical rehabilitation and professional reintegration' (Haase et al. 2002), which the Enzensberg Clinic carried out from 1998 to 2000 in cooperation with the healthcare department of AUDI AG Ingolstadt, the Audi company health insurance fund and the state social insurance board of Upper Bavaria (LVA Oberbayern). Based on the conclusion that rehab physicians frequently lack knowledge of workplaces and work requirements and of the role that company medical officers play in the companies, there was a striving for a closer cooperation between the rehab clinic and companies. The idea was to create a virtually seamless reintegration into the workforce after a person's illness or accident, as well as a reduction of the time that an employee was unable to work. The intervention program therefore focused on a close and coordinated cooperation, with a mutual exchange of information, among the Enzensberg Clinic, the AUDI company medical officers and the relevant funding organizations (Audi BKK and LVA Oberbayern).

The pilot scheme comprised 40 AUDI AG Ingolstadt employees who were patients at the Enzensberg Clinic. During the rehab program the company medical officer of AUDI AG was contacted by the Enzensberg Clinic to clarify important issues regarding the patients' workplace, gradual reintegration or necessary modifications to the workplace. On each worker's discharge from the clinic the company medical officer received a medical report containing the findings and performance profiles of the worker. On this basis the company medical officer was able to initiate the necessary measures within the company. If more comprehensive measures for the employee's participation in working life had to be initiated, the rehab consultants of the funding organizations were also involved in the process.

For a control group, 56 AUDI employees were identified who had also taken part in a rehab program, but outside of the pilot scheme. In the context of the pilot scheme, more than three-quarters of the intervention group, but only half of the control group, were able to recommence full-time employment with the company within the first two months after rehab; a large number did so immediately, i.e., within two days of in-patient rehabilitation. Occupational rehabilitation went faster within the intervention group. While this group took an average of 53 days off due to the inability to work before recommencing employment, the control group took an average of 91 days. This is because of a reduction of the length of the period between the end of the rehabilitation measures and each employee's presentation to the company medical officer and, consequently, until commencement of an occupational workplace program. Furthermore, even after the rehab program was completed, the employees in the intervention program had fewer days off due to inability to work than the control group, thus not only promising a faster, but also a more sustained, occupational reintegration.

Conclusion

The role played, and opportunities offered, by a clinic in disability management need to be evaluated and further developed on an ongoing basis. Currently, a catamnestic evaluation of functional performance study is being conducted at the Enzensberg Clinic, based on the evaluation of functional performance study by Büschel, Greitemann and Schaidhammer (2008). This study is investigating the professional performance and the success (effectiveness) of recommendations by the clinic for people who underwent an evaluation of functional performance.

The health and security of the company's employees depend on the performance profile of each employee. However, for the integration process to be successful it is just as important that all parties involved in the process cooperate well and confidently. Depending on the individual case, network partners outside the company can be involved in the decision-making process in order to ensure success in complex situations. According to the company survey described above, businesses would like to see the following issues addressed in their integration management:

* interdisciplinary examination of the injured or ill employee
* creation of a positive and negative performance profile
* establishment of a injured/ill worker integration plan for the business
* close cooperation between the employees and the business (Schlechter, Riedl & Maier 2008).

With its network, the rehab/case management support by the clinic can contribute greatly to the resolution of the issues identified by the companies. Employees with impaired performance can, on the one hand, be deployed more suitably within the business, with a more constant ability to work, or on the other hand, information can be provided with regard to a disability pension if a lack of competitiveness is medically assessed. Funding organizations involved in the provision of disability management are given decision-making aids that allow them to assess appropriate rehabilitation goals within the company, thus increasing the likelihood of success. In this context, the disability management costs to the company become more calculable. The mutual understanding of company processes and requirements of the different institutions involved in the process promotes respect and thus the development of partnerships, particularly in the area of external provision of disability management. This results in a win-win situation for all parties involved.

Definitions

EFL = Evaluation of functional performance utilizes 29 work-related standardized performance tests to investigate the loading capacity of the activity areas: handling of loads/(hand) strength, posture/flexibility, static posture, locomotion, and hand coordination. The objective of this evaluation is a realistic assessment of the person's work-related, ergonomically safe loading capacity. This enables a comparison with the requirements of the person's previous professional work or with another intended activity. (IGPTR 2007; EFL 2007)

IMBA = Integration von Menschen mit Behinderungen in die Arbeitswelt (integration of people with disabilities into the working environment). This profile system can be used to describe and compare workplace requirements and human skills and abilities on the basis of uniform characteristics. It can be used to deduce preventative and rehabilitation measures. IMBA is a standardized recording and documentation system that consists of nine main complexes that are broken down into a further 70 characteristics. The main complexes comprise: posture, movement of the body, movements of parts of the body, information, complex capacities, environment, workplace health and safety, work organization, and key qualifications (IMBA 2001).

Bibliography

Adlhoch, U., Fankhaendel, K., Magin, J., Seel, H., Weters, B. & Zorn, G. (2005). *Handlungsempfehlungen zum Betrieblichen Eingliederungsmanagement.* Available at: http://ww.hauptfuersorgestelle.de/files/599/Handlungsempfehlungen_BEM_lvr.pdf, accessed 8 August 2011.

Büschel, C., Greitemann, B. & Schaidhammer, M. (2008). Stellenwert der Evaluation der funktionellen Leistungsfähigkeit nach Isernhagen (EFL) in der sozialmedizinischen Begutachtung des Leistungsvermögens, Teil 1 + 2. *MED SACH* (5 & 6): 195–200; 212–19.

Bundesamt für Arbeitsschutz und Arbeitsmedizin (Federal Institute for Occupational Safety and Health). (2007). Available at: http://www.baua.de/Informationen-fuer-die-Praxis/Statistiken/Arbeitsunfähigkeit/Kosten.html_nnn=true, accessed 8 August 2011.

Britschgi, S. (2006). Schwerpunkte der Betriebsratsarbeit. In: S Britschgi, *Krankheit und betriebliches Eingliederungsmanagement.* Frankfurt am Main: Bund-Verlag.

Deutsche Rentenversicherung Bund. (2005). Rehabilitation 159. Berlin: n.p.

Deutsche Rentenversicherung. (2007) Rehabilitation. *Band 159* 3(2007).

Dworschak, B. & Buck, H. (2006). Die Veränderung der Arbeitswelt. In: S. Böttscher, Marie-Luise & Ernst Becker Stiftung (eds), *Generation 60plus* (27–34). n.p.

EFL-Akademie. (2007). Evaluation funktioneller Leistungsfähigkeit nach Isernhagen. Available at: http://www.efl-akademie.de, accessed 12 August 2007.

Federal Institute for Occupational Safety and Health. (2007). Available at: http://www.baua.de/de/Informationen-fuer-die-Praxis/Statistiken/Arbeitsunfäehigkeit/Kosten.html_nnn=true, accessed 14 November 2007.

Froese, E. (2009). *Reha-Management/Das Konzept der Verwaltungs-Berufsgenossenschaft*. Stuttgart: Gentner.

Fuchs, H. & Welti, F. (2005). *Medizinische Rehabilitation im Rahmen des betrieblichen Eingliederungsmanagements – alle können gewinnen!* Bonn: Arbeitskreis Gesundheit e.V.

Gagel A. (2004). Eingliederungsmanagement auf der Basis der Novelle zum SGB IX und der Gemeinsamen Empfehlungen nach § 13 Abs. 2 Nr. 8 und 9 SGB IX. *Forum B – Schwerbehindertenrecht und Fragen des betrieblichen Gesundheitsmanagements*, Info Nr. 2/2004. Available at: http://www.iqpr.de/iqpr/download/foren/B2-2004.pdf, accessed 25 October 2007.

Haase I., Riedl, G., Birkholz, L-B., Schäfer, A. & Zellner, M. (2002). Verzahnung von medizinischer Rehabilitation und beruflicher Reintegration. *Arbeitsmedizin Sozialmedizin Umweltmedizin* (331–35).

Hetzel, C., Flach, T. & Mozdzanowski, M. (2007). *Mitarbeiter krank*. Wiesbaden: Universum.

IGPTR. (2007) Interessengemeinschaft Physiotherapie Rehabilitation. Beurteilungen. Available at: http://www.igptr.ch/ass_igpnr/Beurteilungen/EFL.pdf, accessed 12 August 2007.

IMBA. (2011). Integration von Menschen mit Behinderungen in die Arbeitswelt. Available at: http://www.imba.de, accessed 8 August 2011.

Mehrhoff F. & Schian, H.M. (2009). *Zurück in den Beruf – Betriebliche Eingliederung richtig managen*. Berlin: De Gruyter.

Pressestelle des Bundesarbeitsgerichts. (2007). *Krankheitsbedingte Kündigung – Betriebliches Eingliederungsmanagement nach § 84 Abs. 2 SGB IX, Pressemitteilung Nr. 54/07*. Available at: http://juris.bundesarbeitsgericht.de/cgi-bin/rechtssprechung/document .py?Gericht=bag&Art=pm&sid =151f7dea80fa711753fca89529a8fdd7&nr=11959&pos=0&anz=1, accessed 25 October 2007.

Riedl, G., Klimczyk, K., Kuhnt, O. & Schesser, R. (2009). Schmerz. In: F. Mehrhoff & H-M Schian, *Zurück in den Beruf – Betriebliche Eingliederung richtig managen* (141–53). Berlin: De Gruyter.

Schinkel, S. (2006). Betriebliches Eingliederungsmanagement – eine Chance für Betrieb und Arbeitnehmer. *RV aktuell* (102–05).

Schlechter, K., Riedl, G. & Maier, J. (2008). *Rehab/Case Management Support mit Fahreignungszentrum Allgäu im Betrieblichen Eingliederungsmanagement – Befragung von Maschinenbauunternehmen*. Hopfen am See: Eigenverlag Fachklinik Enzensberg.

Sozialgesetzbuch Neuntes Buch (2005). *Rehabilitation und Teilhabe behinderter Menschen – vom 19.06.2001*.

Stegmann, R., Berger, J-J., Dering, C., Huber, A. & Koss, D. (2005). *Prävention und Eingliederungsmanagement – Arbeitshilfe für Schwerbehindertenvertretungen, Betriebs- und Personalräte*. Frankfurt am Main: Cross Media Konzeption und Produktion.

Zink, P. (2006). Berufliche Wiedereingliederung: Welcher Organisationsstruktur bedarf es im Grossbetrieb, um bei allen beteiligten Personen Vertrauen für ein betriebliches Eingliederungsmanagement (BEM) zu erzielen? *Die BG* 11(2006): 512–15.

Zorn, G. (2006). Betriebliches Eingliederungsmanagement – Rechtsfragen zur praktischen Umsetzung im Betrieb. *BR* (42–46).

14 *Disability Management of Orthopaedic Disorders: A Pilot Project*

LUTZ TROWITZSCH, DÉSIRÉE HERBOLD, BERNHARD KOCH AND BIRGIT-CHRISTIANE LEINEWEBER

Introduction

The already visible economic, social and cultural consequences of recent dramatic demographic changes in Western industrial societies require a reversal of the trend in the age distribution of the labour force so that people remain working for longer. This will require a clear commitment from firms to address problems related to the employment of older and performance-reduced employees. Corporate structures and the behaviour of executives will play important roles in achieving such demographic change. Today, the esteem of the employees, a positive working atmosphere and fulfilling the potential of each employee appear to provide conspicuous advantages in a competitive globalized environment (Hauser, Schubert & Aicher 2005). These are central concerns for occupational health care and disability management, as are behaviour-related and context-related injury prevention. At present, the integration of performance-reduced employees is hindered by their long-term inability to work and delayed access to medical and occupation-oriented rehabilitation (Weber, Weber & Raspe 1999), and, consequently, by doctors' limited understanding of the problems that their patients face at work (Isernhagen 1991). The appearance of chronic pain and the psychosocial stress of affected parties present further serious problems (Waddel 1998; Linton & Nordin 2006). Furthermore, lack of clarity about who is responsible for communications between workplaces and the social welfare system in Germany compounds the difficulties.

Musculoskeletal diseases still rank highest in the disease statistics of health insurance institutions in most Western developed nations. In Germany, musculoskeletal disorders are second on the list, with 16 per cent of those with such problems taking early pensions (DRV-Bund 2007). According to the Quebec Task Force on Spinal Disorders (1987), between seven and ten per cent of all those with unspecified, chronic back pain, despite intensive investigation and treatment, remain disabled for long periods or even permanently, and some suffer intense, chronic disease. According to Linton and Nordin (2006), even this low figure represents 80 per cent of the direct and indirect health expenditures that originate in claims on medical supply and social insurance systems. Forty per cent of the work time lost to disability is connected to a work-related problem (Schmidt & Kohlmann 2005). Mainly in heavy industry, but also in labour-intensive medium and small enterprises, illness increases by up to 25 per cent among employees aged over 55 years (Salzgitter BKK 2009).

As shown in Figure 14.1, the musculoskeletal diseases that cause 600 lost workdays per 100 benefit recipients at Salzgitter AG – with its approximately 9,000 steel workers – are almost twice as high as the BKK statistics, whereas 42 lost workdays per hundred amounts to 24 per cent (Salzgitter BKK 2008).

As is clear from Figure 14.1, musculoskeletal diseases are still the most significant cause of extreme physical difficulties at work (Van Nieuwenhuyse et al. 2006) (though psychosocial problems caused by increased workloads and stress also increasingly cause employee ill-health) (Linton & Nordin 2006; Frachignoni, Oliveri & Bazzini 2006). It would seem reasonable and effective to attend to this small group of long-term disabled people with an early and professional disability management program (Van Nieuwenhuyse et al. 2006). Therefore, strategies of occupational reintegration and integrated health management are being increasingly accepted not only in private companies, but also by service providers in the social and health systems, which are adopting policies to provide constructive solutions to the challenge of demographic changes to the work force. The disability management model developed in the 1990s in Canada and Australia after the establishment of the National Institutes of Disability Management and Research (NIDMAR 1994), is finding growing acceptance worldwide.

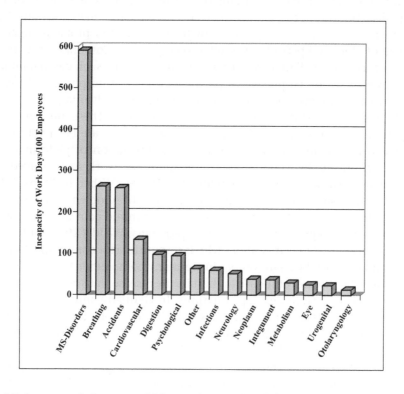

Figure 14.1 Lost workdays per 100 employees (weighting by health problem)

Legislation

Since 1 May 2004, legislation in Germany commits employers, through § 84, Art. 2 of the German social code IX (SGB IX), to put in place an early warning system for the punctual detection, elimination and prevention of work time lost through disability. The research group Niehaus et al. (2008) found that more than 50 per cent of big companies, 38 per cent of medium- and nearly 25 per cent of small-sized companies currently have disability management (DM) programs in place. Of 527 companies surveyed, 32 per cent cooperate in rehabilitation arrangements, though the success and effectiveness is uncertain because so few evaluation studies are available. Based on the results of its model of a medical occupational rehabilitation program (Trowitzsch & Rust 2000; Trowitzsch et al. 2006) the Institute for Work and Social Medicine of the Paraceleus Klinik, Bad Gandersheim, established in 2004, developed an DM program to be provided to large and medium enterprises. Salzgitter AG and its health insurance company, Salzgitter BKK, were the first major concerns to join the project. We developed a pilot scheme together with BKK and medical officers of Salzgitter AG, in which the former took responsibility for the structural and financial aspects of the professional DM scheme for long-term disabled members. After multiple discussions, mutual plant tours and development of a procedures manual, the project proposal was presented to Salzgitter AG management, the human resources office, works councils and at the foremen level.

On 15 September 2005, the first agreement was signed, according to which Salzgitter BKK was instructed to arrange a DM program with our Paracelsus Klinik as the external service provider, on behalf of five affiliated business concerns of Salzgitter AG. Four days later, after preparation of an information flyer, the first patient was admitted into the program.

Aim

The aim of the pilot project was to provide all those involved – employees, employers, occupational physicians, family doctors, specialists, health insurance and pension-fund insurers – with a network of medical, psychological, social and occupational professionals to survey performance-challenged employees and to make recommendations for a professional disability management program. The concept strives for a win-win outcome for all participants. Employees unable to do their usual job are subjected to a substantiated activity-related, functional-capacity testing directly related to the workplace; objective functional disorders are detected; professional socio-medical comments are fed into the DM program, as are comments on illness management and the psychosocial stress factors involved.

As arranged with the local pension fund insurer, in case of need, accommodation was made available in our clinic for a three-week, in-patient medical or occupational rehabilitation, or, if more appropriate, with our project partner, the occupational rehabilitation centre Goslar, for a four-day, occupational orientation. Suggestions for immediate action or recommendations for retraining could be submitted immediately to the company and to the pension fund, according to the guidelines of the state rehabilitation and participation in working life scheme.

Our recommendations to the DM team were incorporated into the companies' own health management procedures which, according to § 84,2 SGB IX, must involve a designated, integrated team that includes occupational physicians. It is expected that the early implementation of a DM plan will abolish or ameliorate the disease-related reduction of employee functionality, provide pain relief, avoid chronification and strengthen the social competence of patients. Moreover, cost-effective rehabilitation and early allocation of a place in the production process that matches the abilities of the disabled is designed to avoid disruption to participation in working life. From existing sociomedical studies in the investigation of social achievement claims (Merten, Friedel & Stevens 2007), we know that we must reckon with an injury aggravation rate of between 36 and 42 per cent for the disabled at work. For this program, we needed an objective performance appraisal to compare with the subjective feelings of stress. Our analysis dealt with the following questions:

1. Is it possible to improve the reintegration of performance-challenged employees by early, intensive cooperation with occupational physicians and thus reduce work hours lost to disability?
2. Which bio-psychosocial factors and processing disorders were presented by performance-challenged employees who use DM programs?
3. What efficiencies and effectiveness can we expect from this pilot project?

Material and Methods

Process-producing statistics were noted continuously during the project. Data was acquired through a questionnaire in order to make an inventory of rehabilitation status (IRES II) (Gerdes & Jäckel, 1995) at the beginning of the project (t0), as well as in a follow-up postal survey six months later (t2). Through statistical measurement of its effects, the success of the disability management program was determined and illustrated from the patients' points of view. We carried out activity-specific evaluation of participants using Isernhagen's functional capacity evaluation (FCE) test (Isernhagen 1988). To assess the potential for reducing work hours lost due to disability and illness, Salzgitter BKK collected statistics using the data and evaluation system from the Berlin company Terranet GmbH's electronic disability-case-management program to detect the days employees were unable to work one year before and one year after FCE testing. The occupational physicians were asked about the implementation of the recommendations of Paracelsus Klinik up to time t2; and in the written surveys, up to t2, the patients assessed their subjective experiences of the DM program. All statistical evaluations were carried out using the statistic package for the social sciences (SPSS).

EXCLUSION CRITERIA

The cases were taken exclusively from the orthopaedic sphere and show chronic diseases of the spinal column, joints or muscle-band accessory, as well as conditions after surgery and post-trauma injuries. Stability of post-operative conditions must be guaranteed; criteria for exclusion were acute inflammatory conditions, myocardial infarctions, strokes and abdominal surgery within the last four months. In such situations, there are too many complexities for occupational physicians to be able to assess the clinical pictures clearly.

PROCEDURE

The Salzgitter BKK case manager extended an invitation to each patient who matched the given criteria, and advised them of the company's responsibility and fiduciary duty according to § 84 Abs. 2 SGB IX, informed the patient about the DM program, handed over the flyer and prepared them for participation. Participation in the program was voluntary; there was a written agreement, and there were no negative consequences for refusing to participate. For the company, secrecy remained a priority throughout the program; internal communication occurred only via the occupational physician. With the employee's approval, the Salzgitter BKK case manager informed the leading occupational physician, who conducted a workplace load analysis, made a video recording of the workplace and sent it to the clinic, then arranged a date for hospitalization. All preliminary findings, such as X-ray images, magnetic resonance imaging and computed tomography imaging, were required by the general practitioners or specialists. Salzgitter BKK bore the cost of the five-day stay at the clinic. Costs were charged to the pension fund at the clinic's usual daily rate for care.

PROCESS

During the five-day stay at the Paracelsus Klinik, a standardized basic program was implemented. An essential element was a multidisciplinary assessment of the illness/injury/disability using specialist orthopaedics, internal medicine, occupational and social medicine and sports medicine, with an objective demonstration of reduced capacity and function according to the bio-psychosocial criteria of the International Classification of Functioning, Disability and Health (ICF). The participant's psychological state was assessed by a psychologist, who conducted a short, structured, diagnostic interview, assessed the context factors of psychological and social stress and made a condition analysis and a validated diagnosis according to the Diagnostic and Statistical Manual of Psychological Disorder (DSM-IV). Impartial examination findings were compared with the patient's subjective assessment of their disabilities. These were analyzed by internationally recognized, target-oriented assessment methods and are demonstrated in the following section.

ASSESSMENT METHODS

The following tests and questionnaires were used to assess program participants.

Evaluation of functional capacity

For impartial development of the activity-related, physical performance profile, the FCE system developed in the United States in 1988 by Susan Isernhagen, whose work in 2004 received an award for the 'best work injury management' in the US, served as a central element (for more detail see Kaiser et al. 2000). It is a semi-quantitative procedure that can be carried out only by qualified physical therapists. The FCE system is based on verifiable and commensurable criteria of the kinesio-physical test methodology under realistic, work-related stress conditions. Over two days, 29 typical occupational processes with workplace-specific additional tests take place. Each test is between two and four hours in the laboratory, and each one is carried out up to the patient's maximum capacity. Reliability tests are also carried out. During the tests, attitudes to work, job safety, cardiopulmonary stress, functional impairment and maximum carrying capacity are analyzed, and pain is noted. The skills profile of each employee was balanced with his or her occupational requirement profile in the ensuing job match. In the case of abnormalities in the profile, a detailed statement demonstrating the functional disorder and lack of adequate job performance was made. The intensity of the work, the capacity of performance, attitudes to work and the quantitative job performance in a normal workday are illustrated by the FCE protocol and demonstrate the basis for the occupational physicians' reintegration activities (Figure 14.2).

Duration of load per 8 hours	Rarely	Occasionally	Frequently	Continuous	Maximum Load
Category	Maximum	Heavy	Medium	Light	General Remarks
Weight/ power (kg, kp =10N)					maximum load (self-limitation)
Floor to waist lift	17.5	15	7.5	5	
Waist to overhead lift	12.5	10	5	2.5	
Horizontal lift (to 1.5 m)	20	17.5	10.5	7.5	
push static kp	30	22.5	15	7.5	dynamic 40 kg
pull static kp	25	18	12	6	dynamic 30 kg

Figure 14.2 FCE: Physical Capacity Profile (Selection of Tests)

Spinal function sort-performance assessment of capacity testing

The FCE test was accompanied by a self-assessment of physical ability, using the spinal function sort-performance assessment and capacity testing (PACT) developed by the Swiss Working Group for Rehabilitation (Matheson & Matheson 1996). The test results were compared with the workload standard of the US Department of Labor *Dictionary of Occupational Titles*. The test uses 50 pictures of daily life, where the client indicates whether they feel able to carry out those activities, would feel slightly restricted, moderately restricted or highly restricted in doing them. The test was customized for German classifications of work, where the critical values are light, light to medium-heavy, medium-heavy, severe and most severe load, of 5, 10, 15, 20, and more than 40 kilograms, respectively. Consistency tests are available and are an excellent impartial parameter for measuring the motivation of the participant. The test was done before the first and the second stress analyses and aligned with the performance profile of the FCE test. One hundred to110 points, predominantly sitting, represent a light physical workload; 195 points represent the maximum capacity. A score of fewer than 100 points before the first and the second tests – without impartial confirmation of functional restriction – indicates the patient's subjective misinterpretation of their own capacity compared with the FCE measurement of their performance. According to Oesch et al. (2003), incidents of chronic behaviour can be indicated here, as well as context factors for below-average self-assessment. On the first and on the second days, and after testing, the pain score was labelled from zero to ten (0 = no pain, 10 = maximum pain) and compared with impartially viewed pain behaviour. A higher pain description and a pain score of more than eight, with missing confirmation of functional disturbance, were assessed as a somatoform disorder, or maladapted pain disturbance, according to the definitions of Matheson (1988) and Oesch et al. (2003). Further analysis of the pain index was carried out using the IRES II questionnaire with basic domain 'pains' and 'symptoms'.

Self-assessment patient questionnaire 'indicators of rehab status' (IRES II)

The IRES self-assessment questionnaire is a measuring instrument, a standardized, multidimensional test based on a representative sample, developed by Gerdes and Jäckel (1995) for the German rehabilitation system. The questionnaire contains 161 items, including subcategories related to pains and symptoms, risk factors, occupational demands, disablement through ageing, psychological stress and social problems, combined into basic domains such as somatic status, functional status and psychosocial status, that come together to form a 'total rehab score'. The data are available for statistical processing, automatically generated by the SPSS program and consulted for calculation of effects. Values below the 75th percentile are assessed as 'inconspicuous'; those between the 75th and 90th percentiles are considered 'conspicuous' and values above the 90th percentile are assessed as 'serious'. According to Schubmann et al. (1997), the calculation of the effect is proved for samples without control groups with a more exact effect size, where effect sizes under 0.4 are valued as 'slight', between 0.4 and 0.8 are valued 'medium' and those of more than 0.8 are considered 'intense' effects. In addition, the IRES questionnaire covers all relevant bio-psychosocio-demographic data of the patients.

Work-related behaviour patterns (AVEM)

AVEM is a multidimensional, personality-diagnostic test procedure developed by Schaarschmidt and Fischer (1996), with which sophisticated self-assessments of behaviour and experience in relation to work and professional life can be made. It measures commitment to work, personal durability and stress management, and attitudes to health. Classifications are clustered according to types: Type G behaviour is consistent with healthy behaviour; Type S behaviour indicates protective behaviour at work; Type A behaviour indicates a high level of engagement with work, increased willingness to perform and a striving for perfection. Type B behaviour is associated with a limited ability to distance oneself from the job, a tendency to give up easily and a reduced tendency for active problem-solving.

DISABILITY MANAGEMENT

After complete analysis of the data, functional disorders were divided into subjective impairments and psychosocial context factors. Recommendations to the disability management team were developed, together with terminal occupational and sociomedical specialist counselling, along with a statement of the functional disorders and prognosis for the condition, and a statement about current capacity to work. If appropriate, immediate return to work was approved, or gradual reintegration was recommended.

Results

Between September 2005 and the beginning of July 2009, a total of 38 severely ill and long-term disabled patients took part in the DM project. In that period, 38 complete datasets for IRES II (t0), and AVEM questionnaires (t0) were available, as well as 38 FCE stress protocols with the subjective self-assessment of the probands according to their capacity (PACT). For technical reasons, in the evaluation of the written follow-up survey up to t2, for the IRES questionnaire we can report only on a sample of 27 out of 32 patients. Five patients did not take part in the first follow-up survey (six months after the testing), for unknown reasons, so we refrained from sending them the second follow-up survey, opting rather to have investigations carried out through a closed, annual follow-up survey with attending occupational physicians in February 2007, 2008 and 2009. This meant that the rate of return after 2006 dropped to 84 per cent. Except for marginally increasing the average age of the participants, the drop out in survey participation produced no further significant differences to the analysis. The average follow-up period of our survey was now 216 +/- 123 days, approximately seven months.

SOCIO-DEMOGRAPHIC DATA

The demographic data of the participant population (N = 38) up to t0 are demonstrated in Table 14.1 and contrasted with the sample up to t2 (N = 27).

As Table 14.1 shows, this project involved only male participants, with an average age of just over 44 years; 75.7 per cent of whom are married; 71 per cent have a secondary-school certificate; and on average, have worked in a Salzgitter enterprise for 20.5 years. The average number of hours worked per week is 39.5 hours. They mostly work on a shift system of early, late and night shifts.

More than half of the participants are categorized as a skilled worker or qualified as a foreman. Twenty-nine per cent of them have a degree of severe disability, and the average is 35 per cent. Also conspicuous is the high number, one quarter of the workers, who have a migrant background. Not shown in the table are their specific occupations, among which metalworker, welder, crane operator and engineer are preponderate – these are the workers who deal with heavy loads, of approximately 20 kg, under strenuous conditions, mainly while crouching and kneeling. The main illnesses and injuries presented are lower-back pain, including disc hernias (among 12 of the 38); slipped disc followed by conservative medical treatment (five people); severe complications following surgery on a herniated disc (three); first- and second-degree spondylolisthesis (two); spondylodesis of the lumbar, and cervical spine trauma (two); gonarthrosis III with ruptured meniscus (six); acromioclavicular (AC) joint arthroscopy with complications (three); Morbus Bechterew (one); endoprothesis, surgery for cruciate ligament rupture, and lower ankle joint rupture. Nearly 30 per cent have had multiple, major operations and more than 18 per cent have had one surgical procedure; more than half were only treated conservatively.

Table 14.1 Socioeconomic and demographic profile

Test intervals	t 0	t 2
Sample group	(n = 38)	(n = 27)
Mean age (standard deviation, SD)	44.3 (+/- 7.7)	46.0 (+/- 8.3)
Seniority, years (SD)	20.5 (+/- 1.7)	20.6 (+/- 0.9)
Marital status (%)		
married	71.9	66.7
single	10.8	18.5
divorced	10.8	11.1
widowed	2.7	3.7
Education (%)		
secondary general school	71.9	66.7
intermediate secondary	18.4	18.5
special upper secondary	5.3	7.4
other	5.2	7.4
Occupational category (%)		
unskilled	7.9	3.7
semiskilled	28.9	29.6
skilled	44.7	44.4
foreman	18.4	22.2
Working hours per week	39.9	39.5
Suffering severe disability (%)	27.0	42.3
degree (mean)	35.5	36.7
Nationality (%)		
German	92.1	92.6
German, migrant background	26.3	25.0
other	7.9	7.4

IRES II DATA

In Figure 14.3, subjective impairments are shown visually by the IRES II questionnaire (t0), with serious stress values on the domains 'pain and symptoms', 'occupational stress', 'impact of work' and 'disability in daily life'.

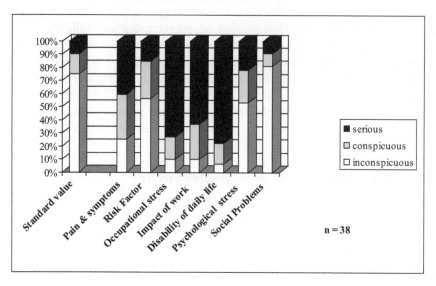

Figure 14.3 Patient self-assessment questionnaire IRES II (main dimensions)

RESULTS OF THE FUNCTIONAL CAPACITY EVALUATION

The two-day FCE test was completed with all patients. Except for a small increase in post-exercise discomfort, no major complications occurred. The results of the FCE testing produced a median stress capacity of 23.6 kg among the 38 patients in the basic test 'ground-to-waist lift', that is, an average 'heavy' stress capacity. This was significantly different from the self-assessments of capacity. The self-assessment in the PACT test was highly reduced, at 136 points, consistent with a capacity assessment between 'light' and 'medium-heavy', that is, between 10 and 12.5 kg. Between the first and the second tests, self-perception of capacity increased marginally, to 146 points, representing a corporal stress severity of between 12.5 and 15 kg. A cognitive behavioural approach was entered, but up to this point in the testing there was no significant change (Mann-Whitney U test; p = 0.06) between the first and second PACT test. After transforming the PACT values and the actual work to an ordinal scale (from 0 = negative pattern to 6 = maximum weight), this difference is shown in Figure 14.4. In contrast, moreover, comparison of the first PACT test and the final work test shows that a significant difference between self-perception and actual capacity was detected (Mann-Whitney U test; p = 0.000). Participants significantly underestimated their own functional capacity.

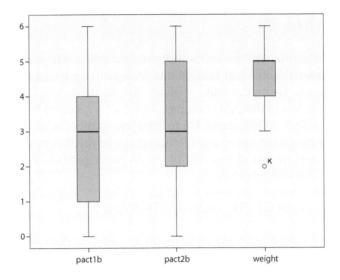

Figure 14.4 Self-perception of physical abilities and actual performance

ANALYSIS OF CORRELATIONS BETWEEN PACT AND AVEM TESTS

To see the relationship between subjectively understood capacity, independent of the injury or disability, and behaviour at work, nominal values of the AVEM test were contrasted with the metric values of the PACT test. As shown in Figure 14.5, the rank correlation test, according to Spearman, demonstrates for non-parametric, two-sided tests a significant, one-dimensional dependence ($r = .43$; $p = .05$) between behaviour type and self-assessment of capacity. Thus, contrary to the work they actually achieve, Type B employees assess themselves as significantly less able than the protective types (S), who in turn see themselves as less able than Type A. The most realistic subjective assessments are made by those who are Type G.

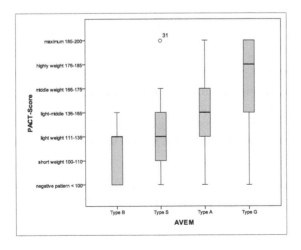

Figure 14.5 Distribution of AVEM type and self-evaluation of functional capacity

DISABILITY DATA (N = 38)

In order to obtain a median follow-up for independent and stable parameters of the data, Salzgitter BKK measured hours lost to disability/incapacity one year before and one year after the DM program. Using the DIAS analysis system, it was calculated that a total of 3,212 workdays were lost to disability (average = 84.5 +/- 67.8 days) before and 2,990 days after DM (average = 78.7 +/-88.8 days). Up to 2009, no significant difference between the sample groups was noted (X^2 test; p = .257); however, the median value shrank from 71.5 days to 36.5 days; and we found that five of the 38 participants lost no working days to disability after the DM intervention.

EFFECTS ON THE DATA OF THE NON-PARTICIPANTS

Table 14.2 shows a sample of 'long-term unemployable' workers who were invited to counselling interviews with the case manager in the first quarters of 2007 and 2008, but who did not want to participate in the DM program; 19 of 42 invited employees returned to full-time work within 14 days of this conversation.

Table 14.2   Outcomes after potential applicants contacted by Salzgitter BKK

Invited to personal meeting	(n = 42)
Participated in FCE DM program	11 (26%)
Able to resume work the following week	11 (26%)
Able to resume work two weeks later	8 (19%)
Continuing inability to work	7 (17%)
In gradual occupational rehabilitation	5 (12%)

Note: 19 of the 42 (45%) employees were able to resume work a fortnight after the personal meeting.

Psychological Co-morbidity

In order to discern coping disorders caused by psychological stress – which perpetuates long-time disability – each patient saw the psychologist, who found the following: six people presented with mild to severe depression and one with agitated depression; five suffered from generalized anxiety and pain-management problems; two showed a tendency to catastrophize; and nine had a maladaptive pain and stress disorder. Altogether, 22 of the 38 suffered partial to severe psychological co-morbidities, which in two cases led to a change of diagnosis in the psychological sphere and entailed psychosomatic in-patient medical treatment.

Recommendations for Disability Management

Recommendations for DM of all the workers in our program were made, as shown in Table 14.3. The disability management statement contains a case-dependent recommendation for the introduction of medical exercise-therapy in the company's physiotherapy department; for the continuation of physiotherapy; or, if appropriate, for out-patient psychotherapy. If required, recommendation was made for immediate – that is, within 14 days – outpatient or in-patient medical or professional rehabilitation in the clinic, or for an application for social benefits (for severe disability, counselling for addiction, financial advice, etc.). According to the performance profile, integration into the former workplace was recommended, or, if necessary, a temporary shift to 'protected' employment, or changes to the workplace. In the event that after in-patient rehabilitation the participant had lost the capacity to work in the job for which they were qualified, application was made to the pension fund for occupational rehabilitation in order that the participant regain a capacity for participation in professional life. The patient confirmed their acceptance of the proposals by signing the short medical report upon discharge. The report with the proposals concerning the diagnosis, functional disability, disability management, laboratory values and the FCE protocol were communicated immediately to all participating physicians. Directly after the testing, the employee presented him/herself to their employer as well as to the occupational physician for further adjustment of the recommended activities.

Table 14.3   Recommendations made for all participants (N = 38)

Recommendations for Rehabilitation	
Outpatient physiotherapy	6 (16%)
Medical exercise therapy	22 (58%)
Psychological therapy	8 (21%)
Occupational therapy	2 (5%)
Inpatient rehabilitation	9 (24%)*
Recommendations for Disability Management	
Return to work at the same workplace	22 (58%)
Internal occupational rehabilitation	10 (26%)
Internal occupational rehab; no night shift	4 (11%)
Occupational rehabilitation with pension	2 (5%)
Application for severe disability status	4 (11%)

Note: * Two psychological inpatient rehabilitations recommended.

EFFECTIVE DISABILITY MANAGEMENT OF THE SAMPLE (N = 27)

After transmission of the reintegration data by the enterprise to time t2, and through a follow-up survey of the employees, we found that reintegration into the former workplace was possible in 15 of the 27 cases, that is, more than 55 per cent of participants. In 10 cases, the integration team arranged – through a change of employment contract by the human resources department of the enterprise – a position in the workplace that matched the relevant employee's capacities according to the FCE performance. For two of the 27, benefits were applied for under the rehabilitation and participation in working life scheme of the German state pension fund. In five cases, in-patient rehabilitation in our clinic was begun immediately.

MEASUREMENT OF EFFECT SIZES BY THE IRES II QUESTIONNAIRE

In Table 14.4, the statistical data for calculating effect sizes are reproduced in the sample group (N = 27).

After the disability management intervention and a mean follow-up period of seven months, significant, permanent, slightly moderate-to-medium long-term effects appear in the participants' subjective views of their workloads. Mainly in the subcategory level 'occupational stress', a slightly moderate-to-medium long-term advance was present, with an effect size of 0.39; in the category 'stress caused by intensity of the work = impact of work' we see a medium effect size of 0.64. The main category 'functional status' was improved, with a slightly moderate-to-medium effect size of 0.37. The domains 'pain and symptoms' and 'disability in daily life' also improved, though not significantly.

Table 14.4 Statistical data: changes to self-assessment questionnaire IRES II (N = 27)

Statistical Data	t-score	fg	p-value	effect size
Domain				
rehab status	.88	26	ins.	.17
Main domains				
somatic status	.93	27	ins.	.18
functional status	1.92	27	.031*	.37
psychosocial status	.33	27	ins.	.08
Sub-domains				
pain & symptoms	1.15	27	ins.	.22
occupational stress	1.87	23	.036*	.39
impact of work^2	3.13	24	.002**	.64
disability in daily life	1.34	27	ins.	.25
psychological stress	.42	27	ins.	.03
social problems	.17	27	ins.	.18

T-testing with hypothesis to = t2; p-value: α=5%;

*p < .05; **p = .01; ins. = insignificant. fg = degree of freedom; effect size: < 0.4 = moderate, 04–0.8 = mean, > 0.8 = high.

^{2} = Item

Participants' Assessments of the DM Program

After the follow-up observations, study participants were asked their views of the program. The rate of return for this survey was 86 per cent. Three-quarters (74 per cent) of respondents agreed (strongly, mostly or partly) that the FCE testing was important to achieving workplace adjustments to suit their abilities. For 78 per cent, the testing was important to their understanding of their own capacities after having experienced injury or illness. Seventy per cent of respondents said that they would actively recommend the DM program. However, 33 per cent of the participants recorded negative responses because their desire for some relief at work were not fulfilled due to misinterpretations and negative work attitude of the workers themselves.

DISCUSSION

Medical occupational rehabilitation benefits in Germany are the responsibility of the state social security administration and employers' liability insurance associations. In a meta-analysis of randomized controlled trials (RCT) of medical rehabilitation among those in very different categories (including pensioners and unemployed), Hüppe and Raspe (2005) proved that the earlier, conservative medical treatment strategy had only a few, slight, long-term effects. In contrast, Streibelt et al. (2006) succeeded for the first time in demonstrating the high predictive value of intensified work-related programs, based on FCE testing and 'work hardening' training for patients with substantial work-related problems, in the context of medical rehabilitation. There is strong evidence that 80 per cent of workers who performed the intensified work-related program were still in their workplace one year later. A favourable cost-benefit effect was also proved in a later study (Streibelt et al. 2008). The first, highly significant, favourable, long-term results of a cluster-randomized study design were presented by Bethge et al. (2010). The aim of Bethge et al.'s study was an evaluation of the implementation and efficacy of an intensified multimodal work-related program using a cognitive behavioural approach, with the involvement of an FCE-related 'work hardening' training program (Bethge & Trowitzsch 2008), and labour and socio-medical experts from our Paracelsus Klinik. Bringing this knowledge to the debate about disability management, we accommodate in our diagnostics, rehabilitation, survey and DM program the new physical and psychological stresses of modern workplaces, as also outlined by Franchignoni, Oliveri and Bazzini (2006). In Germany, evaluations of outcomes from DM programs are currently only sporadic; the analysis presented in this chapter offers the first evidence we have of important data from a disability management program. The high rate of reintegration of performance-challenged employees into their former workplaces (more than 55 per cent) is a key outcome of our project. Furthermore, it is notable that severe chronification was detectable only after an average of 78.7 days off work because of disability in almost one-third of cases. In addition, our data seems to show that work-related behaviour type (according to the AVEM test) is an independent and self-contained predictor of a lower self-assessment of capacity and possibly partially responsible for a psychosocial barrier (low job satisfaction) to getting over the disability more quickly. Further research is needed in this area.

Data gained a year before and after FCE testing appear to show a trend towards reduction of work time lost from a median value 71.5 to 36.5 days. Five employees returned to work and continued to work regularly without any further absence due to health problems. In addition, there were a few highly conflict-driven employees whose long-term absence from work is above-average despite their going through a disability management program. A clear benefit results from this project for the health fund, as well for the enterprise involved, if we also take into account the early recovery from disability of approximately 45 per cent of the non-participants as a result of the DM program. There is an urgent need for research into the effects on those who did not participate in the study, who became employable again immediately after they were invited by the BKK case manager to participate in the program. A reason for this might be that there are 'protective behaviour' Type S people among the non-participants as well as participants, who show no great interest in overcoming their disability speedily and feel forced into doing so by a disability management program. It should be noted here that employees who have worked in any of the Salzgitter AG subsidiaries for 25 years have guaranteed salary security.

Conclusion

In spite of the small numbers in our study group, the following key statements can be made in light of our results:

1. That disability management is a reliable method for the effective and efficient reintegration of performance-challenged employees. It is proven that an intense, professional, disability management program can significantly and effectively reduce the stress of the participants. A positive work environment is necessary to the reintegration of performance-challenged employees.
2. Close collaboration with occupational physicians improves understanding of the actual situation at the performance-challenged employee's workplace and, after work-related FCE testing, leads to realistic recommendations about their capacity for reintegration.
3. A high – more than 50 per cent – presentation of psychological comorbidities among participants indicates the need to include careful psychological diagnosis, as well as a cognitive behavioural therapy module, in rehabilitation.
4. A trend to reduction in work hours lost to disability was seen, but the sample size was too small for this to be considered proven statistically.

Initial positive results from a similar project (*JobReha-Projekt*) have recently been reported by a study group at Gutenbrunner (Schwarze et al. 2008).

The affiliation of other international, heavy-industry companies to our project in 2008 and 2009 demonstrated the need for early, quality assured, functional and occupational capacity testing and rehabilitation, in order to keep older, performance-challenged employees in the workplace and to provide age-appropriate jobs for the future. Disability management appears to be beneficial for all involved. The present daily financing of the DM project cannot be maintained in routine treatment because of the high level of individual deployment; additional funds for the personnel-intensive FCE certificate will be pursued according to the guidelines of the Federal FCE Association.

Acknowledgment: For the translation, we thank Vivian Kley, and for copy-editing, we thank Kathleen Weekley.

Bibliography

Bethge, M. & Trowitzsch, L. (2008). Berufsbezogenes funktionelles Training in der Rehabilitation bei muskuloskelettalen Erkankungen. In A. Hillert, W. Müller-Fahrnow & F. M. Radoschewski (eds), *Medizinisch-beruflich orientierte Rehabilitation. Grundlagen und klinische Praxis*, (163–68). Köln: Deutscher Ärzte-Verlag.

Bethge, M., Herbold, D., Trowitzsch, L. & Jacobi, C. (2010). Berufliche Wiedereingliederung nach einer medizinisch-beruflich orientierten orthopädischen Rehabilitation: Eine cluster-randomisierte Studie. *Rehabilitation* 49: 2–12.

DRV-Bund, Rentenzugangsarten (2007). Available at: http://www.deutsche-rentenversicherung-bund.de/nn_7130/SharedDocs/de/Inhalt/04_Formulare_Publikationen/03_publikationen/Statistiken/Broschueren/rv_in_zahlen_2008_pdf.html, accessed 24 October 2009.

Franchignoni F., Oliveri M. & Bazzini G. (2006). Work Rehabilitation Programs: Work Hardening and Work Conditioning. In Ch. Gobelet & F. Franchignoni (eds), *Vocational Rehabilitation* (95–130). Collection de l'ácadémie. Europénne de medicine de reéadaptation. Paris: Springer-Verlag.

Gerdes, N. & Jäckel, W.H. (1995). Der IRES-Fragebogen für Klinik und Forschung. *Rehabilitation* 34: XIII–XXIV.

Hauser, F., Schubert, A. & Aicher, M. (2005). Unternehmenskultur und Mitarbeiterengagement in den Unternehmen in Deutschland. Abschlussbericht Forschungsprojekt Nr. 18/05. Ein Forschungsprojekt des Bundesministeriums für Arbeit und Soziales.

Hüppe, A. & Raspe, H. (2005). Zur Wirksamkeit von stationärer medizinischer Rehabilitation in Deutschland bei chronischen Rückenschmerzen: Aktualisierung und methodenkritische Diskussion einer Literaturübersicht. *Rehabilitation* 44, 24–33.

Isernhagen, S.J. (1988). Functional Capacity Evaluation. In S.J. Isernhagen (ed.), *Work Injury: Management and Prevention* (139–74). Gaithsburg MD: Aspen Publishers.

Isernhagen, S.J. (1991). Physical Therapy and Occupational Rehabilitation. *Journal of Occupational Rehabilitation* 1, 71–82.

Kaiser, H., Kersting, M., Schian, H.M., Jacobs A. & Kasprowski D. (2000). Der Stellenwert des EFL-Verfahrens nach Susan Isernhagen in der medizinischen und beruflichen Rehabilitation. *Rehabilitation* 39, 297–306.

Korsukéwitz, Ch. & Rehfeld, U. (2006). Medizinische und berufliche Rehabilitation der Rentenversicherung-aktueller Stand und Perspektiven. *RVaktuell* 53(11): 449–60.

Linton, S.J. & Nordin, E.A. (2006). A 5-Year Follow-up Evaluation of the Health and Economic Consequences of an Early Cognitive Behavioral Intervention for Back Pain: A Randomized, Controlled trial. *Spine* 31, 853–58.

Margraf, J. (ed.). (1994). *Diagnostisches Kurz-Interview bei psychischen Störungen*. Heidelberg: Springer-Verlag.

Matheson, L.N. (1988). Symptom Magnification Syndrome. In S.J. Isernhagen (ed.), *Work Injury: Management and Prevention*, (257–82). Gaithersburg MD: Aspen Publishers.

Matheson, L.N. & Matheson, M.L. (1996). Spinal Functional Sort. Performance Assessment and Capacity Testing (PACT). Schweizerische Arbeitsgemeinschaft für Rehabilitation SAR, Arbeitsgruppe Ergonomie, Bellikon. *Journal of Occupational Rehabilitation* 6(3): 159–75.

Merten, T., Friedel, E. & Stevens, A. (2007). Die Authentizität der Beschwerdenschilderung in der neurologisch-psychiatrischen Begutachtung. *Praxis der Rechtspsychologie* 17(1): 140–54.

NIDMAR. National Institute of Disability Management and Research (1994). Available at: http://www.nidmar.ca/index.asp, accessed 20 July 2009.

Niehaus, M., Magin, J., Marfels, B., Vater, E.G. & Werkstetter, E. (2008). Betriebliches Eingliederungsmanagement. Studie zur Umsetzung des Betrieblichen Eingliederungsmanagement nach § 84 Abs.2 SGB IX. *Auftraggeber*. Köln: Bundesministerium für Arbeit und Soziales.

Oesch, P., Bircher S., Kool, J., Knüsel, O. & Bachmann, S. (2003). Reconditioning of Patients with Chronic Back Pain: The Importance of Indicators for Symptom Magnification Syndrom. *Phys Med Rehab Kuror* 13:149–58.

Quebec Task Force on Spinal Disorders (1987). Scientific Approach to the Assessment and Management of Activity-Related Spinal Disorders. A Monograph for Clinicians. *Spine* 12: 9–54.

Salzgitter BKK. (2008). Internal Report.

Salzgitter BKK. (2009). *Gesundheitsreport 2009*. Available at: http://bkk.de/bkk/psfile/downloaddatei/45/BKK_Gesund474c1228ea649.pdf, accessed 20 July 2009.

Schaarschmidt, U. & Fischer, A. (1996). *Arbeitsbezogenes Verhaltens- und Erlebensmuster (AVEM)*. Göttingen: Hogrefe-Verlag GmbH & Co. KG..

Schmidt, C.O. & Kohlmann, T. (2005). Was wissen wir über das Symptom Rückenschmerz? Epidemiologische Ergebnisse zu Prävalenz, Inzidenz, Verlauf, Risikofaktoren. *Zeitschrift für Orthopädie* 143: 292–98.

Schubmann, R., Zwingmann, C., Graban, I. & Hölz, G. (1997). Ergebnisqualität stationärer Rehabilitation bei Patienten mit Adipositas. *Deutsche Rentenversicherung* 9–10: 604–25.

Schwarze, M., Fischer, M., Kreiß, T., Rebe, T., Wribitzky, R. & Gutenbrunner, C. (2008). JobReha-occupational Prevention and Rehabilitation Program for Patients with Musculoskeletal Disorders: Physician- and Patient-Reported Outcomes. *Journal for Rehabilitation Medicine* 47 (Suppl.): 50–51.

Streibelt M., Dohnke B., Rybicki T. & Müller-Fahrnow W. (2006). Verbesserungen der Aktivitäten und beruflichen Teilhabe durch ein EFL-zentriertes MBO-Modell in der MSK-Rehabilitation: Mittelfristige Ergebnisse einer randomisierten Studie. In W. Müller-Fahrnow, T. Hansmeier & M. Karoff. (eds), *Wissenschaftliche Grundlagen der medizinisch-beruflich orientierten Rehabilitation* (323–35). Lengerich: Pabst Science Publishers.

Streibelt, M., Blume, C., Thren, K. & Müller-Fahrnow, W. (2008). Economic Evaluation of Medically Occupationally Orientated Rehabilitation in Patients with Musculoskeletal Disorders. A Cost-Benefit Analysis from the Perspective of the German Statutory Pension Insurance Scheme (MBO). *Rehabilitation* 47: 150–57.

Trowitzsch, L. & Rust, B. (2000). Experience with the Bad Gandersheim Model for Complex Rehabilitation. Building a Lower Saxony Competency Network for Dovetailing of medical and Vocational Rehabilitation in Patients with Chronic Low Back Pain. *Rehabilitation* 39: 291–96.

Trowitzsch, L., Schiller, W., Lindner, S. & Thiele, D.A. (2006). Who Returns to Work? 2-Jahresergebnisse nach berufsorientierenden Maßnahmen im BFW Goslar (1998–2001). Neue Konzeption von MBOR in den drei Paracelsus-Kliniken Bad Gandersheim. In W. Müller-Fahrnow, T. Hansmeier & M. Karoff (eds), *Wissenschaftliche Grundlagen der medizinischen Rehabilitation* (428–36). Lengrich: Pabst Science Publisher.

Van Nieuwenhuyse, A., Somville, P.R., Crombez G., Burgdorf A., Verbeke G.,Johannik K., Van den Bergh, O., Masschelein, R., Mairiaux, P.. & Moens, G.F. (2006). The Role of Physical Workload and Pain-Related Fear in the Development of Low Back Pain in Young Workers: Evidence from the BelCOBack Study; Results after One Year of Follow Up. *Journal of Occupational and Environmental Medicine* 63: 45–52.

Waddell, G. (1998). *The Back Pain Revolution*. London: Churchill Livingstone.

Waddle, G. & Norlund A.I. (2000). Review of Social Security. In A. Nachemson & E. Jonsson (eds), *Neck and Back Pain: The Scientific Evidence of Causes, Diagnosis and Treatment* (427–71). Philadelphia: JB Lippincott.

Weber, A., Weber, U. & Raspe H. (1999). Medizinische Rehabilitation bei Langzeitarbeitsunfähigkeit. *Rehabilitation* 38: 220–26.

15 Occupational Stress and Mental Illness: An Overview for Disability Managers

SHANNON L. WAGNER AND HENRY G. HARDER[1]

Introduction

Workplace mental illness has become an issue of growing concern to the disability community. Recent literature suggests that if mental illness and stress-related claims continue on the current trajectory, they may soon become the leading source of disability costs in Canada (WorkSafeBC 2006). Several potential explanations for the higher costs of stress and mental illness claims have been proposed and include longer duration of such claims as well greater possibility of litigation. Regardless of specific cause, the high cost of stress and mental health disability has resulted in increased attention from affected stakeholders. Accordingly, disability management practitioners (DMPs) are increasingly being called upon to provide information about intervention and accommodation for these types of disabilities. This chapter is intended to provide some background information and suggestions for disability management professionals.

Costs of Occupational Stress and Mental Illness

The financial, human and societal costs associated with occupational stress and mental illness are staggering. Research has demonstrated convincing evidence of a connection between occupational stress and absenteeism, employee turnover, impaired performance and productivity, accident rates, unsafe work practices and disciplinary problems (DeFrank & Ivancevich 1998; Noonan & Wagner 2010; WHO 2004) such that the overall cost of stress on workplace performance has been estimated at US$20–30 billion annually (Tillman & Beard 2001). Furthermore, stress-related workers' compensation claims are increasing at a rate suggesting that they will soon become the prevailing occupational disease (Greenburg et al. 1993). Elkin and Rosch (1990) suggest that approximately 54 per cent of absenteeism is related to workplace stress, and their suggestion is further supported by Coyle's (2005) contention that according to Canadian employers, stress creates the most significant drain on employee productivity. Links between occupational

---

1   The authors gratefully acknowledge the contributions of Kerry Phillips to the completion of this chapter.

stress and health care costs demonstrate that approximately 75–90 per cent of physician visits are stress-related (Sutherland 1991) and that workplace stress accounts for 16 per cent of variance in health care costs and 21.5 per cent of variance in the number of health claims (Manning, Jackson & Fusilier 1996). Moreover, research from the National Institute for Occupational Health and Safety (NIOSH 1999) illustrates that there is a stronger association between health complaints and workplace stress than between health complaints and stresses not linked to the worksite (i.e., family and/or financial stress).

On the topic of costs related to workplace stress, MacQueen, Patriquin and Intini (2007: 2) stated that 'stress is part of an explosion in workplace mental health issues now costing the Canadian economy an estimated \$33 billion a year in lost productivity, as well as billions more in medical costs'. The same article suggested that mental health claims are 'now the fastest-growing category of disability insurance claims in Canada' (p. 2) with approximately one million Canadians afflicted. The conclusions of these authors were further supported by other work suggesting that estimates for the costs of short- and long-term disability claims in Canada range from \$15 to \$33 billion annually, with present estimates for mental health claims estimated at 30 per cent of all disability claims and about 70 per cent of total costs (Stephens & Joubert 2001; Sroujian 2003).

Canada is not the only nation feeling the impact of occupational stress. In the United States, one quarter of employees surveyed by Northwestern National Life (1991) listed their jobs as their most prevalent source of stress, and in a survey of key international stakeholders in the European Union, 90 per cent of respondents suggested that stress was a cause of disease in their country (Iavicoli as cited in WHO 2004). Further, Wagner, Danczyk-Hawley and Reid (2000: 18) stated that, for the US disability insurance industry, psychiatric disabilities 'are the primary diagnosis in 10 per cent to 20 per cent of disability claims and the secondary diagnosis in up to 65 per cent of disability claims, costing \$150 billion annually'. In Germany, 98 per cent of German work councils have reported a recent increase in work pressure and 85 per cent reported an increase in overall working hours (WHO 2004).

For employers, the cost of occupational stress can take many forms, including absenteeism, lost productivity, higher medical costs and staff turnover, as well as indirect costs such as recruitment and training of new workers (Goetzel et al. 2002). Burton and colleagues (2005: 774) demonstrated that occupational stress predicted reduced productivity and efficiency and stated that 'those who were dissatisfied with life report 4.5 per cent lost productivity, those with high stress 4.1 per cent lost productivity, those dissatisfied with their jobs lose 3.0 per cent and those who report poorer health lost 1.9 per cent productivity'. Further, Leontaridi and Ward (2002) found that work stress not only predicted absenteeism, but also predicted a greater intention to resign.

Clearly, one of the most serious consequences of occupational stress is mental illness, an aspect of occupational health that is receiving increasing attention. It can be assumed that the increased interest by employers regarding psychiatric illness is intimately related to the acknowledgement of related costs. Kessler and Frank (1997) found that for employees with psychiatric illness, there was a threefold increase in the number of short-term and cut-back work loss days. Further, they demonstrated that for respondents with a dual diagnosis, this difference increased by a twenty-fivefold magnitude. Mental illnesses that result in longer-term disability claims are also very costly. In 1992, the estimated cost for a mental health claim was approximately US\$12,645 (AWCBC 1996) and it has presumably increased exponentially since that time. Mental injury claims are estimated to be 52 per cent more costly overall than traumatic bodily injury and a portion of this increased total cost can be accounted for by the fact that mental injury claims tend to be of longer duration than physical injury claims – an average of 39 weeks versus an average of 24 weeks, respectively (Elisburg 1994). Other possible explanations for this discrepancy include the fact that mental disability claims are more often appealed and/or contested than are physical injury claims; another factor is the inherently multicausal nature of mental injury claims (Gnam 2000). In many instances, traumatic bodily injury is clearly the result of workplace practice, whereas the links between the workplace and mental injury tend to be blurred by the multitude of other potentially contributing factors.

Plausibly Linked Mental Illness

Case management of mental illness and workplace stress has become a primary function of the DMP role. Consequently, disability managers should become familiar with those mental illnesses most plausibly linked with occupational stress and the working environment. Workplace-related assessments for mental disorders are normally completed by a psychologist or psychiatrist, but can also be completed by a family physician. Assessments for issues related to workplace stress and/or mental disorder will normally be guided by the most current edition of the Diagnostic and Statistical Manual of Mental Disorders (DSM). The DSM provides guidelines of clinical criteria related to diagnosable disorders. Often, a DSM diagnosis is the requisite criteria for disability benefits related to issues of mental health.

Few studies have specifically looked at the link between the workplace and particular mental disorders. However, Gnam (2000) suggests that major depressive disorder, mood disorder (not otherwise specified (NOS)), post-traumatic stress disorder (PTSD) and anxiety disorder (NOS) have the highest plausibility of workplace causation – these disorders are likely most commonly linked to the workplace via the experience of occupational stress and traumatic exposure. This is not an inconsequential link as the costs associated with depression alone are alarming. The World Health Organization (2010) estimates that by the year 2020, depression will be the most common cause of disability in the world.

Major depressive disorder (MDD) is characterized by a group of symptoms lasting a period of two weeks or longer and including as a primary symptom either depressed mood or loss of interest and/or pleasure in normally enjoyed activities; these symptoms must be evident nearly every day for most of the day. A diagnosis of major depressive disorder also requires five or more of the listed symptoms to be evident for a given two-week period, in combination with depressed mood or loss of interest. The seven additional possible symptoms, from which a minimum of five must be present, include a change in body weight (not due to dieting), sleep disturbance, psychomotor agitation or retardation, fatigue or loss of energy, feelings of worthlessness or guilt, diminished ability to concentrate or make decisions and/or suicidal ideation/intent. In addition to these symptoms, a diagnosis of MDD requires that no evidence of mania is present, the symptoms are not better accounted for by another disorder, the symptoms are not related to substance use or a general medical condition and the symptoms are not better accounted for by bereavement. Also, it must be clear that an individual's symptoms are creating clinically significant distress or impairment in important areas of functioning.

MDDs also include a multitude of specifiers such as mild, moderate or severe intensity, with catatonic features, with atypical features, etc. In contrast to the clarity of diagnostic criteria for MDD, the criteria for mood disorder (NOS) is vague in its description and according to the DSM-IV TR (APA 2000: 410) 'includes disorders with mood symptoms that do not meet the criteria for any specific mood disorder and in which it is difficult to choose between Depressive Disorder Not Otherwise Specified and Bipolar Disorder Not Otherwise Specified (e.g., acute agitation)'.

Little additional information is provided with respect to mood disorder (NOS); however, the DSM-IV TR provides substantial additional information with respect to MDD. Specifically, the DSM suggests that MDD is up to twice as common in adolescent and adult females as it is in the same population of males. However, in children these gender differences are not evident. Prevalence estimates for MDD do not appear to be influenced by demographic factors and have generally ranged from 10 to 25 per cent for women and 5 to 12 per cent for men (lifetime prevalence). The average age of onset for MDD is in the mid-20s, with evidence suggesting a higher chance of recurrence subsequent to each separate episode. MDD is estimated to be 1.5–3 times more likely in first-degree family members of an individual diagnosed with MDD, as compared to the general population. An important feature of MDD is its noted relationship with a high rate of mortality and disability. Death by suicide occurs in 15 per cent of individuals diagnosed with MDD, and this disorder is associated with high rates of pain, physical illness and decreased physical, social and role functioning. Particularly important for disability managers is the knowledge that:

> up to 20–25 per cent of individuals with certain medical conditions (e.g., diabetes, myocardial infarction, carcinomas, stroke) will develop Major Depressive Disorder during the course of their general medical condition. The management of the general medical condition is more complex and the prognosis is less favorable if Major Depressive Disorder is present. In addition, the prognosis of Major Depressive Disorder is adversely affected (e.g., longer episodes or poorer responses to treatment) by concomitant chronic general medical conditions. (APA 2000: 371)

Similar to mood disorder not otherwise specified, anxiety disorder not otherwise specified is a catch all category that 'includes disorders with prominent anxiety or phobic avoidance that do not meet criteria for any specific Anxiety Disorder, Adjustment Disorder with Anxiety and Depressed Mood' (APA 2000: 484) and little additional information is provided regarding prevalence, familial linkages, differential diagnosis, etc. In contrast, post-traumatic stress disorder (PTSD) is a well-defined mental disorder with clear diagnostic criteria. A diagnosis of PTSD first requires that an individual experienced, witnessed or was confronted with actual or threatened death, serious injury or threat to physical integrity of oneself or others. During the experience of this event, the individual must have experienced a response involving intense fear, helplessness or horror. Given the experience of a suitable event, a series of additional symptoms must be present in order for the clinical criteria to be considered met. Specifically, the individual must report one symptom that suggests a persistent re-experiencing of the event. For example, such symptoms may include recurrent and intrusive recollections, recurring distressing dreams, acting or feeling as if the event were reoccurring, intense psychological exposure to cues about the event and/or physiological reactivity to triggers related to the event. Other required criteria include a minimum of three symptoms related to avoidance of psychological or physical reminders of the event. That is, an individual must report symptoms such as actively attempting to suppress thoughts, feelings or conversations about the event, actively attempting to avoid people and situations related to the event, a sense of a foreshortened future, a feeling of detachment from others and a restricted range of affect. Other symptoms related to a diagnosis of PTSD very closely resemble the symptoms of MDD, often making differential diagnosis between these two disorders difficult. Similar to MDD, the diagnostic criteria for PTSD includes a marked lack of interest or pleasure in previously enjoyed activities, sleep disturbance and difficulty concentrating. Symptoms that may help distinguish PTSD in the process of differential diagnosis includes increased irritablility and/or hostility, hypervigilance and an exaggerated startle response (APA 2000). In addition to the previously described symptoms, a diagnosis of PTSD requires that the duration of symptoms has been greater than one month. The experience of similar symptoms for a period less than one month should be considered using the diagnostic criteria for acute stress disorder (ASD).

Additional information with respect to PTSD suggests that the prevalence of PTSD in adult populations is approximately 8 per cent with significantly higher rates found in noticeably at-risk populations. The DSM states that for such high-risk groups as rape survivors, military combat victims, etc., the prevalence of PTSD may range between one-third and one-half of affected individuals. There is no average age of onset for PTSD given the requirement for a traumatic event. Symptoms often begin within three months after the trauma; however, symptoms may not appear for many months or even years. In approximately half of individuals presenting with symptoms of PTSD, the symptoms should be expected to resolve within a three-month period. Particularly difficult with respect to the workplace is the fact that 'avoidance patterns may interfere with interpersonal relationships and lead to marital conflict, divorce or loss of job' (APA 2000: 465). In addition to the impact of avoidance symptoms, the irriability and/or anger often displayed by individuals with PTSD may intimately impact workplace functioning and relationships (APA 2000).

Models of Occupational Stress

Given the reported links between issues of mental health and workplace stress/experience, it is important for disability managers to become familiar with accepted models of workplace stress. Knowledge of these models will provide DMPs with the theoretical background necessary to provide guidance to employers on issues related to workplace stress. Generally, occupational stress is viewed as a lack of alignment between the needs, capabilities and/or resources of the employee and the conditions of the worksite (NIOSH 1999). Although little agreement exists in the literature with respect to the precise definition of occupational stress, several important models of workplace stress are available, and knowledge of these models is important from the perspective of developing effective interventions and preventing mental illness.

DEMAND-CONTROL MODEL

Arguably the most well-known model intended to aid in the explanation of workplace stress is Karasek's (1979) job demand-control (JDC) model. The essential nature of this model postulates that high rates of psychological strain can be created by workplace environments where high workplace demand is experienced in interaction with low personal control (Bonn & Bonn 2000; Karasek 1979; Kristensen 1995). The central constructs of this original model were job control and job demand, the psychosocial aspects of work presumed to interact for the creation of Karasek's oft-cited 'job strain'. The description of job control included the degree of decision latitude provided to the employee with respect to completing job tasks. This concept of job control was seen to be a combination of employee skill level and degree of decision-making authority available within the employment position. On the other hand, job demand was described as the amount of psychological load attached to the job tasks as well as other concepts such as competing demands, appropriateness of expectations, work rate, etc. Although each of these concepts is considered to be important individually, the JDC model views the interaction of job demand and job control as the primary determinant of work-related stress/strain. Specifically, Karasek's original model predicted that workers in positions with high demand and low control would experience the greatest amount of job strain. In contrast, the model predicted that workers in positions with low demand and high control would experience the least amount of job strain. Alterations to the original model provide further predictions that high-demand, high-control jobs will encourage motivation, learning and engagement; in contrast, low-demand, low-control jobs are expected to create a sense of resignation in the employee, ultimately leading to low levels of motivation and engagement (Karasek & Theorell 1990).

A primary area of debate surrounding the original description of the JDC model was the interpretation of job strain as a singular construct. That is, Karasek's (1979) description of this model did not clearly describe whether he intended for the contributions of job demand and job control to be entirely additive in nature, or alternately, if these two variables interact in a synergistic fashion to create more job strain together than either one would be responsible for independently. Several authors have discussed this respective interaction term, given its interest with respect to occupational health outcomes (Karasek 1989; Schreurs & Taris 1998). Unfortunately, the literature is inconclusive on this issue as several authors have provided modest support for a synergistic interaction between the variables of job control and job demand (e.g., de Jonge & Kompier 1997; de Lange et al. 2003; Dwyer & Ganster 1991; Terry & Jimmieson 1999) while others have found that the primary relationship between these variables is additive (e.g., Barnett & Brennan 1997; Parkes, Mendham & Von Rabenau, 1994). Van der Doef and Maes (1998) criticized the literature in this area by pointing out the lack of studies investigating these competing hypotheses concurrently, using equivalent measures. Continued investigation regarding the interaction term for job control and job demand continues to be important given the practical implications of the competing interpretations (Pelfrene et al. 2002).

A secondary area of discussion regarding the original model has centred around the type of relation that exists between job conditions and health-related outcomes (Pisanti et al. 2003). Several authors suggest that the relationship between job conditions and health-related outcomes is a nonlinear relationship, one that follows a U-shaped distribution (Warr 1990, 1994). This type of distribution suggests that the interaction of high demand and high control may be valuable up to a certain level and then, when experienced beyond this given level, become detrimental. Several studies have provided data supporting the contention that job demand and control influence outcomes of well-being in this way (e.g., de Jonge & Schaufeli 1998; Pisanti et al. 2003).

In the 1980s, the work of Johnson and colleagues (e.g., Johnson and Hall 1989; Johnson 1989) highlighted the importance of social support as an additional variable in the prediction of workplace stress. In recognition of their work and the additional predictive power provided through the use of social support, Karasek and Theorell (1990) revised their model to become the job-demand-control-social support model (JDCS) model. This more recent model predicts that the highest levels of job strain will be experienced in situations where work environments have high demand and low control in combination with decreased levels of social support. This 'iso-strain' hypothesis generally suggests that the negative effects of high strain can be buffered by the existence of strong social support. The JDCS model has received support in the literature (Johnson & Hall 1989; Kristensen 1995; Pelfrene et al. 2001) and Verhaeghe et al. (2003: 267) contend that 'this three-dimensional model became one of the most influential models in research into the relationship between work stress and health'.

EFFORT-REWARD IMBALANCE MODEL

Another model that has received substantial attention in the literature is the effort-reward imbalance (ERI) model proposed by Seigrist (1996; 2001; Siegrist, Siegrist & Weber 1986). This model suggests that occupational stress is a function of the balance between the amount of effort expended by the worker and the appropriateness of the reward achieved as a result of this effort. Specifically, this theorist suggests that effort is determined by the demands and/or obligations placed upon the worker counteracted by the motivational level of the worker. Reward, on the other hand, is a function of factors related to financial remuneration, esteem and promotion/security, also counteracted by the motivational level of the worker. Seigrist's model proposes that effort and reward interact with one another as if on a teeter-totter whereby a balance between effort and reward is a desired state. Further, this model proposes that imbalance between effort and reward will be maintained despite the undesirability of an imbalanced state if the worker feels no alternative choice is available, if imbalance is maintained for strategic reasons or if the motivational pattern of the worker is consistent with 'over-commitment' (Weyers et al. 2006), and 'a set of attitudes, behaviors and emotions that reflect excessive striving in combination with the strong desire of being approved and esteemed' (Siegrist 2001: 55).

A primary distinction between the ERI model and the JDC model is the ERI's shift from work-related control to the social and economic rewards of work, as well as the suggestion that the greatest degrees of occupational strain will be related to situations where there is a lack of reciprocity between the efforts invested in work and the social and economic rewards resulting from such effort. An important social factor to consider when evaluating the ERI model is the fact that social rewards tend to be unevenly distributed within the marketplace. That is, very exhausting jobs, high in extrinsic effort, are often the positions most poorly rewarded, both in terms of financial and social rewards, i.e., manual labour (Rydstedt, Devereux & Sverke, 2007). The high strain related to such imbalanced positions has been considered as an important predictor for health outcomes (Van Vegchel et al. 2005).

Other research using the ERI as a model of workplace stress suggests that this model may be particularly useful within particular populations. For example, Tsutsumi and Kawakami (2004) suggest that the ERI may be particularly useful when investigating job strain for female workers, given the assumption that women may place more weight on the balance between effort and reward than upon control factors within the workplace. Furthermore, some authors have suggested that for human-service-related positions (e.g., nursing) the ERI may be a particularly appropriate method of investigating job strain (Calnan et al. 2004; Marmot et al. 1999).

PERSON-ENVIRONMENT FIT MODEL

Limitations of the ERI discussed by Van Vegchel et al. (2005) include the tendency to approach the model using dichotomous variables (e.g., balance versus imbalance) in place of a continuum from complete balance to complete imbalance. Further, these authors suggest that the variety of variables involved in both effort and reward may impede the ability to distinguish which particular variables are important for specific occupational groups. Both the ERI and JDC model have also been criticized for a potential lack of applicability across occupational groups (de Jonge & Dorman 2003; Kasl 1996) and lack of recognition for sources of strain other than physical effort and time pressure (Melamed, Kushnie & Meir 1991; Van der Doef & Maes 1999). The person-environment fit (P-E fit) model of stress approaches occupational stress from the perspective of the individual. This model was developed by researchers at the University of Michigan in the early 1970s and was developed on the premise that occupational stress could be reduced by ensuring a match between the worker and the workplace (Schwartz, Pickering & Landbergis 1996). Specifically, this model suggests that occupational stress is a function of the fit between the individual characteristics of the workers (e.g., personality, skill level, etc.) and the required characteristics of the work environment (Caplan et al. 1975; French, Caplan & Harrison 1982; Harrison 1978). The interaction between individuals and their environment is bidirectional. That is, it is characterized by abilities of workers meeting the needs of the workplace and the characteristics of the workplace meeting the needs of the workers (Cooper 1998; Cooper, Dewe & O'Driscoll 2001; Harrison 1985). The primary advantage of the P-E fit model lies in its consideration of individual characteristics as an important predictor of occupational stress (Edwards 1996). Noted issues with the usefulness of this model include difficulty understanding which individual and environmental factors are the most influential in the stress response (Harrison 1978; Schwartz, Pickering, & Landbergis 1996), as well as the lack of recognition for the important role of factors external to the individual and direct work environment, i.e., social context (Cooper, Dewe & O'Driscoll 2001).

Specific renditions of the P-E fit model include the supplies-values (S-V) fit (French, Caplan & Harrison 1982), the demands-abilities (D-A) fit (Edwards 1996) and the isomorphic theory of stress (Quick et al. 2001). The S-V fit approach suggests that occupational stress can be reduced via an appropriate fit between an individual's values and the characteristics of the worksite. In this case, worker strain would be increased if the tasks of the worksite were inconsistent with personal values. In contrast, the D-A fit approach is concerned with the fit between the characteristics of the worksite and the perceived ability of the worker. This model suggests that occupational stress would be at its lowest when an individual feels their personal capabilities are consistent with that which is necessary to adequately complete required tasks. In contrast to the previously discussed two-dimensional models, the three-dimensional isomorphic theory of stress proposes that occupational stress is a function of fit between the individual and the work environment on the dimensions of control, uncertainty and interpersonal relations.

The basic tenant of this theory is that low strain will occur in situations where there is good fit between the individual and the environment on all three dimensions and that increasing strain will occur in situations where there is less fit between the individual and the environment on any of the dimensions.

TRANSACTIONAL MODEL

The final model to be discussed here is the transactional model based upon Lazarus' (1966) transactional theory. This approach views stress from a transactional perspective in which the individual is presumed to engage in dynamic cognitive evaluation of the environment. This model goes beyond the objective stressors and emphasizes process, a process by which the individual is expected to appraise the situation and individual coping mechanisms available for adapting to one's environment (Cooper, Dewe & O'Driscoll 2001). Resources are presumed to be influenced by personal characteristics, such as individual personality factors (e.g., Barnett & Baruch 1985; Kobasa 1982; Maddi & Kobasa 1984; Vebrugge 1983) and personal resources, such as active coping strategies and perceived social support (Baruch, Barnett & Rivers 1983; Billings & Moos 1981; Kobasa 1982; Pearlin & Schooler 1978). In contrast to the previously discussed models, the transactional approach suggests that strain will occur when there is an imbalance between demand and the resources available to manage the demand (Gardner et al. 2005). In addition, previous work suggests that cognitive appraisal related to the demand-resource relationship influences the degree of strain experienced (Folkman & Lazarus 1988; Lazarus 1966).

Lazarus proposes three levels of cognitive appraisal within his transactional theory. Primary appraisal involves the individual making a determination about the significance of the encounter. Specifically, at this stage the environment is evaluated in order to determine whether the situation should be considered irrelevant, benign or stressful. If the event is deemed to be stressful, a secondary appraisal will then occur. This secondary appraisal involves the individual evaluating current coping resources in order to determine whether such resources are sufficient for the demands of the present event. Finally, as the situation unfolds, reappraisal and/or re-evaluation of the relationship between demands and resources will continue (Lyon 2000).

The primary contribution of the transactional model is the recognition that cognitive appraisal mediates the stressor-strain relationship (Haslam, Jetten, O'Brien & Jacobs 2004). This recognition provides some explanation for individual differences in reactions to stressful events – that is, why some events are stressful for some people while they are appraised as benign by others. A criticism of this model, however, also follows from its focus on individual appraisal. Specifically, by focusing on subjective appraisal of stressful events, overarching organizational stressors may be overlooked (Brief & Goerge 1991).

Workplace Accomodations

Within the current workplace, a primary role of DMPs has become intervention and accommodation for workplace stress and mental illness. Armed with knowledge regarding theoretical models of workplace stress, disability managers can make evidence-based suggestions and recommendations to employers. Furthermore, knowledge of costs related to workplace stress/mental illness, as well as familiarity with those mental illnesses most plausibly connected to the workplace, allow DMPs to provide stakeholders with information and advice about managing workplace stress and mental health disability, reducing related costs and providing appropriate workplace accommodations consistent with current legislative requirements.

Due to the competitive nature of today's work environment, many employees may be hesitant to admit to difficulty handling stress in the workplace; even fewer may be comfortable discussing their mental health issues with their employers. Moreover, many individuals may not seek treatment for their illness out of fear related to the associated stigma resulting from a diagnosis of mental illness. Goldberg, Killeen & O'Day (2005) found that employees believed co-workers, employers and others discriminated against them or other people with disabilities and, therefore, participants reported that most often they did not disclose their disability. Individuals with mental illness may fear people will label them as uneducated, indolent, unreliable, unpredictable or unable to cope with workplace pressures/stress if they disclose an experience of mental illness.

Mental ill-health should be recognized and accommodated in the workplace in a manner similar to other forms of illness and disability. Carling (1993) found that employers require education regarding reasonable accommodations in the workplace for persons with psychiatric disabilities in order to be better equipped to serve and retain their employees. Mancuso (1990) reported that prior to the implementation of the Americans with Disability Act, a search of the Job Accommodation Network (n.d.) data banks indicated that only 1 per cent of over 8,000 accommodations documented concerned psychiatric disabilities. Currently, employers report substantial growth in the demand for information regarding appropriate accommodations for people with psychiatric disabilities, which suggests a trend towards increasing accommodation efforts in this area. The Job Accommodation Network (n.d.) provides a more recent list of accommodations that may benefit employees suffering with mental illnesses in the workplace, including:

1. additional time to learn new responsibilities
2. self-paced work load
3. time off for counselling
4. use of supportive employment and job coaches
5. graduated work schedules
6. reduce distractions in the work area.

Similarly, Fabian, Waterworth and Ripke (1993) gathered information from client files kept by service providers on 231 job modifications for 47 jobs among 30 supported employees. In this study the following reasonable accommodations were identified: altering job tasks; adjusting hours or schedule; providing orientation and training to co-workers and supervisors; adapting the non-physical work environment by providing physical assistance at the job site; and modifying workplace social norms. The accommodation most frequently used was providing orientation and training to supervisors and co-workers.

Watson Wyatt (2002) recommended that employers implement the following strategies in order to reduce the impact and costs associated with occupational stress:

1. examine the frequency of short-term disability/long-term disability claims;

2. review return-to-work policies;
3. prepare education programs about causes, symptoms and treatment in order to overcome stigmatization;
4. look at internal culture to determine if there are internal issues such as harassment or conflict between management and employees; and
5. implement employee assistance programs (EAPs).

Marine et al. (2006) conducted a review of 19 studies from various countries looking at different stress management strategies. The interventions listed below all proved to be successful at reducing workplace stress and resulting mental ill-health.

*   cognitive behavioural therapy
*   relaxation training
*   therapeutic massage
*   multicomponent interventions, such as combining communication skill training, stress management training, and practical skills in problem-solving
*   music-making.

It was found that such interventions resulted in significantly reduced stress levels, reduced symptoms of burnout, reduced anxiety and an overall improvement in general health.

According to an article published by *Medical News Today* (2008: 23), 'a variety of studies have shown that for every dollar spent on a Corporate Wellness Program, the returns have been cost savings of up to $10.10 in the areas of decreased absenteeism, fewer sick days, reduced WSIB/WCB claims, lowered health and insurance costs, and improvements to employee performance and productivity'. It was further reported that, 'the Canadian Institute of Stress found that stress control programs alone can result in an 18 per cent reduction in absences, 32 per cent reduction in grievances, 52 per cent reduction in disability time, 7 per cent improvement in productivity, and 13 per cent improvement in service quality' (*Medical News Today* 2008: 24).

Due to the enormous toll unhealthy workplaces are taking on Canadian employers, the Canadian Mental Health Association (CMHA n.d.: 10) has recommended the following steps which employers can take to reduce occupational stress in the workplace:

*   offer flexible hours
*   allow workers to work from home where possible and appropriate
*   offer graduated return-to-work schedule
*   train managers on how to support work/life balance
*   encourage staff to stay home with sick children or elderly relatives when needed
*   eliminate unnecessary meetings
*   communicate expectations clearly to staff
*   allow staff to control their own priorities as much as possible.

Conclusion

In recent years the prevalence of reported occupational stress has increased, and subsequently so too have the costs for companies and organizations. The financial costs of occupational stress/mental illness can take many forms, including absenteeism, lost productivity, higher medical costs and staff turnover, as well as associated costs of recruiting and training new workers. More importantly, the human costs of occupational stress and mental illness may be immeasurable. Workplace stress is a reality in the modern workplace, with the prevalence of mental health and stress-related claims rising dramatically in the last decade. DMPs will be called upon more and more frequently to provide advice and guidance for these types of disabilities. Consequently, it is incumbent upon disability managers to become familiar with the literature in this area so that they can advise employers appropriately and provide awareness/education regarding responsibilities for necessary policies and supports.

Bibliography

Association of Workers' Compensation Boards of Canada (AWCBC). (1996). *Occupational Stress: How Canadian Workers' Compensation Boards Handle Stress Claims*. AWCBC report. British Columbia: AWCBC.

American Psychiatric Associaton. (2000). *Diagnostic and Statistical Manual of Mental Disorders*. (4th Ed.) text revision. Washington DC: APA.

Barnet, R.C. & Baruch, G.K. (1985). Women's Involvement in Multiple Roles and Psychological Distress. *Journal of Personality and Social Psychology* 49: 135–45.

Barnett, R.C. & Brennan, R.T. (1995). The Relationship between Job Experiences and Psychological Distress: A Structured Equation Approach. *Journal of Organizational Behavior* 16: 259–76.

Barnett, R.C. & Brennan, R.T. (1997). Change in Job Conditions, Change in Psychological Distress, and Gender: A Longitudinal Study of Dual-Earner Couples. *Journal of Organizational Behavior* 18: 253–74.

Baruch, G.K., Barnett, R.C. & Rivers, B. (1983). *Life Prints: New Patterns of Love and Work for Today's Women*. New York: McGraw-Hill.

Billings, A.G. & Moos, R. (1981). The Role of Coping Responses and Social Resources Attentuating the Stress of Life Events. *Journal of Behavioral Medicine* 4: 139–57.

Bonn, D. & Bonn, J. (2000). Workplace and Related Stress: Can it be a Thing of the Past? *Lancet* 355: 124.

Brief, A. P. & George, J.M. (1991). Psychological Stress and the Workplace: A Brief Comment on Lazarus' Outlook. *Journal of Social Behavior and Personality* 6: 15–20.

Burton, W., Chen, C., Conti, D., Schultz, A., Pransky, G. & Edington, D. (2005). The Association of Health Risks with On-the-Job Productivity. *Journal of Occupational and Environmental Medicine* 47(8): 769–77.

Calnan, M., Wadsworth, E., May, M., Smith, A. & Wainwright, D. (2004). Job Strain, Effort-Reward Imbalance, and Stress at Work: Competing or Complementary Models? *Scandinavian Journal of Public Health* 32: 84–93.

Canadian Mental Health Association. (n. d.) *Sources of Workplace Stress*. Richmond BC: CMHA.

Carling, P. (1993). Reasonable Accommodations in the Workplace for Individuals with Psychiatric Disabilities. *Consulting Psychology Journal* 45(2): 46–62.

Caplan, R.D., Cobb, S., French, J.R.P., Harrison, R.V. & Pinneau, S.R. (1975). *Job Demands and Worker Health*. Washington DC: National Institute for Occupational Safety and Health.

Cooper, C.L. (1998). *Theories of Organizational Stress*. London: Oxford Press.

Cooper, C.L., Dewe, P.J. & O'Driscoll, M.P. (2001). Organizational Stress: *A Review and Critique of Theory, Research, and Applications*. Thousand Oaks CA: Sage Publications.

Coyle, J. (2005). MP's Flight Sends Wrong Message on Stress. *Toronto Star*. 11 June.

DeFrank, R.S. & Ivancevich, J.M. (1998). Stress on the Job: An Executive Update. *Academy of Management Executive* 12(3): 55–66.

de Jonge, J. & Dorman, C. (2003). The DISC Model: Demand in these Strain Compensation Mechanisms and Job Stress. In M.F. Dollard, A.H. Winefield & H.R. Winefield, (eds), *Occupational Stress and the Service Professions* (43–74). London: Taylor & Francis.

de Jonge, J. & Kompier, M.A.J. (1997). A Critical Examination of the Demand-Control-Support Model from a Work Psychological Perspective. *International Journal of Stress Management* 4: 235–58.

de Jonge, J. & Schaufeli, W.B. (1998). Job Characteristics and Employee Well-being: A Test of Warr's Vitamin Model in Health Care Workers using Structural Equation Modeling. *Journal of Organizational Behaviour* 19: 387–407.

de Lange, A.H., Taris, T.W., Kompier, M.V., Houtman, I.L.D. & Bonger, P.M. (2003). 'The very Best of the Millennium' Longitudinal Research and the Demand-Control-(Support) Model. Journal of *Occupational Psychology* 8: 282–305.

Dwyer, D.J. & Ganster, D.C. (1991). The Effects of Job Demands and Control on Employee Attendance and Satisfaction. *Journal of Organizational Behavior* 7: 595–24.

Edwards, J.E. (1996). An Examination of Competing Versions of the Person-Environment Fit Approach to Stress. *Academy of Management Journal* 39(2): 292–339.

Elkin, A.J. & Rosch, P.G. (1990). Promoting Mental Health at Work. *Occupation Medicine State of the Art Review* 5: 739–54.

Elisburg, D. (1994). Workplace Stress: Legal Developments, Economic Pressures, and Violence. *John Burton's Workers' Compensation Monitor* 6: 12–19.

Fabian, E.S., Waterworth, A. & Ripke, B. (1993). Reasonable Accommodations for Workers with Serious Mental Illness: Type, Frequency and Associated Outcomes. *Psychosocial Rehabilitation Journal* 17(2): 163–72.

Folkman, S. & Lazarus, R. (1988). Ways of *Coping Questionnaire Manual*. Palo Alto CA: Consulting Psychologists Press Inc.

French, J.R.P., Jr., Caplan, R.D. & Harrison, R.V. (1982). *The Mechanisms of Job Stress and Strain*. New York: Wiley.

Gardner, B., Rose, J., Mason, O., Tyler, P. & Cushway, D. (2005). Cognitive Therapy and Behavioral Coping in the Management of Work-Related Stress: An Intervention Study. *Work and Stress* 19(2): 137–52.

Gnam, W. (2000). Psychiatric Disability and Workers' Compensation. In T. Sullivan (ed.), *Injury and the New World of Work* (305–28). UBC Press: Vancouver.

Goetzel, R., Ozminkowski, R., Sederer, L. & Mark, T. (2002). The Business Case for Quality Mental Health Services: Why Employers Should Care About the Mental Health and Well-Being of Their Employees. *Journal of Occupational & Environmental Medicine* 44(4): 320–30.

Goldberg, S., Killeen, M. & O'Day, B. (2005). The Disclosure Conundrum: How People with Psychiatric Disabilities Navigate Employment. *Psychology, Public Policy and Law* 11(3): 463–500.

Greenberg, P.E., Stiglin, L.E., Finkelstein, S.M. & Berndt, E.R. (1993). The Economic Burden of Depression in 1990. *Journal of Clinical Psychiatry* 54: 405–18.

Harrison, R.V. (1978). Person-Environment Fit in Job Stress. In C.L. Cooper & R. Payne (eds), *Stress at Work* (23–52). New York: Wiley.

Harrison, R.V. (1985). The Person Environment Fit Model and the Study of Job Stress. In T.A. Beehr & R.S. Bhagart (eds), Human Stress and Cognition in Organizations: An Integrated Perspective (23–52). New York: Wiley.

Haslam, S.A., Jetten, J., O'Brien, A. & Jacobs, E. (2004). Social Identity, Social. Influence, and Reactions to Potentially Stressful Tasks: Support for the Self-Categorization Model of Stress. Stress and Health 20: 3–9.

Job Accommodation Network (n.d.). Accommodation and Compliance Series: Employees with Mental Health Impairments. Available at: http://askjan.org/media/Psychiatric.html, accessed 1 August 2011.

Johnson, J.V. (1989). Control, Collectivity and the Psychosocial Work Environment. In S.L. Sauter, J.J. Hurrell & C.L. Cooper (eds), Job Control and Worker Health (46–74). Chichester: Wiley and Sons.

Johnson, J.V. & Hall, E. (1989). Job Strain, Workplace Social Support and Cardiovascular Disease: A Cross-Sectional Study of a Random Sample of the Swedish Working Population. American Journal of Public Health, 78, 1336–342.

Karasek, R. (1979). Job Demands, Job Decision Latitude, and Mental Strain: Implications for Job Redesign. Administrative Science Quarterly 24: 285–306.

Karasek, R. (1989). Control in the Workplace and its Health-Related Aspects. In S.L. Sauter, J.J. Hurrell & C.L. Cooper (eds), Job Control and Worker Health (129–60). Chichester: Wiley.

Karasek, R. & Theorell, T. (1990). Healthy Work: Stress, Productivity, and the Reconstruction of Working Life. New York: Basic Books.

Kasl, S.V. (1996). The Influence of the Work Environment on Cardiovascular Health: A Historical, Conceptual, and Methodological Perspective. Journal of Occupational Health Psychology 1(1): 42 –56.

Kessler, R.C. & Frank, R.G. (1997). The Impact of Psychiatric Disorders on Work Loss Days. Psychological Medicine 27: 861–73.

Kobasa, S.C. (1982). Stressful Life Events, Personality and Health: An Inquiry into Hardiness. Journal of Personality and Social Psychology 42: 707–17.

Kristensen, T.S. (1995). The Demand-Control-Support Model: Methodological Challenges for Future Research. Stress Medicine 11:17–26.

Lazarus, R. (1966). Psychological Stress and the Coping Process. New York: McGraw-Hill.

Leontaridi, R. & Ward, M. (2002). Work-Related Stress, Quitting Intentions and Absenteeism. IZA Discussion Papers 493. Institute for the Study of Labor (IZA), 1–26.

Lyon, B. (2000). Stress, Coping, and Health. In V. Rice (ed.), Handbook of Stress, Coping, and Health: Implications for Nursing Research, Theory, and Practice (3–23). Thousand Oaks CA: Sage Publications.

Maddi, S.R. & Kobasa, S.C. (1984). The Hardy Executive: Health Under Stress. Homewood IL: Dow Jones-Irwin.

MacQueen, K., Patriquin, M. & Intini, J. (2007). Workplace Stress Costs the Economy Billions. MacLean's Magazine. 15 October. Available at: http://www.thecanadianencyclopedia.com/index. cfm?PgNm=TCE&Params=M1ARTM0013158, accessed 12 March 2009.

Mancuso, L.L. (1990). Reasonable Accommodation for Workers with Psychiatric Disabilities. Psychosocial Rehabilitation Journal 14(2): 3–19.

Manning, M.R., Jackson, C.N. & Fusilier, M.R. (1996). Occupational Stress and Health Care Use. Journal of Occupational Health Psychology 1(1): 100–09.

Marine, A., Ruotsalainen, J., Serra, C. & Verbeek, J. (2006). Preventing Occupational Stress in Healthcare Workers. Cochrane Database Syst Rev 18 Oct; (4): CD002892.

Marmot, M., Siegrist, J., Theorell, M. & Feeney, A. (1999). Health and the Psycho-social Environment at Work. In M. Marmot & R.G. Wilkinson (eds), *Social Determinants of Health* (105–31). Oxford: Oxford University Press.

Medical News Today (2008). Mentally Unhealthy Workplaces taking an Enormous Toll in Canada. 5 May. Available at: http://www.medicalnewstoday.com/articles/106140.php, accessed 4 April 2009.

Melamed, S., Kushnie, T. & Meir, E. (1991). Attentuating the Impact of Job Demands: Added is an Interactive Effects of Perceived Control and Social Support. *Journal of Vocational Behavior* 39: 40–53.

National Institute for Occupational Health and Safety (NIOSH). (1999). *Stress at Work*. DHHS Publication No. 99–101. Available at: http://www.cdc.gov/niosh/stresswk.html, accessed 10 October 2005.

Noonan, J. & Wagner, S.L. (2010). Workplace Stress: Theory and Recommendations. *Journal of Vocational Evaluation and Work Adjustment.*

Northwestern National Life. (1991). *Employee Burnout: America's Newest Epidemic*. Minneapolis MN: Northwestern National Life Insurance Company.

Pearlin, L. & Schooler, C. (1978). The Structure of Coping. *Journal of Health and Social Behavior* 19: 2–21.

Quick, J.C., Nelson, D.L., Quick, J.D. & Orman, D.K. (2001). An Isomorphic Theory of Stress: The Dynamics of Person-Environment Fit. *Stress and Health* 17: 147–57.

Parkes, K., Mendham, C.A., Von Rabenau, C. (1994) Social Support and the Demand-Description Model of Job Stress: Tests of Additives and Interactive Effects of Two Samples, 44: 91–113.

Pelfrene, E. Vlerick, P., Mark, R.P., De Smet, P., Kornitzer, M. & DeBacker, G. (2001). Scale Reliability and Validity of the Karasek 'Job Demand-Control-Support' Model in the Belstress Study. *Work on Stress* 15: 297–313.

Pelfrene, E., Vlerick, P., Kittel, F., Mak, R.P., Kornitzer, M. & De Backer, G. (2001). Psychosocial Work Environment and Psychological Well-being: Assessment of the Buffering Effects in the Job Demands-Control (-Support) Model in BELSTRESS. *Stress and Health* 18: 43–56.

Pisanti, R., Pia Gagliardi, M., Razzino, S. & Bertini, M. (2003). Occupational Stress and Illness among Italian Secondary School Teachers. *Psychology and Health* 18(4): 523–36.

Rydstedt, L.W., Devereux, J. & Sverke, M. (2007). Comparing and Combining the Demand-Control-Support Model and the Effort Reward Imbalance Model to Predict Long-Term Mental Strain. *European Journal of Work and Organizational Psychology* 16(3): 261–78.

Schreurs, P.J.G. & Taris, T.W. (1998). Construct Validity of the Demand-Control Model: A Double Cross-Validation Approach. *Work Stress* 12: 66–84.

Schwartz, J.E., Pickering, T.G. & Landbergis, P.A. (1996). Work-Related Stress and Blood Pressure: Current Theoretical Models and Considerations from a Behavioral Medicine Perspective. *Journal of Occupational Health Psychology* 1(3): 287–310.

Siegrist J. (1996). Adverse Health Effects of High-Effort/Low-Reward Conditions. *Journal of Occupational Health Psychology* 1:27–41.

Siegrist, J. (2001). A Theory of Occupational Stress. In I.J. Dunham (ed.), *Stress in the Workplace: Past, Present and Future* (34–51). London: Whurr Publishers.

Siegrist, J., Siegrist, K. & Weber, I. (1986). Sociological Concepts in the Etiology of Chronic Disease: The Case of Ischemic Heart Disease. *Social Science and Medicine* 20: 247–53.

Sroujian, C. (2003). Mental Health is the Number One Cause of Disability in Canada. *Insurance Journal* August: 8.

Stephens, T., & Joubert, N. (2001) The Economic Burden of Mental Health Problems in Canada. *Chronic Diseases in Canada* 22(1): 18–23.

Sutherland, J.E. (1991). The Link between Stress and Illness. Do Our Coping Mechanisms Influence our Health? *Postgraduate Medicine* 89(1): 159–64.

Terry, G. & Jimmieson, N. (1999). Work Control and Employee Well-being: A Decade Review. In C.L. Cooper & I.T. Robertson (eds), *International Review of Industrial and Organizational Psychology* (vol. 14), (95–148). New York, NY: John Wiley and Sons.

Tilmann, J.N. & Beard, M.T. (2001). Manager's Healthy Lifestyles, Coping Strategies, Job Stressors, and Performance: An Occupational Stress Model. *The Journal of Theory Construction and Testing* 5(1): 7–11.

Tsutsumi, A. & Kawakami, N. (2004). A Review of Empirical Studies on the Model of Effort-Reward Imbalance at Work: Reducing Occupational Stress by Implementing a New Theory. *Social Science and Medicine* 59: 2335–359.

Van der Doef, M. & Maes, S. (1999). The Job Demands-Control-Support Model and Psychological Well-being: A Review of 20 Years of Empirical Research. *Work and Stress* 13(2): 87–114.

Van Vegchel, N., de Jonge, J., Bosma, H. & Schaufeli, W. (2005). Reviewing the Effort-Reward Imbalance Model: Drawing Up the Balance of 45 Empirical Studies. *Social Science and Medicine* 60: 1117–131.

Vebrugge, L.M. (1983). Multiple Roles and Physical Health of Women and Men. *Journal of Health and Social Behavior* 24: 16–30.

Verhaeghe, R., Mak, R., Van Maele, G., Kornitzer, M. & De Backer, G. (2003). Job Stress Among Middle-Aged Healthcare Workers and its relation to Sickness Absence. *Stress and Health* 19: 265–74.

Wagner, C., Danczyk-Hawley, C. & Reid, C. (2000). The Progression of Employees with Mental Disorders through Disability Benefits Systems. *Journal of Vocational Rehabilitation* 15: 17–29.

Warr, P.B. (1990). Decision Latitude, Job Demands, and Employee Well-being. *Work and Stress* 4: 285–94.

Warr, P.B. (1994). A Conceptual Framework for the Study of Work and Mental Health. *Work and Stress* 8: 84–97

Weyers, S., Peter, R., Boggild, H., Jeppesen, H.J. & Siegrist, J. (2006). Psychosocial Work Stress is Associated with Poor Self-Rated Health in Danish Nurses: A Test of the Effort-Reward Imbalance Model. *Scandinavian Journal of Caring and Science* 20(1): 26–34.

WorkSafe BC. (2006). *Demand Safety: Safety is a Shared Responsibility*. British Columbia: WorkSafe BC. Available at:

http://www.worksafebc.com/publications/reports/annual_reports/pub_10_20.asp, accessed 15 July 2011.

World Health Organization. (2004). *Mental Health and Working Life*. Available at: http://www.euro. who.int/document/mnh/ebrief06.pdf, accessed 10 October 2005.

World Health Organization (WHO). (2010). *Depression*. Available at: http://www.who.int/mental_health/management/depression/definition/en/, accessed 20 January 2010.

Wyatt, W. (2002). *Improving Workforce Productivity through Integrated Absence Management: Sixth Annual Survey Report 2001/2002,Watson Wyatt Worldwide and Washington Business Group on Health.* Available at:s http://www.watsonwyatt.com/research/resrender.asp?id =W-499&page=1, accessed 13 June 2009.

16 Type 2 Diabetes in the Workplace: Perspectives in Canada and the United States

MAMDOUH SHUBAIR

Introduction

Type 2 Diabetes (T2D), formerly known as non-insulin dependent diabetes mellitus (NIDDM), is a serious clinical and public health problem in Canada, the United States, and across the globe. T2D is a serious and costly disease, the prevalence of which is increasing at alarming rates. In the USA, it is the most common endocrine disorder of adults in the workforce (Akinci, Healey & Coyne 2003; Burton & Connerty 2002).

According to the Canadian Diabetes Association (CDA), more than 2 million Canadians had T2D in 2005 (quoted in Beuemann-King 2005). The estimate for 2009 was that 3 million Canadians had the disease. As T2D is rising in epidemic proportions, T2D will affect 3.7 million Canadians by 2020 (Canadian Diabetes Association 2009a). Worldwide, an estimated 285 million people are affected by diabetes; this number is expected to reach 438 million by 2030 (Canadian Diabetes Association 2009a). Diabetes is a leading cause of death – people with diabetes are four times more likely than those without to have complications or comorbidities, such as cardiovascular disease (CVD). T2D is also a leading cause of visual impairment leading to blindness (diabetic retinopathy), end-stage kidney disease (diabetic nephropathy) and non-traumatic lower-extremity amputation (Akinci, Healey & Coyne 2003; Eastman et al. 1997; Goldfarb et al. 2004; Resnick & Howard 2002). People with T2D suffer many psychological problems and mood disorders, and the rate of depression is three times higher than that for their non-diabetic counterparts (Anderson et al. 2001; Colagiun et al. 2006).

Each year, more Canadians and Americans are diagnosed with T2D. Many studies and reports have stated that the costs for managing this debilitating disease, when it is associated with comorbidities such as CVD, kidney disease (nephropathy), eye disease (retinopathy) and lower-limb amputations, are very high. The American Association of Clinical Endocrinologists, in a report, note that health care costs directly related to medical expenditures are three times higher for people with T2D than for those without the disease.

Most notably, T2D impacts workplace productivity (indirect costs). Current estimates of indirect costs include work absences (workers' absenteeism), disability leave and/or workforce exit – all these factors lead to diminished or lost productivity (Goldfarb et al. 2004; Lavigne et al. 2003). A December 2009 report, commissioned by the CDA, presents a 'Canadian diabetes cost model' which details the significant increase in the cost and prevalence of T2D in Canada, both of which have risen sharply over the past decade and are expected to continue to rise to epidemic proportions in the foreseeable future (Canadian Diabetes Association 2009b). The Canadian diabetes cost model is the first such model using Canadian data and is utilized to determine the economic burden of T2D on Canadian society, both now and in the future.

According to the CDA 2009 report (Canadian Diabetes Association 2009b), the total population with T2D has increased from 4.2 per cent in 2000 to 7.3 per cent in 2010 and will increase to 9.9 per cent by 2020. Today, one in four Canadians either has diabetes or prediabetes. Prediabetes is a condition where a person's blood sugar levels are higher than normal, but not high enough to be diagnosed as T2D (fasting plasma glucose levels of 7.9 mmol/L or higher). The CDA 2009 report (Canadian Diabetes Association 2009b) estimates that nearly six million Canadians today are living with prediabetes. Prediabetes is of concern to clinicians and health care professionals since almost 50 per cent of those with the condition will ultimately develop T2D. A number of studies have mentioned that comorbidities or complications associated with T2D, such as CVD and neuropathy, begin during the prediabetic stage (CDA 2009b; Cohn 2008; Public Health Agency of Canada 2007).

The Economic Burden of Prediabetes and T2D in Canada and the USA

In Canada, more than 20 people are diagnosed with T2D every hour of every day (CDA 2009b). T2D is a serious disease affecting the quality of life of people with the disease, as well as that of their families. T2D is leading to a financial crisis for the Canadian healthcare system (CDA 2009b). The 2009 CDA report predicted that T2D would place an approximated $12.2 billion burden in the Canadian healthcare system in 2010, an increase of $5.9 billion or nearly double its level in 2000. The direct healthcare expenditures related to T2D accounts for 3.5 per cent of public healthcare spending in Canada – this percentage is likely to continue to rise given the projected increase in the number of people living with prediabetes and T2D in Canada (CDA 2009b).

The CDA 2009 (Canadian Diabetes Association 2009b) report makes an important argument in relation to interventions that would potentially reduce the prevalence of T2D. A reduction in the incidence rates by two per cent per year, together with better and effective disease prevention and management approaches, would lead to substantial medical care cost savings of 9 per cent in direct costs and 7 per cent in indirect costs.

In the USA, in 2008, the American Diabetes Association (ADA 2008) published an article, 'Economic Costs of Diabetes in the U.S. in 2007', in the journal *Diabetes Care*. In that study it was estimated that the total cost of diabetes in 2007 was US$174 billion, including US$116 billion in excess medical expenditures and US$58 billion in reduced national productivity. In the US, the medical expenditures on behalf of people with diagnosed T2D are approximately 2.5 times higher than those of their non-diabetic counterparts

(ADA 2008). For the employed population, indirect medical costs incurred due to reduced productivity amounted to US$20 billion, and $26.9 billion for lost productivity due to premature death. This study is unique and noteworthy since it combined research findings from the health economics literature, public health, and medical evidence with new, empirically derived analysis to provide thorough information on T2D costs by sociodemographic group, health care services setting, comorbid conditions (associated with T2D) treated, and cost-effectiveness analysis. Major data sources analyzed and referenced in that study include the National Health and Nutrition Examination Survey (NHANES), the National Health Interview Survey (NHIS), National Ambulatory Medical Care Survey (NAMCS), Medical Expenditure Panel Survey (MEPS), National Nursing Home Survey (NNHS) and National Home and Hospice Care Survey (NHHCS).

Effect of Diabetes on Workplace Productivity

Some of the most recent evidence citing the economic burden of T2D in Canada and the US was reviewed above. Next is a critical review of the substantial impact of T2D on workers, their employers in general and the workforce. Implications for workplace health promotion, T2D prevention and management and policy will be discussed subsequently.

The link between health and workforce productivity has been recognized for centuries as a foundation for a healthy economy (Berger et al. 2001; Goetzel & Ozminkowski, 2000; Holland et al. 2001; Stewart et al. 2004). In addition to the issue of disability and workers' compensation, employers recognize that health conditions affect their active workforce and the ability of employees to get to and function at work. Health conditions such as obesity and T2D currently represent a national, public health crisis in North America and around the world. However, there is increasing evidence that obesity and T2D (and associated comorbid conditions) are related, at least in part, to adverse work conditions. In particular, the risk of obesity and T2D may increase in high-demand, low-control work environments. The risk also increases among shift workers or those who work long hours during night-time (Schulte et al. 2007). Employed workers spend a quarter to a third of their lives at work, and the pressures and demands of work do affect their eating habits and activity patterns, which can lead to obesity and T2D.

There is a paucity of research that examines the nature and scope of complex interactions among workers' lifestyle patterns, workers' occupational health and safety, stress at work and risk of obesity/T2D. Some of the important questions related to that complex network include whether obesity (and T2D) is an 'individual' problem or a 'societal/environmental' health issue/condition. Moreover, should workers' obesity/T2D be given any more consideration than other behavioural, modifiable risk factors, such as smoking, blood pressure and alcohol use, when one is addressing workplace health promotion issues.

Workplace Health Promotion and Type 2 Diabetes Prevention and Management

The Canadian Diabetes Association developed the Healthy Workplace Initiative in 2003. This initiative is still viewed as an opportunity to encourage employers and corporations to adopt the principles of comprehensive, workplace health promotion. Moreover, the CDA developed the 2008 clinical practice guidelines for the prevention and management of diabetes in Canada (CDA 2008).

In the US, the Centers for Disease Control and Prevention (CDC) developed specific guidelines for employers to help them assist their employees with diabetes management (CDC 1999). The suggested guidelines include developing a supportive work environment so that employees with T2D feel comfortable adopting and performing behaviours that promote good diabetes control; providing encouragement and opportunities for all employees to adopt healthier lifestyles that reduce the risk of chronic diseases such as obesity and T2D; coordinating all corporate diabetes control efforts to make them more efficient as well as accountable within an organization; and demanding the highest quality medical care for people who are suffering from T2D and its comorbidities. In addition, the new American Diabetes Association clinical practice guidelines published as a supplement in the January 2010 issue of *Diabetes Care* focus on maintenance of glycaemic control and secondary prevention in the form of screening using the glycosylated haemoglobin (HbA1c), in an attempt to prevent onset and further complications/comorbidities from T2D (ADA 2010).

While there is abundant literature on the economic burden and costs of T2D in the American and Canadian literature, I would like to emphasize that there is no information related to the effectiveness of comprehensive interventions targeted toward T2D management in patient populations or employees. A few publications have been identified which are pertinent to the rights and responsibilities of employees with T2D in the workforce. Most of these publications were developed to give employers information about diabetes to assist them to support a person with T2D in the workplace. For example, the Americans with Disabilities Act is a federal law that prohibits discrimination against individuals with disabilities. Title I of the Americans with Disabilities Act covers employment by private corporations with 15 or more employees, as well as local government and state employers. The Americans with Disabilities Act requires employers to provide 'reasonable' adjustments or accommodations to enable employees with disabilities stemming from T2D to enjoy equal access to employment opportunities. A question arises, however, in relation to when and under what conditions does the Americans with Disabilities Act consider T2D a disability. The Americans with Disabilities Act was amended in 2008 to strengthen the language relation to diabetes. T2D is a disability when it 'substantially limits one or more of a person's major life activities. Major life activities are basic activities that an average person can perform with little or no difficulty, such as eating or caring for oneself. T2D is also a disability when it causes side effects or complications that substantially limit a major life activity' (The US Equal Employment Opportunities Commission 2008).

Other jurisdictions, such Canada and Australia, also call for 'reasonable' adjustments for employees with T2D. These can include any or all of the following measures:

- flexibility within the work environment to allow regular short breaks of time throughout the day for small snacks or to manage medication needs;
- allowing a safe location for medication storage within the workplace (may require refrigeration);
- provision of a private location in which blood sugar levels can be checked and medication self-administered;
- education for colleagues or first aid officers regarding what to do in case of complications such as, hypoglycaemia or low blood sugar; and/or
- provision of occupational health and safety aids if needed.

It is important to note that most people/employees with T2D do not require significant accommodations or adjustments in their respective workplace. Many of the activities needed to achieve glycaemic control can be carried out by diabetics themselves, such as monitoring of blood glucose levels, medicating, exercising and dieting. For that reason, enhancing patients' capacities and education for the self-management of T2D has become an important priority in current diabetes care. In addition, the employee with T2D has responsibilities. One of the most important responsibilities is that an employee declares their diabetes status to their employer (but not necessarily to all staff). Failure to do so may make a person ineligible for workers' compensation – this is important particularly when the condition of T2D is severe enough to interfere with the daily and normal functioning or productivity of an employee, or when the job is considered a safety hazard or poses a significant health risk for an employee. When it comes to safety concerns, an employer should be careful not to act on the basis of fears or stereotypes about T2D. The employer should evaluate each employee on their knowledge, skills, experience and how having T2D affects their work and quality of life. In other words, an employer should determine whether a particular employee would pose a direct threat or significant risk of substantial harm to themselves or others that cannot be reduced or eliminated by reasonable accommodation.

Type 2 diabetes is a serious debilitating chronic disease that affects people of all ages. It is increasing alarmingly among children and teenagers, which will result in future workers entering the workforce with pre-existing T2D. This fact has important implications for policy related to prevention and management of T2D in the workplace. One of the policy implications is that there needs to be improved and effective communication between physicians (or health care professionals) and workers with T2D. Physicians and other health care professionals are in a very good position to provide support for diabetic persons based on the latest clinical guidelines published by the ADA and CDA. However, these clinical practice guidelines provide little information on how health care providers may support patients in the effective prevention and management of T2D in the workplace.

Disability researchers have noted that the development of any intervention to improve working conditions for sick workers requires information about the direct experiences of the immediate stakeholders themselves, and particularly the patients (Detaille et al. 2006). There is a paucity of research into what employees with T2D need to cope with and manage their diabetic status at work. Future research should examine views, attitudes, beliefs and perceptions of workers with T2D, in addition to in-depth exploration of the different perspectives of physicians (and health care providers) and patients regarding the experience of having T2D. Being more than just a physiological disease, T2D has broader psychosocial effects that affect the quality of life of diabetic workers. Future research and policy should be directed towards developing instruments/questionnaires focused on workers with T2D, something that is currently lacking. Policymakers should pay particular attention to the social and emotional aspects of T2D in the workforce, as this is relatively a new focus area in T2D care and management.

Proposed Comprehensive Health Promotion Programs for Prediabetes and T2D in the Workplace

In relation to a given job, questions are sometimes raised by employers about the safety and effectiveness of individuals with T2D. It was common practice to restrict individuals with T2D from certain employment categories or jobs solely because of the diagnosis of T2D or the use of insulin or oral hypoglycaemic agents, with no regard to the abilities and circumstances of such individual. From a health promotion perspective, an increasing number of employers have introduced health promotion activities for their employees in recent years. Health promotion programs typically comprise three approaches to employee health: health education, preventive medicine and physical fitness. Some of these activities/programs are run directly by employers and some others, such as self-management and educational interventions, are primarily based on efforts undertaken by employees themselves. Self-management interventions include instruction in weight loss/management, medication management, physical activity, blood glucose monitoring, as well as other tasks specific to T2D management.

Conclusions

In conclusion, there follow some recommendations for employees with prediabetes and T2D in relation to prevention and self-management of these conditions under the umbrella of a comprehensive worksite health promotion program. First, such employees should be considered individually for employment, based on the requirements of the specific job and the individual's medical history, medical condition and treatment strategy. Second, medical assessments by treating physicians should always be included as part of the case-by-case individualized assessment by an endocrinologist with expertise in assessment and treatment of prediabetes and T2D. Third, subjective evaluations of potential employees should not be performed; objective methods of screening for prediabetes and T2D should be based on the latest evidence and scientific knowledge about these conditions and their prevention/management. Fourth, evaluation of any safety concerns or risks posed by employees with T2D should include determining whether such concerns are justifiable in relation to the job functions/duties the employee has to perform. A single occurrence of severe hypoglycaemia should not in itself preclude an individual from employment. However, if such an individual has recurrent episodes of hypoglycaemia then concerns about safety are justifiable and such an individual may not be able to safely perform the job.

Finally, a significant aspect of prevention and management of prediabetes and T2D in the workplace that is lacking is the psychosocial assessment of workers. There is a paucity of research into coping strategies and the impact of adverse psychosocial factors that stem from dealing with T2D on a daily basis on physical functioning and quality of life for individuals. Future research studies should evaluate psychosocial factors in workers with T2D and effective programs should be designed for stress management.

Before a workplace health promotion program is designed, employees with prediabetes or T2D must be asked to determine their knowledge, attitudes and beliefs towards overall wellness, and their current individualized level of action. The major purpose of a health promotion program is to influence the health attitudes of individual workers so that they will make personalized choices in their day-to-day decisions which will lead to a positive and healthy lifestyle. Components of an effective comprehensive workplace health promotion for prediabetes/T2D should include the following objectives. The first and foremost objective should be to assist employees to cope better with their prediabetes/ diabetic status. This objective can be achieved through providing psychological assessment and counselling for such individuals. Depression is common with a chronic condition such as T2D. Mental health assessment and provision of counselling services and psychiatric treatment should be individualized based on a worker's level of psychological and physical functioning. Second, employees should be encouraged to adopt and maintain a physically active lifestyle, including cardiopulmonary fitness and skills in cardiopulmonary resuscitation. Provision of recreational facilities, for example, gyms or fitness clubs, within corporations/workplace settings and allowance for break times during working hours for employees to exercise is of utmost importance. Third, workers should be influenced to adopt and maintain proper eating habits that optimize nutritional requirements and weight. A potentially effective strategy is to design and implement healthy cafeteria programs within corporations/workplace settings, not just for prediabetic/diabetic workers but also for all employees. And fourth, as a method of primary prevention and as health promotion strategy in relation to prediabetes and T2D among employees, smoking, alcohol, and use of recreational drugs should be strictly discouraged.

In conclusion, individuals with prediabetes or T2D can and do serve as highly productive members of the workforce. Senior management and middle management in corporations or workplace settings should tailor their efforts towards designing comprehensive workplace health promotion and wellness programs that integrate all employees, but more specifically provide opportunities and encouragement for prediabetic and diabetic patients to be successful at work. Stress management, provision of mental health counselling and treatment, particularly when coexistent conditions such as depression, anxiety or other mental health conditions, should be given priority. Health education and reasonable accommodations for T2D employees should also be a priority. Type 2 Diabetes can be a disabling health condition; however, most cases when detected early can be managed effectively. Therefore, workers with prediabetes/T2D should not be discriminated against as long as they are able to perform their jobs in a safe and appropriate manner.

Bibliography

Akinci, F., Healey, B.J. & Coyne, J.S. (2003). Improving the Health Status of US Working Adults with Type 2 Diabetes Mellitus. *Disease Management and Health Outcomes* 11(8): 489–98.

American Association of Clinical Endocrinologists (AACE). (2008). *State of Diabetes Complications in America: A Comprehensive Report*. Available at: http://harrisschool.uchicago.edu/News/press-releases/media/Diabetes%20Complications%20Report_FINAL.PDF, accessed 1 August 2011.

American Diabetes Association (2008). Economic Costs of Diabetes in the US in 2007. *Diabetes Care* 31: 596–615.

American Diabetes Association (2009). American Diabetes Association's New Clinical Practice Recommendations Promote A1C as Diagnostic Test for Diabetes. Available at: http://www.diabetes.org/for-media/2009/cpr-2010-a1c-diagnostic-tool.html#, accessed 3 January 2010.

American Diabetes Association. (2010). *Diabetes Forecast Consumer Guide 2011: The Latest Tools for a Healthy Diabetes Lifestyle*. Available at: http://www.diabetes.org/for-media/2010/diabetes-forecast-consumer.html, accessed 1 August 2011.

Anderson R.J., Freedland, K.E., Clouse, R.E. & Lustman F.J. (2001). The Prevalence of Comorbid Depression in Adults with Diabetes. *Diabetes Care* 24: 1069–078.

Berger, M.L., Murray, J.F. & Xu, J. et al. (2001). Alternative Valuations of Work Loss and Productivity. *Journal of Occupational and Environmental Medicine* 43: 18–24.

Beuemann-King, B. (2005). Diabetes in the Workplace. Available at: http://www.worksmartlivesmart.com/, accessed 29 June 2009].

Burton, W.N. & Connerty, R.N. (2002). Worksite-based Diabetes Disease Management Program. *Disease Management* 5(1): 1–8.

Canadian Diabetes Association. (2007). *Prediabetes: The Chance to Change the Future*. Available at: http://www.diabetes.ca/files/Prediabetes-Fact-Sheet_CPG08.pdf, accessed 2 January 2010.

Canadian Diabetes Association (2008). The 2008 Clinical Practice Guidelines for the Prevention and Management of Diabetes in Canada. *Canadian Journal of Diabetes* 32 (Suppl 1): S1–S201.

Canadian Diabetes Association (2009a). The Prevalence and Costs of Diabetes. Available at: http://www.diabetes.ca/documents/about-diabetes/PrevalanceandCost_09.pdf, accessed 1 January 2010.

Canadian Diabetes Association (2009b). An Economic Tsunami: The Cost of Diabetes in Canada. Available at: http://www.diabetes.ca/get-involved/news/new-canadian-diabetes-cost-model-paints-a-sobering-view-of-diabetes-in-cana/, accessed 1 January 2010.

Centers for Disease Control and Prevention (1999). *Making a Difference: The Business Community Takes on Diabetes*. Report No.: NPDP pub #33. Atlanta GA: US Department of Health and Human Services Public Health Services, National Center for Chronic Disease Prevention and Health Promotion..

Cohn, R. (2008). Economic Realities Associated with Diabetes Care: Opportunities to Expand Delivery of Physical Therapist Services to a Vulnerable Population. *Physical Therapy* 88: 1417–424.

Colagiun, R., Colagiun, S., Yach, D. & Pramming, S. (2006). The Answer to Diabetes Prevention: Science, Surgery, Service Delivery, or Social Policy? *American Journal of Public Health* 96: 1562–569.

Detaille, S.I., Haafkens, J.A., Hoekstra, J.B. & van Dijk, F.J.H. (2006). What Employees with Diabetes Mellitus Need to Cope at Work: Views of Employees and Health Professionals. *Patient Education and Counseling* 64: 183–90.

Eastman R.C., Javitt, J.C. & Herman, W.H. et al. (1997). Model of Complications of NIDDM. II. Analysis of the Health Benefits and Cost-Effectiveness of Treating NIDDM with the Goal of Normoglycemia. *Diabetes Care* 20: 735–44.

Goetzel, R.Z. & Ozminkowski, R.J. (2000). Health and Productivity Management: Emerging Opportunities for the Health Promotion Professional in the 21st Century. *American Journal of Health Promotion* 14: 211–14.

Goldfarb, N., Weston, C. & Hartmann, C.W. et al. (2004). Impact of Appropriate Pharmaceutical Therapy for Chronic Conditions on Direct Medical Costs and Workplace Productivity: A Review of the Literature. *Disease Management* 7(1): 61–75.

Holland, J., Holland, C. & Anstadt, G. et al. (2001). *Impact of the Workforce Environment on Worker Health and Productivity*. Socttsdale AZ: The Institute for Health and Productivity Management.

Lavigne, J.E., Phelps, C.E., Mushlin, A. & Lednar, W.M. (2003). Reductions in Individual Work Productivity Associated with Type 2 Diabetes Mellitus. *Pharmacoeconomics* 21(15): 1123–134.

Resnick, H.E. & Howard, B.V. (2002). Diabetes and Cardiovascular Disease. *Annual Reviews of Medicine* 53: 245–67.

Schulte, P.A., Wagner, G.R., Ostry, A., Blanciforti, L.A., Cutlip, R.G., & Krajnak, K.M. et al. (2007). Work, Obesity, and Occupational Safety and Health. *American Journal of Public Health* 97: 428–36.

Stewart, W.F., Ricci, J.A., Leotta, C. & Chee E. (2004). Validation of the Work and Health Interview. *Pharmacoeconomics* 22(17): 1127–140.

The US Equal Employment Opportunities Commission (2008). Questions and Answers about Diabetes in the Workplace and the Americans with Disabilities Act (ADA). Available at: http://www.eeoc.gov/facts/diabetes.html, accessed 2 January 2010.

Index